Descriptosaurus: Ghost Stories

C000257948

Descriptosaurus: Ghost Stories builds on the vocabulary and descriptive phrases introduced in the original bestselling *Descriptosaurus* and, within the context of ghost stories, develops the structure and use of the words and phrases to promote colourful cinematic writing. This essential guide will enable children to take their writing to the next level, combine their descriptions of setting and character and show how the two interact. Children can then experiment with their own ghost stories, armed with the skills, techniques and vocabulary necessary to describe their ghostly scenes in a way that allows the reader to feel the characters' fear and visualise the source of their terror within the setting.

This new system also provides a contextualised alternative to grammar textbooks and will assist children in acquiring, understanding and applying the grammar they will need to improve their writing, both creative and technical.

Alison Wilcox has extensive teaching experience in schools in England and Scotland. Colleagues describe her methods as 'innovative and inspirational to even the most reluctant of writers'.

Descriptosaurus

Ghost Stories

Alison Wilcox

Routledge
Taylor & Francis Group

LONDON AND NEW YORK

First published 2016
by Routledge
2 Park Square, Milton Park, Abingdon, Oxon OX14 4RN

and by Routledge
711 Third Avenue, New York, NY 10017

Routledge is an imprint of the Taylor & Francis Group, an informa business

British Library Cataloguing in Publication Data
A catalogue record for this book is available from the British Library

Library of Congress Cataloging-in-Publication Data
Wilcox, Alison.
    Descriptosaurus : ghost stories / Alison Wilcox.
        pages cm
    1. Creative writing (Elementary education) 2. Literary form—
    Study and teaching (Elementary) 3. Ghost stories. I. Title.
    LB1576.W48758 2016
    372.62'3—dc23   2015008741

ISBN: 978-1-138-85872-5 (hbk)
ISBN: 978-1-138-85873-2 (pbk)
ISBN: 978-1-315-71775-3 (ebk)

Typeset in Myriad Pro
by Keystroke, Station Road, Codsall, Wolverhampton

Contents

Introduction

BACKGROUND

When I first decided to write *Descriptosaurus* it was because my experience of teaching creative writing to children had revealed that many had great imaginations and lots of ideas, but did not have the descriptive vocabulary to communicate these effectively. This was partly due to a lack of reading or a passive involvement with a text so that the techniques and vocabulary were not absorbed. I have been delighted with the response to the original work and have seen many fabulous examples of descriptive writing.

After writing *Descriptosaurus,* I returned to the classroom to conduct further research on different ways to use the resource. It became evident that one of the weaknesses in children's texts was the way they connected their writing. Often the pace of their writing was dramatically slowed by lengthy, unnecessary detail because they didn't have the vocabulary to move the story on to another scene. I also found that displaying the text on the whiteboard and modelling the process was extremely effective. This was why the second edition included a CD and a section on connectives and adverbs.

NATIONAL LITERACY TRUST – DESCRIPTIVE WRITING COMPETITION

In 2013, I collaborated with the National Literacy Trust on a descriptive writing competition. I was astounded by the response and the quality of the entries. I think that too much attention is given to the apparent decreasing standards in schools, particularly in literacy, and not enough media attention given to the outstanding young writers and teachers in our classrooms today. The work and support of the National Literacy Trust are vital in maintaining and improving these standards.

WHY WRITE *DESCRIPTOSAURUS: GHOST STORIES?*

As part of the process, the National Literacy Trust analysed the genres children chose in their descriptive pieces. It is important that children are given the opportunity to develop their interests and passions. To ensure that children are engaged and enthused with creative writing, it is vital that they are, where possible, given a choice. The four genres that stood out as by far the most popular were: ghost stories; adventure; fantasy; and myths & legends, which is why we have decided to concentrate on these four areas.

It was also evident that, for a lot of children, 'scary' meant that the setting had to be scary and the ghost gruesome. Ghost stories are an ideal way of illustrating that it is the building up of suspense and atmosphere that can make a story truly gripping. Ghost stories are, therefore, an excellent genre to show how depth and colour can be brought to a piece of writing by using senses, and this book aims to provide the vocabulary and techniques to develop this skill. The chapters have been deliberately organised to demonstrate how drip-feeding information to the reader builds up suspense – for example, the vocabulary to describe the ghost has purposely been left to the last chapter.

S/C-I-R: SETTING/CHARACTER, INTERACTION, REACTION

It was also evident that only the setting or ghost were used to create the 'scary' element of the writing, with little suspense included. To paint a cinematic picture the text must have suspense, but that suspense is only felt by the reader if the character's reaction and interaction are also included. For example, a creaking door can add atmosphere, but the reader needs to feel the character's fear about what is making the noise, lurking in the shadows. To develop this skill, I have been experimenting with a new system I have called 'S/C-I-R' (Setting/Character-Interaction-Reaction) which has resulted in cinematic writing of an exceptional standard.

The resulting work has described the setting, moved the character through the setting, and described their reactions to what they see or the events in which they are involved. A model of the S/C-I-R structure is included at the beginning of each chapter.

CONTEXTUALISED GRAMMAR LEARNING

Another benefit of this system has been to provide a contextualised alternative to the prescriptive, repetitive focus on textbook grammar in response to the introduction of the SPAG tests. Taking a number of sentences or phrases for setting, interaction and reaction, combining them into a descriptive paragraph of a scene, and then experimenting with different ways of combining the sentences, openers and length is a very engaging way of learning about grammar and its impact on the flow, sense and expression. I have also noticed that the discussion that results from this experimentation has a dramatic impact on the quality of responses to comprehension tasks.

The exercise can be extended to changing tenses, including adverbs, or even using it to write a scene for a playscript. These exercises can be done as extended sessions, as part of the planning, or as warm-up exercises. They are also excellent for modelled and collaborative learning. Different focuses can be used. For example:

★ Giving the class three sentences all starting with pronouns, and setting them the challenge of using different ways to open their sentences.
★ Asking them to use the three sentences to produce a paragraph of five or more sentences.
★ Blending the sentences, but changing them into the first person and present tense.

PLANNING AND EDITING

The age-old problem of ineffective planning and cursory editing still remains. To aid in this process, I have included a section in the Appendix on the structure and planning of a ghost story, breaking it down into manageable parts. A plot planning sheet is also included in the Appendix. Developing a habit of using a planning sheet to brainstorm ideas will, as we all know, greatly enhance the final piece of text. Hopefully, the structure of the planning sheet will also aid in the structure of the story.

To help with the development of strong characterisation, I have also included a planning sheet for a hero/heroine and the ghost. A planning sheet for the various elements that can be used to indicate the presence of the ghost and build suspense has also been included. For example, a lingering smell, sudden drop in temperature.

To combat cursory editing, planning sheets are provided for scenes, whether it be for Setting, Suspense or the appearance of the Ghost. If phrases and sentences are collected for Setting/Suspense/Ghost, Interaction and Reaction for each of the scenes, and the process of blending, altering, reducing, practised in warm-up activities, is used, hopefully the editing will become more focused and effective.

NON-FICTION

Ghost stories can be the focus for a lengthy unit, which can include many and varied non-fiction tasks. For example:

- ★ Newspaper article about a past tragic event that occurred in the setting.
- ★ An estate agent sales advert describing the house. This can be extended to include a floorplan, which is useful when planning where and how the ghost appears etc.
- ★ Diary entries from a previous, dead inhabitant.
- ★ Discursive historical piece on an event in history.

I have had so much fun writing this book, it has been hard to stay focused on the brief, as I constantly found myself writing lengthy scenes, which expanded into short stories. I hope all those who use *Ghost Stories* enjoy using it as much as I enjoyed writing it.

Alison Wilcox

Key elements

The history of ghost stories stretches back to the time when people relied on oral storytelling to entertain and scare each other. Charles Dickens and M.R. James made the idea of telling ghost stories at Christmas fashionable, and the genre was at the height of its popularity in the latter part of the 1800s until the Second World War. They remain very popular today, and the oral ghost-storytelling tradition is still honoured at Halloween.

FORM OF ENTERTAINMENT

The success of the ghost story lies in providing a sense of excitement and dread, relying on the fear of the unknown, the fear of the dark, fear of what lurks in the shadows. They are designed to have the reader jumping at every creak or flicker, footstep or shadow.

The tales often include

- ★ A mysterious presence in an attic, cellar, eerie corridor, ruins, medieval castle, dungeons, graveyards or tombs
- ★ Something lurking behind the door
- ★ A fleeting glimpse of a misty, ghostly shadow
- ★ A faint eerie light in a dark corridor
- ★ Lights flickering in a deserted part of a building
- ★ The creak of a door as the rusty hinges groan
- ★ Whispered calls that drift through the air
- ★ The sound of shuffling footsteps, clanging chains when nobody is about

★ Wolves baying, hooves thundering, owls hooting, rooks cawing
★ A flutter of a curtain
★ A cold touch like a breath of wind
★ A painting which has eyes that appear to move
★ Doors that seem to open by themselves.

(See the planning sheet in the Appendix.)

WHAT MAKES A GREAT GHOST STORY?

1. A ghost!
2. A sinister setting;
3. Atmosphere;
4. Suspense and mystery;
5. Emotion (reaction and interaction);
6. A killer last sentence with a spooky twist!

1. THE GHOST

Tips for creating a mysterious ghost

1. The presence of the ghost may be heard or felt, but not seen.
2. A ghost may be seen but not make a sound.
3. A ghost may be standing right in front of the character but cannot be touched.
4. It may be accompanied by sounds, smells, or sensations of cold to indicate its presence.
5. The ghost may be capable of:

★ moving, lifting, and breaking objects;
★ opening and closing doors and windows;
★ turning lights on and off;
★ causing objects to fall from shelves;
★ interfering with electrical appliances (turning on the television);
★ interfering with a phone's reception causing a crackling noise on the line;
★ causing power surges;
★ moving through and around walls and objects.

Most hauntings involve:

Sounds

- ★ Mysterious footsteps
- ★ Rustling
- ★ Whispering
- ★ Animal sounds and howling
- ★ Thumps, bangs, tapping and rapping.

Smells

- ★ Flowers
- ★ Perfume
- ★ Rotting flesh.

If the ghost was a witch, she may be accompanied by the smell of burning flesh.

Touch

- ★ A cold prickling of the skin
- ★ Cold breezes
- ★ Feelings of being touched by an invisible hand.

Why is the ghost haunting the setting?

It has unfinished business. It is not going to go away until it resolves this business. There are three types of *unfinished business*:

(A) Revelation – the ghost bears messages about:

- ★ an imminent event
- ★ death
- ★ family secrets
- ★ a crime.

(B) Revenge – the ghost seeks revenge for:

- ★ murder
- ★ theft.

(C) Recovery – the ghost wants to recover a lost object:

- ★ a will
- ★ treasure
- ★ a family heirloom.

Decisions

When planning your ghost story you will need to make a number of decisions about the ghost, its identity, background, motivations and actions:

- ★ What is the unfinished business?
- ★ Adult, child or animal ghost?
- ★ Male or female ghost?
- ★ When did they live?
- ★ How did they die?
- ★ When and where does the ghost appear, and to whom?
- ★ What is the signal to the reader that the ghost is present if it is not initially visible? Is it because there is a change in temperature, a movement, unexplained sounds, or smell?
- ★ What does the ghost look like, sound like, move like?
- ★ What can the ghost do?
- ★ Can they help or hurt you?
- ★ How do you feel about the ghost – love or fear it?
- ★ Will the main character help the ghost or defeat it?

2. THE SETTING

The setting in a ghost story is where the:

- ★ ghost appears
- ★ action takes place
- ★ unfinished business is resolved.

Key points

1. Decide why the setting is important to the story.

- ★ Was it the scene of a crime or death? What happened here and in which part of the setting?
- ★ Was it the place where the lost object has been hidden/stored? What obstacles are there to retrieving it, e.g. a hidden passage that has to be discovered?

2. Think of words and phrases to help you build up the description of the setting.

Imagine you have a camera and move it around the location, then zoom in to pick up extra details.

3. Be descriptive.

Use figurative language such as similes and metaphors.

4. Use senses to bring the setting to life for your reader.

As well as sight, think about what your character can:

- ★ hear
- ★ smell
- ★ touch
- ★ possibly taste.

It is not essential for the setting to be a haunted castle or graveyard. Normal settings and actions can be scary. Bedrooms late at night or a dark, dusty attic, a haunted school or hospital can also be frightening.

A story can be truly terrifying if the plot can happen to anyone, anywhere. It is the *atmosphere* that is created that makes the setting scary – a fluttering curtain, a flickering light, doors slamming shut when there is no breeze. The setting must have *eerie* and *mysterious* elements.

3. ATMOSPHERE

An essential part of a good ghost story is a:

- ★ scary atmosphere
- ★ build-up of tension.

An atmosphere of **gloom, doom**, and **threat** is often a feature of a ghost story. Placing characters in a dark or ill-lit room will immediately create a feeling of unease. *What or who is lurking in the shadows?*

The key to writing a gripping ghost story is to withhold some information:

- ★ Rather than the character seeing the ghost early on in the story, it is more effective for it initially to be heard, smelt, felt.
- ★ At the beginning, the ghost should be an eerie presence, a shadow, a faint light, a chilling presence.

Weather can be used to great effect to create a scary atmosphere and tension:

- ★ Howling winds
- ★ Mist or fog
- ★ Ferocious storms
- ★ Relentless rain.

There may be:

- ★ Unexplained noises in the night
- ★ Lights going out when there is no wind
- ★ The howl of wolves in the distance; the screech of an owl.

Examples

The howling thunder rolled away, leaving the room eerily quiet after the storm. His heart thumped in his chest as he peered into the dark, aware of an icy chill in the room. He clutched the duvet . . . held his breath. Out of the shadows, the sound of a wheezy breath hung in the air.

Add detail and description to paint a picture in the reader's mind. Giving a setting an atmosphere is more than stating that it is dark or cold outside. For example, 'It was dark outside' doesn't enable the reader to feel the atmosphere and the tension. Adding more descriptive detail could give you:

> The moon was covered in heavy clouds like a torn, black veil. Below, the ground was full of flitting shadows.

4. SUSPENSE

To create a sense of mystery and suspense:

(a)   Don't reveal everything at once. Instead, hint that the character saw something, heard, felt, smelt something, e.g. 'The temperature dropped for no apparent reason.'

(b)   Gradually revealing what it was later adds to the mystery and suspense and is much more effective than a detailed description of a hideous ghoul.

(c)   Hint that something unusual is going to happen, e.g. 'This was only the start of the day's strange events.'

(d)   Raise questions to hook the reader, e.g. 'Why had/ did . . .?'

(e)   Slowly feed bits of information to the reader to keep them guessing and anxious to find out what happens next.

(f)   Use the 'ticking clock' effect.

(g)   Use word order and punctuation to add suspense:

   ★   Include a sentence that holds back essential information from the reader until its ending.
   ★   Use colons, commas and repeated full stops to delay the revelation, e.g. 'When he turned on the torch the sight that met his eyes made him gasp; behind the door was . . .'

(h)   Sprinkle the story with mysterious words:

   ★   unusual
   ★   strange

* curious
* odd
* peculiar
* bizarre
* weird
* abnormal
* freakish
* unnatural
* eerie
* creepy
* spooky
* fishy
* baffling
* mysterious
* mystifying
* bewildering
* perplexing
* unaccountable
* inexplicable.

(h)   Build a sense of urgency and panic by:

* Making frequent references to time:
    * He checked his watch again.
    * It was ten minutes to midnight. He had to get out by midnight.
    * Could he make it in time?
    * He searched desperately for a way out. Frantic now . . . time was running out.
    * He checked his watch again; his heart sank as he saw that there was now only one minute to go and he was still trapped inside and no closer to finding a way out.
* Varying the length of the sentences. Place several short sentences consecutively. Include one-word or two-word sentences, e.g. 'Oh no!' or 'Banging again, again.'
* Using pronouns (he, she, it) to refer to any mysterious characters before revealing their names and history.

★ Giving them something unusual about their appearance, e.g. 'He was tall and slim with dark shoulder-length hair. As he walked, his feet barely seemed to touch the ground.'

5. EMOTION

Emotion is vital in ghost stories. The basic rule is the same as in any other genre – 'show not tell'.

Reaction

Describing how a character reacts to events in the setting brings the scene to life for the reader and enables them to empathise with the character's situation. For example, 'He was terrified as the footsteps moved down the corridor and stopped outside his door' *tells* the reader that the character is terrified, but does not *show* how the character reacts to the situation.

If the character encounters the ghost, describe:

★ how he is feeling inside using, for example, heart or pulse
★ facial expressions
★ eyes
★ voice.

For example, the same situation could be expanded to describe the character's reaction to the footsteps as they neared his door:

He wrapped the duvet tighter around him and held his breath. His chest was tight, his heart pounding against his ribs. As the footsteps shuffled down the corridor, he clutched his duvet up around his head and screwed his eyes shut tight. The footsteps stopped outside his door. Winding the duvet around his fist, he rammed it into his mouth to stem the scream that was building inside his throat.

Note: Fear isn't the only emotion you can use when writing a ghost story. The character may experience sadness, anger or even hope and excitement. The same principles apply to describing the character's reaction to their situation.

Interaction

To add a cinematic quality to your writing it is essential that the character's movements are described as they react to the event in the setting and their situation.

A character may:

- ★ be frozen to the spot;
- ★ move nervously, cautiously;
- ★ move quickly;
- ★ frantically look for a way of escape;
- ★ move forward to defend himself.

Apart from enabling the reader to visualise the character's movements, their interaction is a signpost to the reader as to the degree of danger and the closeness of the threat, e.g.,

She kept her eyes fixed to the floor, unable to bring herself to look at the vision in front of her. Rooted to the spot, paralysed by fear, terrified of raising her head.

She darted behind the couch, crouched low, and covered her head with her hands.

Part 1
The setting

1

Hooks to build suspense

Note: Apart from aiding the flow of your writing, this chapter can also be used to stimulate quick, brainstorming activities to get your creative juices flowing by asking the questions – Why? How? When? Where? Who? What happened next? It is amazing how many stories can be created as a result of these quick activities.

OPENINGS

★ If you had asked him whether or not he believed in ghosts, he would have said no . . . a couple of months ago. But not now!

★ How different things would have been if they had never:
  ☆ inherited that house;
  ☆ won that holiday;
  ☆ visited the church/hotel/house/ruins/great uncle;
  ☆ opened that diary/box/door.

★ He should have followed them, or run the other way, but he stood frozen in shock as the door opened. And that was when everything started to go wrong.

★ As soon as she opened the door to the cellar and stepped inside, she knew. She knew that she had made a terrible mistake.

★ *Nobody had come this way for a long, long time.*

★ Something terrible had happened here – she could feel it – sense something ominous, menacing . . . wanted to get away, to run from whatever waited for her.

- ★ He sensed that something was wrong here. Very wrong. Why had he come? Was it too late to turn back?
- ★ She looked up at the dark, unblinking eyes of the (house) and she got the weirdest feeling; a feeling of unease and a sense of a threatening, malignant presence.
- ★ As soon as he had stepped into the house, an eerie sensation had enveloped him and would not go away. At night, in particular, he felt very uneasy. The feeling was getting stronger by the day. It was like the house was watching, waiting, biding its time.
- ★ As soon as he had entered the hotel, he'd been fighting an underlying sense of panic and as night approached and the shadows lengthened, the hotel suddenly felt full of dark secrets.
- ★ The abbey felt as if it had been destroyed by tragedy. Sadness and despair were trapped in its walls, cemented into the fabric of the building, locked behind its doors.

WARNING OF DANGER TO COME

- ★ Foreboding buzzed along his limbs like an electric current pulsing just beneath the skin.
- ★ She had a strange feeling – a premonition that something bad was about to happen.
- ★ He felt a sudden shiver. He tried to shake off his tension, but in vain. He began to have a growing awareness of impending evil.
- ★ A sense of foreboding crept through her, and sweat trickled down her forehead. Something wasn't right!
- ★ Sometimes it was a chill, other times an odd feeling that she couldn't quite place.
- ★ He began to feel cold. Icy dread prickled his neck as the clock struck midnight, warning him that danger was near.
- ★ His heart was thudding in his chest. He didn't know why. There was no obvious reason for his fear.
- ★ A peculiar sensation had gripped the back of his neck, like a cold, skeletal hand tugging at his hair.
- ★ There was no one else there. She knew that. But something was urging her to run.

- ★ A strange sensation had gripped the back of his neck, like a cold, skeletal hand pinching his nerves, sending a shiver down his spine.
- ★ His pulse was racing but he didn't know why. Fear clawed at him like a wintry breeze, as cold as the freezing air that had descended on the room.

AN OMINOUS PRESENCE

- ★ Those were nervous days while he waited for the smell to return, the sudden chill, the vaporous tentacles, but they didn't come. Not then.
- ★ Something was coming. She felt its presence. It was as if it was waiting. But for what?
- ★ She sensed something – some kind of eerie presence coming through the wood. She sensed it reaching out to her, drawing her nearer.
- ★ Her eyes flew open in the darkness. She was wide awake now, and too tense to breathe. This was no dream. She was not alone in the house.
- ★ It was as if the unseen watchers were everywhere, circling, moving closer with each passing moment.
- ★ He felt as if he was being watched. But when he scanned the hall, there was no one there.
- ★ She had a sensation of being watched, of an accompanying presence close by her side.
- ★ He was suddenly aware of another presence, of something watching him, its eyes boring into him like a searing heat on his back.
- ★ Had she heard something? Had she really felt a presence? Was there someone in the corridor? All these questions tumbled frantically through her head as she clutched the duvet above her head.
- ★ There was someone lurking in the dark; someone who had no reason for being there.
- ★ The presence was closer, moving nearer, still invisible, but there and reaching towards her, and soon would be close enough to touch her.
- ★ She searched the darkness for any sign, any sound. There was nothing. Just that lingering stench.
- ★ There was no warning, no tell-tale creak or footsteps.
- ★ Before he had taken more than a few steps, he was aware of a mysterious presence.

★ Someone had walked into the room when she was asleep. That was why she had woken. Every nerve in her body screamed at her that they were still there.

★ For a brief second, she thought the light caught someone, lurking behind the curtains. She opened her mouth to cry out, but when she looked again . . . there was no one there.

★ An uneasy feeling of being watched settled over her. There was no one there. It didn't make sense!

★ He had an uncomfortable feeling of someone or something lurking in the shadows: someone or something watching him.

★ He sensed something dark moving in the shadows, waiting for him.

★ She had a creeping certainty that there was something, someone in the room with her, breathing on her, resting icy cold fingers on her pillow.

★ Something deep in her mind told her that it was no ordinary visitor outside her door.

★ The camera was pointing straight at her, jerking back and forth following her every movement. The building was empty, so who was operating the camera?

TOO CLOSE FOR COMFORT

★ Something was coming closer. She could feel its presence.

★ The footsteps were louder. Another creak, another shuffle just down the corridor. Only seconds away.

★ The clanging of chains was getting closer. Whoever it was had almost reached the top of the stairs. In seconds, they would be close enough for him to see.

★ The shuffling footsteps edged nearer. Soon they would be on the landing and heading straight for her room.

★ The footsteps were growing louder and getting closer. He could hear the creak of boot leather and then, one foot dragging along the floor.

DON'T DO IT!

★ It was as if she was being pulled into something dark and dangerous by a hand she couldn't see, couldn't stop even if she wanted to.

★ There was no reason why she was so desperate to go up into the attic; she just knew she had to. It was as if she was being drawn by an invisible force.

★ Despite her fear, she was seized with an urgent need to open the door and check.

★ Something urged him on. Every nerve in his body screamed at him to get out. But before he knew what he was doing, his legs seemed to move of their own accord, and he edged towards the door.

★ She didn't want to look but she couldn't seem to stop herself.

★ The broken door summoned him like a dark, unblinking eye.

★ She always had to dig deeper – search for answers. She just couldn't let things go, even when she knew she should.

★ Gripped by an urge to turn and run, he knew he couldn't. It was like an invisible thread was pulling him towards the cellar door.

★ Something strange was happening. Something strange and deeply disturbing. She couldn't understand what, but she was determined to get to the bottom of it.

★ There had to be another way out. There was, but the only way he could get to it meant going deeper into the house, through the inky blackness of the hall and down into the basement.

THE CLOCK IS TICKING: THE BELLS ARE TOLLING!

★ The minutes dragged past.

★ The seconds crawling by seemed like hours.

★ The seconds ticked away, agonisingly slowly.

★ An hour passed, and then another, and after a while . . .

★ In the long, agonising moments that followed . . .

★ *On every hour and half hour, the church clock chimed.*

★ She didn't sleep the rest of the night. In the background, the grandfather clock ticked off each minute.

★ *He saw that it was just after midnight.*

★ The grandfather clock boomed loudly, twelve times – midnight already!

★ Just as the town clock struck midnight . . .

★ She glanced nervously at her watch. And saw that it was just after midnight. And then it started. Bells. A cacophony of sound. One after another. Ringing, clanging, ringing, clanging – warning her to get away.

★ *Time was ticking away; she could feel it beating everywhere.*

★ Time wound itself around her, creeping, ticking, winding on and on.

★ There was just enough time to turn back and find another way out. She knew time was running out and she had to make a decision soon or it would be too late.

★ There was no time to worry. No time to think. He had to act now. Time had run out.

★ He had less than a second to make a decision.

★ She knew she didn't have long to act. It had to be soon.

★ She couldn't afford to wait any longer.

★ Hurry! The house seemed to whisper. Time is . . . ticking . . . tickticking . . . ticktickticking.

★ The grandfather clock beat an anxious tick, tick, tick.

2

Woods

Ahead of him, he saw a flash of white. A torch? It flashed again. He headed towards it. Suddenly, he realised that he had been drawn further into the wood. **It was almost as if it had been done on purpose; some eerie presence tugging him forward.**

He was now in the middle of the wood, and surrounded by blackness on all sides. It was as if the trees and bushes had closed in on him, deliberately preventing him finding his way back.

Unable to shake the feeling of being watched, he kept looking over his shoulder. In his mind, every shadow in the wood grew eyes. Suddenly, his pulse started to race. He had caught sight of a movement out of the corner of his eye. It turned out to be no more than a swaying branch, but he **couldn't shake off his unease. A strange sensation had gripped the back of his neck, like a cold, skeletal hand tugging at his hair.**

He quickened his pace, but the ground was uneven and he stumbled, crashing to the ground. His flailing hand caught on something hollow as he fell, which rolled down the path, briefly shattering the silence that had descended on the wood.

All the way through the woods, birds had fluttered through the trees, squirrels scampered from branch to branch, but as he had entered the clearing, there was an eerie silence – a throbbing silence, which had wrapped around him like a thick blanket.

Resting on his hands and knees, shocked and winded, his shoulders heaving as he sucked in air, he raised his head. **A shiver charged down his spine like an electric shock.** In front of him in the clearing was a semi-circle of gravestones, leaning together as if whispering secrets of the past. Every root, every branch, every leaf gave off a feeling of abandonment – forsaken even by the animals and birds.

As he staggered to his feet, the trees began to whisper. It grew louder . . . more insistent . . . then louder still, until it seemed to engulf the wood. **A tingling sixth sense made him look up. As he turned his head, he shuddered and went rigid.**

SECTION 1 – SETTING

WORDS	
Nouns	**Clearing**, track, path, trail, roads
	Telephone lines, electricity cables
	Shelter, houses, hunting lodge, cottage, ruins, graveyard, gravestones, skull, skeleton
	Trees, bushes, canopy, trunks, branches, boughs, twigs, leaves, roots, undergrowth, bogs, swamps
	Thorns, brambles, creepers
	Owls, crows, bats, birds, squirrels
	Wind, breeze, gust, gale
	Silence, whisper, rattle, creak, crack
	Mist, fog, shadows, blackness
Similes/ Metaphors	**like tiny white hands**; like long, bony fingers; like barbed wire; arm-like tentacle; as if whispering secrets of the past; like a pistol shot
Adjectives	**Dark**, gloomy, moonlit
	Unseen, invisible
	Cold, chilly, icy
	Thick, dense, impenetrable, claustrophobic
	Tall, high, vast
	Gnarled, twisted, interlocking, drooping
	Wild, ancient, ruined
	Strange, eerie, silent
	Bare, bony, rotting, matted, decayed

Vicious, barbed, ankle-twisting, dangerous, treacherous

Yew, oak, elm, willow

Verbs	**Surrounded**, circled, wrapped around, swallowed, engulfed

Grew, narrowed

Shrivelled, worn away

Stood, leaned, bowed, climbed, littered, strangled, blocked

Sheltered, hid, concealed

Tugged, grasped, clasped, clutched, tripped

Darkened, cut out, steeped, shrouded, glowed

Ran, headed, plunged

Imagined, realised, discovered

Peered, saw, picked out, looked like

Shivered, stopped, ceased

Fluttered, scampered

Hooted, cawed, cracked

PHRASES – NOUNS AND ADJECTIVES

- ★ Within minutes . . .
- ★ Without warning
- ★ *All the way through the woods*
- ★ In the clearing
- ★ Behind them . . .
- ★ Ahead of him . . .
- ★ Through the leaves . . .
- ★ On either side of the track . . .
- ★ Below the moonlit clouds . . .
- ★ *Not a place for humans*
- ★ No houses . . . no roads
- ★ No telephone lines; no electricity cables
- ★ Nothing but a dense wood
- ★ A few, ancient, leaning gravestones
- ★ *Vast gnarled oak tree*
- ★ Under the drooping canopy of a weeping willow
- ★ Tight interlocking branches
- ★ Twisted boughs
- ★ Impenetrable walls of thorns and brambles

- ★ Matted creepers
- ★ Dense undergrowth
- ★ Bare branches
- ★ Every root, every branch, every leaf . . .
- ★ *Cold and claustrophobic woods all around them*
- ★ Gloomy corridors between the tall yew trees
- ★ Black void full of wild and ancient trees
- ★ Darkened spaces between the trees
- ★ *Unseen owls*
- ★ Something invisible . . . an eerie presence
- ★ *An eerie silence*
- ★ Whole wood of trees – silent – not a rustle, not a creak
- ★ Utterly silent, save for the cawing of a murder of crows
- ★ Sound of the wind among the trees
- ★ Leaves rustling as if whispering secrets to one another
- ★ Sound of a snapping twig
- ★ Crackling in the canopy above their heads

PHRASES – VERBS

- ★ *Secrets hidden in its black depths*
- ★ Where anything could be hidden
- ★ *As if the trees and bushes were . . .*
- ★ As if they didn't want to let him through;
- ★ Climbed almost horizontally out of the ground
- ★ Seemed to get narrower with every step
- ★ Closed in on him
- ★ Blocked the path
- ★ Prevented him finding his way back
- ★ *Headed towards it*
- ★ Plunged into the wood
- ★ Wound their way through the wood
- ★ *Realised that he had been drawn further into the wood*
- ★ Discovered that he was in the middle of the wood
- ★ *Dotted with vicious thorns*
- ★ Ran through the semi-darkness like barbed wire
- ★ Littered with treacherous bogs
- ★ Bowed low, their leaves shrivelled
- ★ *Wrapped around the ruined cottage*
- ★ Seemed to be tied together
- ★ Strangled the trees
- ★ Tangled together as if it had been struck by a violent storm
- ★ Reached an arm-like tentacle over the wall

- ⭐ *Tugged at her feet*
- ⭐ Tried to trip her up
- ⭐ Threw up ankle-twisting, gnarled roots
- ⭐ *Steeped in shadow*
- ⭐ Swallowed them whole
- ⭐ Seemed to engulf the wood
- ⭐ Formed a gloomy vault
- ⭐ Darkened the already gloomy evening
- ⭐ Surrounded by blackness on all sides
- ⭐ Peered into the black spaces between the trees
- ⭐ Could see only blackness
- ⭐ *Shrouded in mist*
- ⭐ Saw a flash of white
- ⭐ Glowed through their branches
- ⭐ Glowed in the moonlight like hundreds of tiny white hands
- ⭐ *Could conceal any number of dangers*
- ⭐ Suddenly grew eyes
- ⭐ Picked out branches like long bony fingers
- ⭐ Looked like faces sneering from gnarled tree trunks
- ⭐ Took on strange, shifting shapes
- ⭐ *Caught a movement on the edge of his vision*
- ⭐ Turned out to be no more than a swaying branch
- ⭐ *Stood in the centre of the clearing*
- ⭐ Leaned together as if whispering secrets of the past
- ⭐ Had long been worn away
- ⭐ *Forsaken even by the birds*
- ⭐ Gave a feeling of abandonment
- ⭐ *Circled above the trees*
- ⭐ Fluttered through the trees
- ⭐ Scampered from branch to branch
- ⭐ *Began to whisper*
- ⭐ Couldn't hear anything above the rattle of the branches
- ⭐ Hooted from the treetops
- ⭐ Grew louder . . . more insistent . . . then louder still
- ⭐ Cracked out like a pistol shot

SENTENCES

The woods wrapped around the old hunting lodge.

Matted creepers strangled the trees.

The leaves and branches seemed to be tied together as if they didn't want to let him through.

It was as if the trees and bushes had closed in on him, deliberately preventing him finding his way back.

A vast gnarled oak tree climbed almost horizontally out of the ground; its twisted boughs blocking the path.

The dense undergrowth tugged at her feet, trying to trip her, throwing up ankle-twisting, gnarled roots and impenetrable walls of thorns and brambles.

Vines dotted with vicious thorns ran through the semi-darkness like barbed wire.

All the woodland was tangled together as if it had been struck by a violent storm.

The cold and claustrophobic woods around them did nothing to ease their fear and unease.

The gnarled bough of the yew tree reached an arm-like tentacle over the ancient wall that surrounded the graveyard.

Every root, every branch, every leaf gave a feeling of abandonment – forsaken by the animals and birds.

There were no houses. There were no roads or tracks which could lead to houses; no telephone lines; no electrical cables. Nothing but a dense wood littered with treacherous bogs.

The trees bowed low, their branches shivered, their leaves shrivelled and began to fall. Within minutes, all the branches were bare.

They sheltered against the rain under the drooping canopy of a weeping willow. Through the leaves they could see only blackness.

The corridors between the tall yew trees were steeped in shadow.

Behind them, the dense wood was shrouded in mist.

The tight interlocking branches formed a gloomy vault.

The trees took on strange, shifting shapes. The branches glowed in the moonlight like hundreds of tiny white hands.

The track seemed to get narrower with every step until the wood swallowed them whole; the branches darkening the already gloomy evening.

The wood to either side of the track was a black void full of wild and ancient trees. The moonlit clouds above glowed through their branches.

She tried to peer into the black spaces between the trees. Anything could be hidden there. It was definitely not a place for humans.

The wood seemed huge with secrets hidden in its black depths.

It was easy to imagine someone or something watching her from the darkened spaces between the trees.

He discovered that he was in the middle of the wood, and was now surrounded by blackness on all sides. Ahead of him, he saw a flash of white. A torch? It flashed again. He headed towards it. Suddenly, he realised that he had been drawn further into the wood. It was almost as if it had been done on purpose.

The torch picked out branches like long bony fingers and what looked like faces sneering from gnarled tree trunks.

They plunged into the wood. Immediately, the light was cut out behind them.

There was a growing unease among them as they wound their way through the wood, for its dark recesses could conceal any number of dangers.

In his mind, every shadow in the wood suddenly grew eyes. He caught a movement on the edge of his vision, but it turned out to be no more than a swaying branch.

Unseen owls hooted from the treetops.

Everything was still. A whole wood of trees that were so silent it made a shiver run up and down his spine.

The sound of the wind among the trees ceased abruptly.

The trees began to whisper. A crackling in the canopy above their heads. It grew louder . . . more insistent . . . then louder still, until it seemed to engulf the wood.

The trees stood tall and dark, their leaves rustling as if whispering secrets to one another.

The wood was utterly silent, save for the cawing of a murder of crows circling above the trees.

He couldn't hear anything above the rattle of the branches in the wind and his own ragged breathing.

All the way through the woods, birds had fluttered through the trees, squirrels scampered from branch to branch, but in the clearing, there was an eerie silence. A few gravestones stood in the centre of the clearing, leaning together as if whispering secrets of the past. The names had long been worn away.

Then the sound of a snapping twig cracked out like a pistol shot.

SECTION 2 – INTERACTION

Nouns	**Drive**, house, graves
	Direction
	Tree, branches, bark
	Snow, wind, rain
	Pain, fright, fugitive
	Mind, body, shoulders, chest, lungs, knees, toes, hands, face, eyes, ears
Similes/ Metaphors	**As still as a statue**
Adjectives	**Hollow**, rubbery, gnarled
	Heaving, flailing
Verbs	**Imagined**, expected, realised
	Pressed, twisted, ducked, crept
	Rose, ran, darted, bolted
	Slowed, rested
	Slipped, skidded, scrambled
	Clenched, grasped, thudded
	Shocked, winded, gasped, reeled
	Looked, glanced, blinded
	Rolled, whizzed, rushed, caught

PHRASES – NOUNS AND ADJECTIVES

* ⋆ Away from the house rather than towards it
* ⋆ *Something smooth, round and hollow*
* ⋆ Gnarled branches
* ⋆ *On the tips of his toes . . .*
* ⋆ Flailing hand
* ⋆ Like fugitives
* ⋆ Head down, arms pumping, legs a blur of movement

PHRASES – VERBS

- ⋆ Reeling with fright, he . . .
- ⋆ Kept looking over her shoulder
- ⋆ Looked from side to side and over her shoulders
- ⋆ *Crept from tree to tree like fugitives*
- ⋆ Crawled over the ground, keeping low
- ⋆ Crouched on the ground, afraid to move
- ⋆ *Terrified of raising her head*
- ⋆ Hardly dared to raise his head
- ⋆ *Slithered to a halt*
- ⋆ Shuddered and went rigid
- ⋆ Rooted to the spot like a rabbit caught in the headlights
- ⋆ Stood perfectly still
- ⋆ Frozen to the floor and paralysed by fear
- ⋆ Lingered in the shadows, motionless, alert
- ⋆ Crouched behind the hedge, motionless
- ⋆ Stood with his hands on his hips, head bowed
- ⋆ Sat, corpse-like, frozen and motionless
- ⋆ Huddled in the darkness
- ⋆ *Listened for any sound that might guide him*
- ⋆ Strained for any sound
- ⋆ *Pressed their backs into the tree*
- ⋆ Twisted himself around
- ⋆ Rose to take another look
- ⋆ Ducked behind a tree
- ⋆ *Bolted for the nearest tree*
- ⋆ Scrambled up the muddy bank
- ⋆ Scrabbled against the bark
- ⋆ Ran with his bottom in the air
- ⋆ Scuttled like a rabbit in a warren
- ⋆ Darted and dodged through the trees
- ⋆ Blundered and slipped
- ⋆ Fought his way through the undergrowth
- ⋆ Quickened her pace until her feet appeared to be flying
- ⋆ Started to run, faster and faster
- ⋆ *Grasped at his arms as he pounded past*
- ⋆ Caught on a buried branch
- ⋆ Caught something as she went down
- ⋆ Caught a shoulder on a tree
- ⋆ *Whizzed by him*
- ⋆ Rolled down the path
- ⋆ *Slowed as his legs grew heavy*
- ⋆ Kept slipping, unable to get a grip

* Buckled under her
* Quickened his pace, but the ground was uneven
* Skidded onto his knees through the dust
* Stumbled and flung her hand out in front of her
* Groped for something to stop her falling
* Stumbled, crashing to the ground
* Collapsed on her knees
* Rested on her hands and knees
* Clenched his fists and ran

SENTENCES

It was as if time had stopped. She shuddered and went rigid, as if rooted to the spot.

He stood as still as a statue, like a rabbit caught in the headlights.

Perfectly still, she was frozen to the floor, paralysed by fear.

Motionless and alert, they lingered in the shadows, ready to move quickly.

He crouched behind the tree, motionless, his ears straining for any sound, his eyes peering into the shadows.

Finally, slithering to a halt, he stood with his hands on his hips, head bowed, gasping for breath.

She sat, corpse-like, frozen and motionless.

They crept from tree to tree like fugitives, pressing their backs into the tree.

On the tips of his toes, he rose to take another look.

She couldn't shake the feeling of being watched, and kept looking over her shoulder.

Frantically looking from side to side and over her shoulders, she ducked behind a tree.

He crawled over the ground, keeping low, hardly daring to raise his head.

Terrified of raising her head, she crouched on the ground, afraid to move.

She scrambled up the muddy bank, chest heaving and gasping for breath.

Robert bent over and ran with his bottom in the air, scuttling like a rabbit in a warren.

He darted and dodged through the trees. Blundering and slipping, he fought his way through the undergrowth grasping at his ankles.

Her steps quickened until her feet appeared to be flying.

He started to run, faster and faster, his head down, his arms pumping and his legs a blur of movement.

Clenching his fists, he ran. The trees whizzed by him, their gnarled branches clutching at his arms as he pounded past.

Bolting for the nearest tree, her feet scrambling against the bark, she tried to heave herself up into the branches, but she kept slipping, unable to get a grip.

She stumbled and flung her hand out in front of her, groping for something to stop her falling.

The ground was uneven, so when he tried to quicken his pace, he stumbled, crashing to the ground.

His boot caught a buried branch, and he skidded onto his knees through the dust. Momentarily, he was blinded as it blew into his face, stinging his eyes.

Catching a shoulder on a tree, she grunted with pain.

Her flailing hand caught something as she went down. Something hollow rolled down the path.

As the torch flickered and died, he was left floundering with his outstretched hands clutching at the branches.

Her pace slowed as her legs grew heavy. Eventually, her legs stopped working altogether. Her knees went rubbery. Her mind screamed at her to keep running, but her body was exhausted. She had nothing left. Her legs buckled under her and she collapsed on her knees.

SECTION 3 – REACTION

WORDS	
Nouns	**Instant**, moment, pauses
	Instinct, feeling, thoughts, senses, sensation, nerves
	Panic, urgency
	Shock, fear, dread, terror
	Brain, heart, pulse, temples, chest, breath, cheeks
	Shoulder, spine, neck, arm, forearm, hand, face, eyes
	Voice, whisper, sob, shout, scream, howl, shriek
	Light, torch, shadow
	House, wood, branches, leaves
	Sound, footsteps

Similes/ Metaphors	**Tide**, wave, fist, electric
Adjectives	**Raw**, blind, sheer
	Sixth sense, tingling, shivering, shuddering
	Strange, low, slow, halting, shuffling
	Chilly, icy, steely
	Alert, wide, staring, urgent
	Pounding, thudding, hammering
	Desperate, frantic, rasping, jagged
Verbs	**Knew**, realised, remembered, recalled
	Repressed
	Felt, sensed, imagined
	Sent, rose, quickened, charged, surged
	Held, sucked, blew, gasped, grunted, winded
	Looked, flickered, darted, swept, strained
	Spoke, dropped, lowered, whispered
	Heard, crunched, crackled, snapped
	Slithered, stopped, halted, froze, paralysed, rooted
	Stood, turned, twisted, spun, whirled
	Floundered, flailed, clutched, grasped

PHRASES – NOUNS AND ADJECTIVES

★ In that one instant . . .
★ But the next moment . . .
★ Long pauses in between
★ From a little way off
★ *Something in the desperate urgency of the shout . . .*
★ As the flickering torch . . .
★ Away from the house, deeper into the woods
★ *Raw instinct*
★ Blind instinct
★ Sheer panic
★ Utterly alert
★ Every nerve in his body

- ★ Tingling sixth sense
- ★ Like an electric shock
- ★ Even though his heart . . .
- ★ *Wide and staring*
- ★ Urgent and twisted with terror

PHRASES – VERBS

- ★ Realised he had run in the wrong direction
- ★ Seemed to pull at her, tugging her forward
- ★ *Tried to remember the way back to the house*
- ★ Could not afford to get lost in the wood
- ★ *Knew he had to remain calm*
- ★ Repressed the rising tide of panic
- ★ Forced herself to keep moving
- ★ All her senses were on high alert
- ★ *Felt a chill, steely fist squeeze her heart*
- ★ Clenched and thudded in her chest
- ★ Sent a shivering wave of terror down his spine
- ★ Pounded in her temples
- ★ Made a shiver run up and down his spine
- ★ Charged down his spine like an electric shock
- ★ Strained to breaking point
- ★ *Shivered at the thought of being there alone*
- ★ Felt as if there were eyes everywhere following his every move
- ★ Imagined someone or something watching her from . . .
- ★ Afraid something or someone was following her
- ★ Couldn't shake off the strange sensation that she was being followed
- ★ *Blew out her cheeks*
- ★ Shocked and winded
- ★ Drew a rasping, jagged breath
- ★ Held their breath
- ★ Gasped for breath
- ★ Sucked in air
- ★ Could hardly breathe, the glacial air burning his lungs
- ★ Grunted with pain
- ★ *Darted to and fro*
- ★ Darted wildly from side to side
- ★ Flickered nervously left and right
- ★ Swept the scene in front of her
- ★ Strained to pierce the darkness
- ★ Made her look up
- ★ Looked furtively over her shoulder

- ✶ Constantly looked from side to side
- ✶ *Dropped to an urgent whisper*
- ✶ Spoke in a low, halting voice
- ✶ Caught his breath in a sob
- ✶ *Strained for the sound of footsteps*
- ✶ Heard very slow, shuffling footsteps
- ✶ *Slithered to a halt*
- ✶ Froze her to the spot
- ✶ Turned her head, and froze
- ✶ Stood, hands on hips, head bowed
- ✶ *Rubbed his sweating brow with his forearm*
- ✶ Floundered with his outstretched hands
- ✶ Clutched at the branches

SENTENCES

Something invisible seemed to pull at her, tugging her forward.

Her heart clenched and thudded in her chest. She had to force herself to keep moving.

Reeling with fright, he realised that he had run in the wrong direction – away from the house, deeper into the woods.

A shiver charged down his spine like an electric shock.

In that one instant, she felt a chill, steely fist squeeze her heart and freeze her to the spot. But the next moment, blind instinct took over from sheer panic as she desperately tried to remember . . .

There was something in the desperate urgency of the shout that sent a shivering wave of terror down his spine.

Even though his heart was pounding, he knew he had to remain calm and repress the rising tide of panic. He could not afford to get lost in the wood.

Raw instinct took control. She was utterly alert. Every nerve in her body straining to breaking point.

A tingling sixth sense made her look up. As she turned her head, she froze.

Kitty couldn't shake off the strange sensation that she was being followed. All her senses were on high alert as she strained for the sound of footsteps.

She looked furtively over her shoulder, as if she was afraid something or someone was following her.

He felt as if there were eyes everywhere, following his every move.

Blowing out her cheeks, she drew a rasping, jagged breath.

They all held their breath. From a little way off, they heard very slow, shuffling footsteps, crunching through the autumn leaves, with long pauses in between.

Her eyes darted to and fro, sweeping the scene in front of her, trying to find the source of the whispers.

Rubbing his sweating brow with his forearm, Rob's eyes flickered nervously left and right.

Her eyes were wide and staring and her face urgent and twisted with terror.

His wide eyes strained to pierce the darkness and darted wildly from side to side – he was certain he was being followed.

His voice dropped to an urgent whisper.

He spoke in a low, halting voice, constantly looking from side to side.

He caught his breath in a sob; the whispers had begun again.

He slithered to a halt, and stood, hands on hips, head bowed, gasping for breath.

Shocked and winded, shoulders heaving as she sucked in air, her eyes darted wildly around the rows of graves.

His heart thudded in his ears. He could hardly breathe, the blast of glacial air was burning his lungs.

3

Grounds

As she turned into the drive, Kitty was stopped by two elaborate, stately gates of wrought iron. On top of stone pillars stood huge, black marble griffins, clutching the family's coat of arms in their outstretched claws.

Kitty got out of the car. Arms folded tightly across her chest, neck disappearing into her hunched shoulders, she looked through the twisted railings, and stared at the ghostly shadow of the house beyond the gates. Above her, a camera was pointing straight at her, moving with her, jerking back and forth. The building had been empty since her great uncle had died. So who was operating the camera?

She looked again at the dark, unblinking eyes of the house and got the **strangest feeling: a sense of unease, a sense of a threatening, malignant presence. She shook her head impatiently. Her imagination was getting the better of her again. Cautiously, she reached out towards the gate, her hand shaking and adrenalin surging through her veins.** And that's when it all started to go wrong.

Beyond the gate, a stone path, almost hidden by overgrown shrubs and choked with a creeping chaos of nettles and weeds, wound its way to the front steps of the house.

Robert pushed his way through until the dark house loomed above him. In front of the manor, was a strange bare patch, where nothing grew, not even weeds. Suddenly, he remembered that this was where a young girl had been pushed to her death by the Roundheads during the Civil War, hundreds of years ago.

As he bent down over the grass, Robert's **heart was thudding in his chest. He didn't know why. There was no obvious reason for his fear. There was no one else there. He knew that. But every nerve in his body was urging him to run.**

Something made him look up, and as he did, **the blood stopped in his veins. His heart felt like it had ceased beating. His mouth was dry and his tongue felt swollen.** He was being watched from one of the upper windows.

SECTION 1 – SETTING

WORDS

Nouns	**Drive**, path, wall, fence, railings, gateway, gate, arches
	Barbed wire, spikes, bolts
	Griffins, lions
	Hedge, bushes, shrubs, trees, fruit trees, raspberry canes, black-currant bushes, rose garden
	Brambles, moss, lichen, ivy, nettles, weeds, grass
	Thicket, tunnel
	Pillars, terrace, steps, staircase
	Ruins, summer house, sundial, weathervane, well, gravestones
	Shadows
Adjectives	**Long**, thin, narrow, wide, high
	Straight, winding, twisted, leaning, arched, studded
	Huge, vast, heavy
	Grand, elaborate, stately
	Wild, overgrown, high, knee-high
	Prickly, thorny, needle-sharp, razor-sharp, tangled, gnarled
	Dark, strange, gloomy, sinister, ghostly, eerie, mysterious
	Bare, dead
	Stone, wood, oak, marble, metal, steel, iron, ancient, electric
Verbs	**Surrounded**, lined, flanked, guarded
	Led, ran, bent, curved, wound
	Grew, crept, wriggled, spread, swept, extended, overflowed, choked, strangled
	Pushed, thrust, scraped, clutched
	Crumbled
	Hidden, shadowed, shrouded, steeped, loomed

PHRASES – NOUNS AND ADJECTIVES

- ★ Beyond the gates . . .
- ★ Beyond the sweeping lawns . . .
- ★ In an overgrown part of the garden . . .
- ★ *Long, winding drive*
- ★ Straight drive
- ★ *Huge, stone pillars*
- ★ High, stone wall
- ★ *Twisted, metal railings*
- ★ Needle-sharp, steel spikes
- ★ *Arched gateway*
- ★ Heavy iron gate
- ★ Two elaborate, stately gates of wrought iron
- ★ Heavy gates studded with iron bolts
- ★ Behind the high, wooden gates
- ★ *Tangled thicket*
- ★ Sinister hedge of prickly, tangled branches
- ★ Grabbing claws of branches
- ★ Vast limbs of an ancient, gnarled tree, like some prehistoric beast
- ★ Wild, overgrown bushes
- ★ Gnarled fruit trees and old raspberry canes
- ★ Prickly branches with rapidly spreading suckers
- ★ Knee-high grass
- ★ Creeping chaos of nettles and weeds
- ★ Fallen branches and rotten stumps
- ★ *An air of neglect and misery*
- ★ No longer a garden, more like a jungle
- ★ *No pathway from the foot of the steps*
- ★ Narrow stone terrace
- ★ Several wide grey steps
- ★ A grand staircase
- ★ *Mostly dead grass*
- ★ Strange bare patch in front of the house
- ★ Rose gardens on one side and a clipped lawn on the other
- ★ Silhouettes among the trees

PHRASES – VERBS

- ★ Where the trees ended . . .
- ★ Where the young girl had fallen to her death . . .
- ★ Surrounded by twisted, metal railings
- ★ . . . guarded the gate

- ★ Guarded the entrance to the tunnel
- ★ Led up from the beach to the gardens above
- ★ *Followed the wall around the edge*
- ★ Pushed through a small gap in the bushes
- ★ *Appeared through the trees*
- ★ Came to a fortified gate in a long wall
- ★ Found herself standing in front of the mansion
- ★ Reached a high stone wall
- ★ Stood the ruins of the summer house
- ★ *Hidden in the shadows*
- ★ Steeped in shadow
- ★ Loomed the ghostly shadow of the house
- ★ *Stumbled across a shrouded corner of the garden*
- ★ Studded with arched gravestones
- ★ *Supported by stone pillars on whose summits . . .*
- ★ Guarded by stone lions
- ★ Stood griffins of black marble embracing the family coat of arms . . .
- ★ *Ran a broad drive*
- ★ Lined on either side by a row of gnarled oak trees
- ★ Led up to a terrace and a Tudor mansion
- ★ Wound its way all the way up to the front steps of the house
- ★ Swept all around the main house
- ★ Disappeared in different directions
- ★ Ran along the front of the garden
- ★ Bent round so that there was only darkness ahead
- ★ Led up to the imposing front door of solid oak
- ★ *Hidden by overgrown shrubs*
- ★ Crept and wriggled over the drive
- ★ Choked with rank growth
- ★ Strangled by bushes grown wild
- ★ Crept over the sundial
- ★ Clutched it in their thorny fingers
- ★ Fought with the brambles
- ★ *Blew the old branches of the yew tree towards the house*
- ★ Thrust its shrivelled bony arms up against the window
- ★ Extended long thin, gnarled branches into the air
- ★ Waved wildly with every breath of air
- ★ Scraped the glass with every gust
- ★ *Ate into the house like a virulent disease*
- ★ Reclaimed by nature
- ★ Choked in ivy and brambles like something out of a fairy tale

A moment later, the house appeared through the trees.

A rusting iron gate guarded the entrance to the tunnel, which led up from the beach to the gardens above.

The gate was set in the wall and cunningly hidden in the shadows down a narrow, side alley.

She saw a gateway ahead with great iron gates standing open. The drive bent round so that at first there was only darkness ahead.

Several wide grey steps led up to the imposing front door of solid oak.

To his right were two elaborate, stately gates of wrought iron, supported by stone pillars on whose summits stood black marble griffins, clutching the family's coat of arms in their outstretched claws.

Beyond the sweeping lawns, a grand staircase guarded by stone lions led up to a terrace and a Tudor mansion.

The garden was a creeping chaos of nettles and weeds.

Bushes crept and wriggled over the drive, which was now just a thin strip, steeped in shadow.

The prickly branches, with their rapidly spreading suckers, made a sinister hedge.

The drive was paved, but grass grew in every crevice and moss clung to the surface like mould on bread.

They looked through the twisted railings and spread in front of them in the gloom were dark, leaning, crumbling gravestones, thorny bushes and knee-high grass. Beyond, loomed the ghostly shadow of the house.

The manor house was almost hidden by overgrown shrubs, and the drive was choked with rank growth. They pushed their way through it until the dark house loomed above them.

What had once been a beautiful garden had been reclaimed by nature and the whole property had an air of neglect and misery.

Gnarled fruit trees and old raspberry canes were all choked in ivy and brambles like something out of a fairy tale.

It was no longer a garden, more like a jungle. Rose trees extended long thin, gnarled branches into the air, waving wildly with each breath of wind.

There was no pathway from the foot of the steps except the low tunnels created by the wild shrubbery.

The garden was a tangled thicket. Brambles crept over the sundial, clutching it in their thorny fingers.

She stumbled across a shrouded corner of the garden, studded with arched, crumbling gravestones.

The wind blew the old branches of the yew tree towards the house where it thrust its shrivelled, bony arms up against the window, scraping the glass with every gust.

Beyond the gate, a stone path wound its way between rose gardens on one side and a clipped lawn on the other, all the way up to the front steps of the house.

There was a strange bare patch of grass in front of the house. It was where the young girl had been pushed to her death by the Roundheads during the Civil War, hundreds of years ago.

The garden swept all around the main house, disappearing in different directions. In an overgrown part of the garden stood the ruins of the summer house.

SECTION 2 – INTERACTION

WORDS	

Nouns	**Garden**, hedge, bushes, undergrowth, ground, trees, branches, brambles, thorns, moss
	House, cottage, hotel, castle, moat, ruins, graveyard
	Railings, gates, path, steps, gravel, entrance
	Griffins, lions
	Darkness, shadow, movement
	Shoulder, chest, muscles, legs, feet, fingernails, mouth, eyes
Similes/ Metaphors	**Statue**, cement
Adjectives	**Dark**, gloomy, murky, ghostly, sinister, foreboding
	Cracked, twisted, gnarled, entangling
	Slippery, treacherous
	Metal, iron, stone
Verbs	**Found**, emerged, remained
	Wanted, urged
	Waited, stayed, stopped, halted, rooted, froze, paralysed
	Paused, hesitated, stiffened, tensed, twitched

Looked, gazed, glanced, peered, peeped, darted, flickered

Watched, stared, strained, squinted, searched, swept, probed, settled

Gnawed, folded, raised, fumbled

Edged, eased, crouched, hunched, ducked

Crept, crawled, slithered, struggled, wriggled, writhed, twisted

Pushed, climbed, advanced, dived

Whispered, winced, groaned, crunched

Listened, heard

PHRASES – NOUNS AND ADJECTIVES

- ★ On the edge of the wood
- ★ *Dark, foreboding house*
- ★ Ghostly shadow of the house beyond the gates
- ★ *Metal railings towards the gate*
- ★ Sinister griffins
- ★ Entangling branches or the edge of a path
- ★ *No matter how much she . . .*

PHRASES – VERBS

- ★ Found herself standing in front of the mansion
- ★ Emerged next to . . .
- ★ Stayed close to the walls
- ★ Edged round the . . .
- ★ *Peered nervously through the gates*
- ★ Looked up at the . . .
- ★ Looked round furtively
- ★ Looked through the twisted railings
- ★ Raised his eyes above the . . .
- ★ Peered over the top at the . . .
- ★ Peered through the leaves screening the . . .
- ★ Allowed his gaze to rake from end to end
- ★ Glanced over her shoulder again
- ★ Peered out and squinted into the darkness
- ★ Darted left and right
- ★ *Watched and waited*
- ★ Stared at the entrance to the . . .
- ★ Settled on the moat

- ★ Probed the garden for a flicker of movement
- ★ *Gnawed at her fingernails*
- ★ Folded tightly across her chest
- ★ Disappeared into her hunched shoulders
- ★ Raised her head cautiously
- ★ Eased the gate open
- ★ Swept his hands through the leaves, searching for the key
- ★ *Did not know which way to run*
- ★ Did not know where there would be . . .
- ★ Couldn't have turned round if she had wanted to
- ★ Didn't want to know what was behind her
- ★ Wanted to run, but she couldn't move
- ★ Rooted to the ground
- ★ Had frozen like a statue
- ★ Urged her legs and feet to move
- ★ Remained locked in place as if trapped in cement
- ★ Hadn't moved a muscle for ten minutes
- ★ As if someone had glued her feet to the mud
- ★ Stiffened slightly as he looked up at the stone lions
- ★ *Crouched behind the huge, gnarled oak tree*
- ★ Fought with the brambles
- ★ Writhed and twisted
- ★ Crawled through the gap
- ★ Pushed through a small gap in the bushes
- ★ Twitched from one foot to the other
- ★ Edged inside and then paused again
- ★ Climbed the cracked stone steps gingerly
- ★ Avoided the slippery moss where she could
- ★ Stumbled back onto his feet
- ★ Advanced, hunched over in a crouch
- ★ Dived into the murky water
- ★ *Covered her mouth and whispered through her fingers*
- ★ Winced against the burning of his fingers
- ★ *Listened for any unnatural sounds*
- ★ Crunched over the gravel

SENTENCES

He raised his eyes above the hedge, peering over the top at the dark, foreboding house.

She wanted to run. But she couldn't move. She had frozen like a statue, and no matter how much she urged her legs and feet to move, they ignored her pleas and remained locked in place as if trapped in cement.

She couldn't have turned round if she had wanted to. She didn't want to know what was behind her.

He was rooted to the ground as if someone had glued his feet to the mud. Did not know which way to run. Did not know where there would be entangling branches or the edge of a path to trip him up.

He stiffened slightly as he looked up at the stone lions. Twitching from one foot to the other, he peered nervously through the gates.

Trembling nervously, she gnawed at her fingernails and looked up at the sinister griffins.

Arms folded tightly across her chest, neck disappearing into her hunched shoulders, she looked through the twisted railings and stared at the ghostly shadow of the house beyond the gates.

Staying close to the walls, Rob edged round the metal railings towards the gate. He paused . . . nothing stirred. He eased the gate open, his hand trembling, edged inside and then paused again to listen for any unnatural sounds.

She pushed through a small gap in the bushes, fighting with brambles, to find herself standing in front of the mansion.

Writhing and twisting, Kitty crawled through the gap and emerged at the side of the ruins.

She went crunching over the gravel and gingerly climbed the cracked stone steps, avoiding the slippery moss where she could.

Raising her head cautiously, she peered through the leaves screening the hotel.

She looked round furtively, covered her mouth and whispered through her fingers.

Glancing over her shoulder again, she caught sight of a shadow.

He watched and waited. Slowly, he peered out and squinted into the darkness. His eyes darted left and right, probing the garden for a flicker of movement.

Keeping in the shadow of the hedge, she crept past the gate, until she reached the shade of the oak tree. Dropping to her knees, she peered through the hedge at the house.

Tom stared at the entrance to the castle, allowing his gaze to rake from end to end, and then settling on the moat. He was crouched behind the huge, gnarled oak tree on the edge of the wood. He hadn't moved a muscle for ten minutes. Senses fully alert, he advanced, hunched over in a crouch – and dived into the water.

He lingered in the shadows, motionless, alert and ready to move quickly.

He ducked behind the wall, where he remained motionless, his ears straining for any sound, his eyes peering into the shadows, his heart hammering against his ribs.

He glanced behind him, slithered to a halt, and stood with his hands on his hips, head bowed, gasping for breath.

She sat, corpse-like, frozen and motionless, not daring to raise her head.

He huddled in the darkness, listening for any sound that might guide him.

Tom waited for a moment and then followed. He peeped around the corner of the building. There was no one there.

Staying close to the walls, Rob edged round the summer house, paused . . . nothing stirred, moved closer, paused again to listen for any unnatural sounds, then sprinted across to the hedge for cover.

Quickly rolling onto her side, Katie strained her neck upwards to peer through the window.

He came to the corner and cautiously peered around it, not knowing what he was going to find on the other side.

Frantically looking from side to side and over her shoulders, she ducked behind a tree.

He crawled over the ground, keeping low, hardly daring to raise his head.

She crouched on the ground. She was afraid to move. Terrified of raising her head.

She scrambled over the wall, chest heaving and gasping for breath.

He darted and dodged through the garden. Blundering and slipping, he ran to the gate.

He started to run, faster and faster, his head down, his arms pumping and his legs a blur of movement.

She stumbled and flung her hand out in front of her, groping for something to stop her falling.

He quickened his pace, but the ground was uneven and he stumbled, crashing to the ground.

His boot caught on something buried in the long grass, and he skidded onto his knees.

Her flailing hand caught on the barbed wire fence as she went down. Clutching her bleeding hand, she crouched on her hands and knees, shocked and winded, shoulders heaving as she sucked in air, her eyes darting wildly around the garden.

Her legs buckled under her and she collapsed on her knees.

SECTION 3 – REACTION

WORDS	

Nouns	**Presence**, feeling, sense, sensation, instinct, urge
	Fear, dread, panic, anxiety, adrenalin
	Voice, silence
	Muscles, nerves, skin, sweat, bones
	Heart, veins, pulse, neck, chest, spine, spinal column, stomach, fingers, palms, hair, mouth, tongue
	Knot, throb
	Sixth sense
Adjectives	**Tingling**, prickling, quivering, spider-like
	Chilly, icy, cold
	Evil, menacing, ominous, threatening
	Tight, cautious, alert
	Dry, swollen
Verbs	**Felt**, sensed, realised
	Warned, urged, fought, repressed
	Moved, seeped, crept, crawled, slithered, tingled, prickled, buzzed, shot, charged, surged
	Stopped, ceased
	Gripped, grasped, clutched, hugged, rubbed
	Strained, glanced, flickered, darted, swept
	Drew, swallowed, blew, lowered, trailed off
	Whispered, murmured, sobbed, howled

PHRASES – NOUNS AND ADJECTIVES	

* *Chilly feeling*
* A tingling sixth sense of . . .
* Cold, spider-like sensation
* Prickling sensation
* Tight knot in the pit of her stomach

- ★ Every muscle in her body
- ★ Every nerve in her body
- ★ Skin on the back of his neck
- ★ Surge of adrenalin
- ★ *An evil presence lurking in the shadows*
- ★ Quivering dread of something he could not see
- ★ *Dry mouth*
- ★ Tongue felt swollen
- ★ Sound of his own breathing
- ★ Constantly alert for any sound

PHRASES – VERBS

- ★ Something was very wrong
- ★ As if time had stopped
- ★ Before he had gone a few paces . . .
- ★ Had the distinct feeling that . . .
- ★ Sensed something behind her
- ★ *Warned that she was walking into trouble*
- ★ Warned him not to go any further
- ★ Deepened with every step
- ★ Shuddered as she fought back the urge to flee
- ★ *Shot through her*
- ★ Surged through her veins
- ★ Tingled with dread
- ★ Slithered around her like a dark fog
- ★ Crept up his spinal column
- ★ Crawled down her spine
- ★ Went up on the back of her neck
- ★ Brought a damp chill that gradually crept over her
- ★ Moved to her fingers
- ★ Prickled as he looked at the building
- ★ Buzzed when the shadow shifted once more
- ★ Seeped through her veins and lodged in her bones
- ★ Felt the terror like a red throb in her head
- ★ Pounded in her temples
- ★ Stopped in her veins
- ★ Felt like it had ceased beating
- ★ *Felt a cold sweat break out above her upper lip*
- ★ Broke out on the palms of his hands
- ★ Started from the root of every hair on her head
- ★ Rubbed them dry on his trousers
- ★ *Glanced round nervously*

- ★ Flickered from side to side
- ★ Strained to pierce the darkness
- ★ Darted wildly from side to side
- ★ *Lowered his voice*
- ★ Swallowed a wave of anxiety and kept moving
- ★ Trailed off as she realised what lay ahead
- ★ Drew in a deep breath
- ★ Blew it out hard to stop herself howling

SENTENCES

As a surge of adrenalin shot through her, every nerve in Katie's body was on high alert.

As he stood in the grounds of the abbey, he was suddenly overcome with sadness.

Something was very wrong. He could feel it. A tingling sixth sense of an evil presence lurking in the shadows.

Every muscle in her body tensed. She was constantly alert for any sound.

His nerves were on edge, and he jumped when he heard a noise up on the roof. A bat flitted into the light. Another and another swooped and fluttered as fast as his eye could follow.

A cold, spider-like sensation crawled down her spine. The prickling sensation moved to her fingers. She felt a cold sweat break out above her upper lip.

The skin on the back of his neck prickled as he approached the entrance. The place felt evil.

Cautiously, she reached out towards the gate, her hand shaking and adrenalin surging through her veins.

Every nerve in his body warned him not to go any further.

She sensed someone behind her and felt the hairs go up on the back of her neck.

He felt uneasy. The hairs on the back of his neck tingled with dread.

Her nerves buzzed when the shadow shifted once more. It wasn't the same shadow she had been watching. She swallowed a wave of anxiety and kept moving.

His dread deepened with every step.

It was a quivering dread of something he could not see.

Fear seeped through her veins and lodged in her bones.

A tight knot in the pit of her stomach warned Gail she was walking into trouble. Shuddering, she fought back the urge to flee.

She was frightened. She felt the terror like a red throb in her head. As the blood pounded in her temples, her brain quickened and all her senses were alert.

Fear slithered around her like a dark fog, bringing a damp chill that gradually crept over her, even though she was sweating and drenched in sweat.

As she turned, the blood stopped in her veins. Her heart felt like it had ceased beating. Her mouth was dry and her tongue felt swollen.

Sweat started from the root of every hair on his head. Before he had gone a few paces a chilly feeling crept up his spinal column.

Tom had the distinct feeling they were being watched from one of the upper windows. Sweat broke out on the palms of his hands and he had to keep rubbing them dry on his trousers.

She crept into the graveyard and moved down the narrow path. Her face showed a horrified but morbid fascination as she leant over the stones, searching for his grave.

He glanced round nervously as he heard the snap of a twig behind him. His eyes flickered from side to side and he lowered his voice.

His voice trailed off as he realised what lay ahead.

The sound of his own breathing was deafening in the silence.

Drawing in a deep breath, she blew it out hard to stop herself howling.

She was frozen to the spot, unable to move, the darkness swirling around her.

He lingered in the shadows, motionless, alert and ready to move quickly.

4

Buildings (outside)

The outline of the old manor house filtered through the trees. Katie **looked up at the dark, unblinking eyes of the house, at the triangular turrets like teeth that ran along its roof, and got the weirdest feeling; a feeling of unease and a sense of a threatening, malignant presence. She wondered whether it was too late to turn back. Why had she allowed Tom to persuade her to come here?**

Before she could change her mind, Tom made a stirrup with his hands, took her weight and hoisted Katie up to the top of the wall. She straddled the wall with ease, swinging her trailing leg over swiftly and landing on the other side nimbly and without a sound. Quickly, Tom scrambled over the wall and landed beside her.

Staying close to the walls, they edged round the house, paused for a moment . . . nothing stirred . . . moved closer to the main entrance, paused again to listen for any unnatural sounds. They came to the corner of the house leading to the front door and cautiously peered around it, not knowing what they were going to find on the other side.

Tom had the distinct feeling they were being watched. Sweat broke out on the palms of his hands and he had to keep rubbing them dry on his trousers. Eyes darting rapidly to and fro, he searched the area for any movement. Beside him, he heard Katie gasp. As he glanced in her direction, he saw that she was staring up at the wall above them. **His heart skipped a beat.** Gazing down menacingly on them were elaborate stone carvings and grisly gargoyles.

Tom was suddenly gripped by an urge to turn and run. He knew he couldn't. It was like an invisible thread was pulling him towards the house.

As the torchlight flickered unsteadily, it cast dancing shadows in front of her. **Kitty's heart kept skipping a beat, squeezed like a vice by her fear – fear of** any rustle or creak; fear of any slight movement. Blowing out her cheeks, she drew a rasping breath. She had to suppress the rising tide of panic. She couldn't turn back now. It was too late. She had to find out the truth.

A long row of stone pillars was all that was left of the ancient cloister. To the left, the ruins of a vast arch revealed where the church had once stood. Eventually, she found the entrance to the graveyard.

As she moved nearer, she noticed that ancient symbols had been carved into the metal gate. Shining the torch onto the symbols, she leaned closer. **Her eyebrows knitted together as she tried to remember where she had seen those symbols before. For some reason, they made her feel very uneasy.**

With a quaking hand, she reached out towards the handle – but before she could touch it, the gate swung open of its own accord. **Her pulse stopped, her heart stood still, her outstretched arm was paralysed.**

Out of the corner of her eye, she saw something move. **She took a sharp intake of breath.** In the furthest corner, ornate, wrought iron doors stretched across the entrance to the family tomb; the coat of arms welded into the centre. Someone was standing by the doorway! When she looked again, there was no one there. **Her heart hammered in her chest, her mind reeling** as she stared at the door. It was now open!

SECTION 1 – SETTING

A. Buildings

WORDS	
Nouns	**Countryside**, area, place, site, boundary
	Town, village
	Graveyard, cemetery, burial site, mounds, gravestones, headstones, church, churchyard
	Building, house, mansion, manor, town house, cottage, lodge, hotel, outbuildings
	Spire, cloisters, archways, arches, pillars, statues, carvings, gargoyles
	Clock, weathervane, well
	Fortress, castle, buttresses, towers, turrets, battlements, moat

Walls, gateway, entrance

Roof, rafters, chimneys, gables, gutters

Windows, frames, sills, glass, panes, grilles, shutters

Door, hinges, lock, socket, key

Shell, ruins

Ivy, creepers, trees, branches, vegetation, undergrowth

Damp, mould, moss, weeds

Dust, cobwebs, rubbish, dirt, grime

Rats, spiders, bats, owl

Similes/ Metaphors

Colander, spears, like a mailed fist, like an eagle's nest, like vacant eyes, like worms through the eyes of a skull, like rows of broken, chipped teeth, prying ivy fingers, flaked like dandruff, like portholes

Adjectives

Old, ancient, medieval, Norman, Tudor, Georgian, Victorian

Tall, high, towering, hulking

Long, large, huge, vast, massive

Great, grand, imposing, carved, ornate, elaborate

Small, tiny, narrow

Grey, black, green

Stone, red-brick, metal, iron, wooden

Triangular, diamond-shaped

Stained, leaded, diamond-leaded

Wild, overgrown

Empty, bare, dead, deserted, lifeless, desolate, abandoned

Derelict, ramshackle, rickety, ruined, pitted, peeling, decaying, rotten

Leaning, hanging, broken, torn, crumbling, shattered

Sharp, chipped, ragged, broken, gaping, caved-in

Dark, gloomy, eerie, deathly, haunted, strange, sinister, desolate, forbidding, grotesque, grisly, guarded, evil

Dirty, grimy, dusty, streaked, musty

Visible, hidden, boarded-up

Verbs	**Surrounded**, rose, stood, towered, loomed, soared, thrust
	Hung, perched
	Revealed, filtered, marked, enclosed, guarded
	Shrouded, shadowed
	Spread, stretched, crept, crawled, curled, clung, clasped, wrapped, covered, carpeted, trailed
	Leaned, jutted, gaped, peeled, leaked, smashed, shattered
	Decayed, rotted, pitted, blotched, patched, gnawed, crumbled, flaked
	Clogged, blocked, lodged, trapped, jammed
	Lifted, dislodged
	Spun, whirled, waved, belched
	Swooped, scurried

PHRASES – NOUNS AND ADJECTIVES

* ★ Ahead of them on the edge of the . . .
* ★ Through a break in the trees
* ★ In the shadow of an ancient fortress . . .
* ★ *Along the side of the house . . .*
* ★ In front of the main entrance . . .
* ★ High in one of the buildings . . .
* ★ In the far corner . . .
* ★ *Boundary of the burial site*
* ★ A gravelled forecourt with a circular lawn
* ★ Number of outbuildings
* ★ *Medieval castle*
* ★ Huge grey castle
* ★ Grand Tudor mansion with gables and towers
* ★ Sprawling mansion
* ★ Tall red-brick town house
* ★ Imposing house with a number of huge chimneys
* ★ Rambling old house
* ★ Rickety, old cottage
* ★ *Huge grey castle like a mailed fist above the village*
* ★ Great Norman towers and frowning buttresses
* ★ Large, forbidding castle with turrets and battlements
* ★ Triangular turrets like teeth along its roof
* ★ Towers and turrets and stone staircases

★ Jumble of huge, high chimneys and jagged archways
★ Huge chimneys
★ Foul-smelling moat
★ *Towering grey walls*
★ Forbidding gateway
★ Lookout towers
★ Hulking towers
★ *Long row of stone pillars*
★ Ancient cloister
★ Row of arches
★ Stone arch
★ Clock tower
★ Church spire
★ *A succession of grotesque gargoyles*
★ Elaborate stone carvings
★ Two stone statues
★ Broken stone carvings
★ *Hundreds of tiny panes of stained glass*
★ Elaborate stained-glass window
★ Two diamond-shaped window panes
★ Diamond-leaded windows
★ Rows of small, leaded windows
★ Round windows like portholes
★ Narrow sash windows
★ Metal grilles on the windows
★ *Nobody there*
★ Almost dark
★ No lights anywhere
★ Deathly, haunted place
★ Desolate and eerie place
★ Guarded, evil place
★ Ruined, ghost village
★ Abandoned buildings
★ Derelict building
★ Ruins of a vast arch
★ Empty shells
★ *Huge, ramshackle place*
★ Wild, overgrown feel to the place
★ In a terrible state of decay
★ Old, rotten and in a state of disrepair
★ Pile of stones and shattered walls
★ *Crumbling chimneys and hanging gutters*
★ Broken stone carvings on the row of arches
★ Shattered walls

* Crumbling bricks
* Like rows of broken, chipped teeth
* *Empty, gaping, window frames*
* Rotting sills
* Peeling paint
* Broken windows
* Only ragged traces of glass in the windows
* Sharp spears of glass
* Like worms through the eyes of a skull
* Black holes of caved-in windows like vacant eyes
* Glimpses of black gaps between the cracked glass
* Nearly black with grime
* *Almost invisible under the vegetation*
* Barely visible through the overgrown grass
* Amidst the piles of rubbish, grass and weeds . . .
* *Crawling damp and mould*
* Green patches of mould
* Dark, green moss
* Vines of dead, leafless ivy
* Moss-covered headstones
* *Great black spider*
* Layer upon layer of cobwebs

PHRASES – VERBS

* Surrounded by strange, sinister countryside
* Surrounded by a dense wood
* Caused people to quicken their step as they passed
* *Hung above the town like an eagle's nest*
* Set on a high hill
* Soared into the clouds
* Rose up a mile from the village
* Thrust like a mailed fist above the surrounding woods and fields
* Towered above the surrounding countryside
* *Marked with a dilapidated wooden fence*
* Enclosed within a circle of high, stone walls
* Revealed where the medieval church had once stood
* Guarded the entrance either side of the door
* Carved into the stone above the entrance
* *Visible through the trees*
* Filtered through the trees
* Loomed out of the shadows
* Loomed into sight
* Came across . . .

- ★ Could make out the jagged outlines of . . .
- ★ Wrapped in shadow
- ★ Cast jagged shadows along the ground
- ★ *Stood empty and lifeless*
- ★ Looked like it had been deserted for years
- ★ *Imagined the spirits of the dead haunting it*
- ★ Imagined eyes watching him, ears listening
- ★ Did not seem to welcome entry by humans
- ★ Rumoured to contain the skeletons of those who had attempted to escape
- ★ *Falling down*
- ★ Hidden beneath the dripping slime and mould
- ★ Leaked like a colander
- ★ Clogged with rotting leaves
- ★ Gnawed by hundreds of starving rats
- ★ Reclaimed the blackened ruins of the once great house
- ★ Jutted out of rotting sills
- ★ Gave a faint chink of light
- ★ Hung limp from the window
- ★ Gaped like haunted eyes
- ★ Gaped like open mouths
- ★ Had long since shattered
- ★ *All that was left was . . .*
- ★ Had rotted and nothing remained but . . .
- ★ *Clasped the walls of the house*
- ★ Spread from the ground
- ★ Curled through the roof
- ★ Trailed through the empty windows
- ★ Covered all over with dying creepers
- ★ Crept around the door and up into the stonework above
- ★ Wrapped in ivy
- ★ Waved in the wind
- ★ Looked like the creeping vine was holding the building together
- ★ *Missing off the roof*
- ★ Had been dislodged
- ★ Lifted by prying ivy fingers
- ★ *Crawling with damp and mould*
- ★ Blotched with green moss and yellow lichen
- ★ Spread across the walls like mould on bread
- ★ Could barely make out the words on the stones
- ★ *Trapped in cobwebs*
- ★ Hung from the walls
- ★ Stretched from every surface
- ★ Carpeted the floor
- ★ Spun a web from a broken pane of glass

* Clung to his mouth and nose
* *Peeled from the main door*
* Flaked like dandruff from the . . .
* *Hung askew on its hinges*
* Turned the key and the whole lock came away from the rotten socket
* Lodged the bottom of the door on the floor
* Could only force it open a little way
* *Jutted out of the wall*
* Leaned drunkenly on the roof
* Whirled wildly in the breeze
* Sent the weather vane whirling
* Belched out grey smoke
* *Swooped down from the rafters*
* Scurried across the wall
* Gnawed great holes in the floor
* Lay the bleached bones of a rat

SENTENCES

Through a break of the trees, he saw a huge, grey castle that thrust like a mailed fist above the surrounding woods and fields.

The castle loomed into sight. Hulking towers and turrets and stone staircases soared into the clouds. A succession of grotesque gargoyles jutted out from the tower, casting jagged shadows along the ground.

The castle with its turrets and battlements was large and forbidding. It was set on a high hill and surrounded by a dense wood. Surrounding the building was a foul-smelling moat that was rumoured to contain the skeletons of those who had attempted to escape.

Two enormous stone statues guarded the entrance either side of the door.

The hotel was a grand Tudor mansion with gables and towers, a jumble of huge, high chimneys and jagged archways.

The house was enclosed within a circle of high, stone walls. The building was covered in elaborate stone carvings and grisly gargoyles.

The outline of the impressive manor house filtered through the trees. Triangular turrets like teeth ran along its roof. Grey smoke belched out from the tall chimney on one of the two wings.

They arrived at a rambling old house with huge, leaning chimneys and diamond-leaded windows.

It was a rickety, old cottage with dark, green moss spreading across the walls like mould on bread.

The skin on the back of his neck prickled as he approached the entrance. The building was wrapped in shadow. The place felt evil – the type of place that made people quicken their step as they passed.

There was a wild, overgrown feel to the place, which made it easy to imagine the spirits of the dead haunting it. He imagined eyes watching him, ears listening.

The name of the hotel had been carved into the stone above the entrance, but it was now hidden beneath the dripping slime and mould.

It was a guarded, evil place that did not seem to welcome entry by humans.

Along the side of the house were a number of crumbling outbuildings approached through a row of arches that had broken stone carvings jutting out of the wall.

Metal grilles barred the rows of small leaded windows.

The house had strange, round windows like portholes.

The boundary of the graveyard was marked with a dilapidated wooden fence and moss-covered headstones marked the plots, but she could barely make out the words on the stones.

The village was no more than a pile of stones and shattered walls.

The ruined, ghost village was hidden in the wood in the shadow of an ancient fortress, which hung above it like an eagle's nest.

It was a ghost town of deserted houses crawling with mould and damp – empty shells with gaping windows like haunted eyes.

The manor looked like it had been deserted for years.

It was a desolate and eerie place, in a state of decay, but enough remained to show how impressive the building would have once been.

The house had been unoccupied for more than five years and was slowly falling into decay.

The ruins were like rows of broken, chipped teeth.

Nobody lived there now. Some of the windows were broken and others boarded up, and although it was almost dark, no lights were showing in any of the houses.

A long row of stone pillars was all that was left of the ancient cloister. To the left, the ruins of a vast arch revealed where the church had once stood.

Nature had reclaimed the blackened ruins of the once great house.

The house was nearly derelict. Its stonework was decayed and crumbling, its windows boarded up, paint peeling and sills rotting.

The derelict building stood lifeless. Its crumbling chimneys and hanging gutters were clogged with rotting leaves, and the walls were pitted, as if they had been gnawed by hundreds of starving rats.

The walls were wrapped in ivy, the windows covered, the gutters blocked, the slates lifted by prying ivy fingers, waving in the wind.

Several slates had been dislodged and the chimney pot leaned drunkenly on the roof.

The door hung askew on its hinges and the bottom edge lodged on the floor so that they were only able to force it open a little way.

Ivy trailed through the empty windows like worms through the eyes of a skull.

Vines of dead, leafless ivy crept around the door and up into the stonework above.

The ivy clasped the walls of the house and curled through the roof.

He could make out the jagged outlines of what remained of an elaborate stained-glass window.

The abandoned buildings loomed out of the shadows, the black holes of caved-in windows and doors gaping like open mouths and vacant eyes.

Two windows still showed above the balcony. Some panes were missing and the rest were heavily curtained with layer upon layer of cobwebs.

Many of the windows revealed glimpses of black gaps where the glass had cracked or shattered.

Only ragged traces of glass remained in the windows – sharp spears jutting out of rotting frames.

B. Doors

WORDS

Nouns	**Path**, yard, courtyard, gate, porch, wall
	House, hall, graveyard, tomb
	Entrance, exit, way out
	Door, doorway, panels, panelling, knocker, bell, handle, ring, hoop, lock
	Bolts, nails, symbols, coat of arms, gargoyles
Adjectives	**Wooden**, oak, glass, metal, iron, wrought iron, steel, brass, silver, gold
	Front, back, side
	Heavy, solid, thick
	Low, small, narrow

High, vast, huge, massive

Black, dark, stained

Carved, arched, ornate, elaborate

Odd, misshapen

Old, ancient, rotting

Verbs

Led, stretched, blocked, towered, loomed

Opened, closed, swung

Rattled, thudded, creaked, groaned, echoed

Studded, carved

Rung, knocked, pounded, hammered

PHRASES – NOUNS AND ADJECTIVES

* Where the path . . .
* In the distance . . .
* In front of him . . .
* In the furthest corner
* To the right
* *Entrance to the graveyard*
* Heavily carved stone porch
* *Heavy, oak door*
* Huge, wooden door
* Solid oak door
* Ancient, oak door
* Low, ancient-looking door
* Metal gate
* Ornate, wrought iron doors
* *Large, brass handle*
* Iron hoop
* Heavy iron knocker
* Huge, black knocker in the shape of a lion's head
* Coat of arms
* *As the rusty lock . . .*
* Sudden gust of wind

PHRASES – VERBS

* ★ Studded with sharp, black nails
* ★ Carved with ancient symbols
* ★ Cast in the shape of a serpent's head
* ★ *Difficult to spot the door*
* ★ Stared intently at the wall
* ★ Spotted a crack, then a handle, then the shape of a door
* ★ *Blocked by a metal gate*
* ★ Faced by a low, ancient-looking door
* ★ Stretched across the entrance to the family tomb
* ★ Set deep in the wall
* ★ Towered above them
* ★ *Led to a door with stained-glass panels*
* ★ Led from the courtyard into the main part of the house
* ★ Opened out onto a vast, wood-panelled medieval hall
* ★ Opened onto a dark spiral staircase
* ★ *Rung the bell*
* ★ Knocked on the door
* ★ *Rattled in the wind*
* ★ Opened with an echoing thud
* ★ Before he could touch the handle, the door . . .
* ★ *Opened . . . slowly at first . . . then with more force*
* ★ Swung open slowly
* ★ Creaked and swung open behind her
* ★ Closed behind him with a thud as . . .

SENTENCES

In front of him was a huge wooden door studded with iron.

The squat wooden door opened onto a dark spiral staircase.

They went through a heavy, oak door, which led from the courtyard into the main part of the house.

Where the path ended, they were faced by a low, ancient-looking door studded with sharp, black nails.

The entrance to the graveyard was blocked by a metal gate carved with ancient symbols.

In the furthest corner, ornate, wrought iron doors stretched across the entrance to the family tomb; the coat of arms welded into the centre of the doors.

The front step was set deep in the wall and led to a huge door with elaborate, stained-glass panels of various battle scenes.

A huge, brass knocker cast in the shape of a serpent's head glinted from the wooden door.

SECTION 2 – INTERACTION

WORDS

Nouns	**Ground**, undergrowth, tree, branch, bushes, grass
	Gap, crack
	Path, fence, gate, courtyard, house, building, corner, edge, entrance, wall, window
	Door, frame, keyhole, key, bolts, handle, doorknob, hoop, ring, hinges
	Silence, sounds, noises, whispers, rustles, squawks, howl
	Darkness, shadow, light, torch
	Seconds, minutes, hours, eternity
	Senses, movement
	Pace, footing, direction
	Shoulder, hands, fingers, legs, knees, feet, haunches, head, ear, eye
Adjectives	**Old**, old-fashioned, ancient, rusty, worn-out
	Metal, silver, gold, iron
	Cautious, careful, tentative, nervous, stealthy, furtive
	Quiet, silent
	Alert, quick, fast, swift
	Shaking, trembling, quaking, flailing, floundering
	Terrifying
Verbs	**Found**, located, approached, ventured, emerged
	Climbed, clambered, hoisted, sprung, leaped, launched, vaulted, straddled, landed
	Crawled, crept, wriggled, slithered, crouched, huddled, rolled, writhed, dropped, dived, ducked
	Stopped, waited, paused, halted, hesitated, hovered, twitched, poised

Hugged, brushed, pressed

Moved, inched, edged, eased, stepped, shuffled

Slipped, shifted, skirted

Felt, touched

Looked, peered, peeped, craned, strained, searched, shone, checked

Reached, fumbled, groped, scrabbled, jerked

Pulled, tugged, yanked, turned, twisted, gripped, grasped, clutched, thrust

Opened, pushed, swung, slid, swished

Listened, heard, spoke, clicked, hissed, squeaked, rattled

Quickened, ran, sprinted, scampered, scurried

Adverbs **Cautiously**, carefully, gingerly, quietly

Quickly, swiftly

PHRASES – NOUNS AND ADJECTIVES

- For a few minutes
- *In the direction of . . .*
- Just to her left . . .
- To the side . . .
- Above the door . . .
- On the other side of . . .
- *Towards the house*
- Back of the building
- Wall straight ahead of them
- *As quickly and as quietly as possible*
- Like a panther
- Careful of their footing
- Nearly at a full run
- In one swift movement
- *Top of the wall*
- Side window
- Shadow of the courtyard
- *Through the undergrowth*
- Clumps of ivy
- Behind the tree
- Up a steep slope
- *Pitch black beyond*

- ☆ Flickering light in the darkness
- ☆ *Ancient handle*
- ☆ Iron hoop
- ☆ Rusty hinges
- ☆ Ring of old-fashioned keys

PHRASES – VERBS

- ☆ Made a stirrup with his hands
- ☆ Hoisted her up to the . . .
- ☆ *Climbed up the . . .*
- ☆ Sprung upwards
- ☆ Vaulted the fence
- ☆ Eased himself over . . .
- ☆ Clambered over . . .
- ☆ Leaped over the side of . . .
- ☆ Launched himself over the fence
- ☆ Poised to leap
- ☆ *Leapt down onto the . . .*
- ☆ Landed in a crouch
- ☆ Curled herself into a ball
- ☆ Rose up from his haunches
- ☆ *Crept to the wall on hands and knees*
- ☆ Crept cautiously through the derelict building
- ☆ Wriggled through the undergrowth
- ☆ Writhing and twisting, crawled through the gap in the walls
- ☆ *Inched closer*
- ☆ Inched towards the . . .
- ☆ Eased through the . . .
- ☆ Edged deeper into the darkness
- ☆ Felt her way along
- ☆ Felt his way cautiously
- ☆ Stepped carefully to avoid the slates that had been dislodged
- ☆ *Shuffled quickly sideways*
- ☆ Shuffled blindly in the direction of . . .
- ☆ Stepped gingerly to the edge of . . .
- ☆ *Moved in total silence*
- ☆ Spoke in whispers
- ☆ *Shone her torch*
- ☆ Checked what lay ahead with his torch
- ☆ Emerged from the shadow of the gateway
- ☆ *Halted at every rustle and squawk*
- ☆ Waited before he moved again

- ★ Waited a moment and then followed
- ★ Paused on the other side
- ★ Paused . . . nothing stirred . . . moved on
- ★ Paused frequently to listen for unnatural sounds
- ★ Began to move forward . . . paused again
- ★ Hesitated outside the entrance to the graveyard
- ★ For what seemed like an eternity
- ★ Listened underneath the window . . .
- ★ *Slipped around the side*
- ★ Shifted round the house to the front door
- ★ Moved to the corner of . . .
- ★ Approached the back of . . .
- ★ Skirted the rear of . . .
- ★ Hugged the wall
- ★ Brushed his shoulder against the walls
- ★ Pressed himself against the wall
- ★ Kept close to the shadows
- ★ *Peered inside*
- ★ Peered over the wall
- ★ Peered furtively around corners
- ★ Strained his neck to peer upwards
- ★ Craned their necks to see what was inside
- ★ Leaned forward just enough to see around the . . .
- ★ Peered cautiously round the corner
- ★ *Felt around for the window*
- ★ Parted the ivy
- ★ Probed deep inside with his fingers for the opening
- ★ Fumbled through vines of dead, leafless ivy
- ★ *Closed up behind him*
- ★ Kept contact with him by a hand on his shoulder
- ★ *Quickened their pace*
- ★ Crossed the lawn quickly
- ★ Sprinted around the corner
- ★ Scampered across the . . .
- ★ Scurried off round the . . .
- ★ Plunged through the gap
- ★ *Edged closer to the door*
- ★ Hovered outside the door
- ★ Ventured a step closer to the door. Then another . . .
- ★ *Stood at the heavy, oak door*
- ★ Turned and walked up to a wooden door
- ★ Twitched from one leg to the other
- ★ *Shifted the pile of crates*
- ★ Revealed an ancient-looking door set in the wall

* *Stood poised at the handle*
* Turned the knob
* Tugged on the handle
* Yanked on the handle
* Eased down the handle, a fraction at a time
* Took hold of the handle, paused, turned it swiftly and entered
* Reached out towards the door, hand shaking
* *Gave the door a cautious push*
* Eased the door open a crack
* Eased the door ajar
* Opened the door a couple of centimetres . . . opened it a bit more
* Let the door drift open slowly
* Swung open of its own accord
* Squeaked open
* Started to swing inwards
* *Stepped through the door*
* Slipped through the door into the darkness
* *Reached in his pocket*
* Took out a ring of old-fashioned keys
* *Reached out with a quaking hand*
* Reached out her hand to try the door
* Took hold of the handle, paused briefly before . . .
* *Grasped the iron hoop*
* Turned the knob, but hesitated to open the door
* *Waited a few minutes before going inside*
* Stepped through the door
* Edged through the doorway
* Ducked sideways
* *Put his foot on the first rung*
* Took his weight
* Climbed the ladder until he was level with the window
* *Eased open a wooden shutter*
* Peered gingerly through . . .
* Pushed the sash window upwards
* Slid his penknife into the gap and eased the window open
* *Climbed inside*
* Climbed through the gap
* Slid the window shut behind him

SENTENCES

Tom made a stirrup with his hands, took her weight and hoisted her up to the top of the wall surrounding the church.

She straddled the wall with ease, swinging her trailing leg over swiftly and landing on the other side nimbly and without a sound.

Senses fully alert, they backed away from the rambling old house, hunched over in a crouch and vaulted over the fence.

Writhing and twisting, Katie crawled through the gap in the hedge and was faced by a row of moss-covered headstones.

They crept cautiously through the long row of stone pillars, which was all that was left of the ancient cloister, and eventually found the entrance to where the ruins of the church had once stood.

Tom waited for a moment and then followed. He peeped around the corner of the building. There was no one there. No sign of the ghostly figure. It had vanished into thin air.

Staying close to the walls, Tom edged round the house, stepping carefully to avoid the slates that had been dislodged from the roof. He paused for a moment . . . nothing stirred . . . moved closer to the main entrance, paused again to listen again for any unnatural sounds, then sprinted across the courtyard, and dived behind a wall for cover.

Pressing himself against the wall, he made his way towards the window where he had caught a glimpse of a black gap where the glass had cracked or shattered.

Katie skirted the rear of the outbuilding, hugging the shadows, peering furtively around corners and halting at every rustle.

Quickly rolling onto her side, Katie strained her neck upwards to peer through the stained-glass window.

He came to the corner and cautiously peered around it, not knowing what he was going to find on the other side.

Keeping low, Tom scampered across the courtyard to the door where two enormous stone statues guarded the entrance either side of the door.

She fumbled through vines of dead, leafless ivy for a door knob. When she eventually found the knob and turned it, the whole lock came away from the rotten socket and her wrist plunged through the gap.

The whole of the side of the house was wrapped in thick ivy. He had to feel around for the window, parting the ivy and probing deep inside with his fingers for the opening.

He pulled away the ivy and pushed open the old wooden door of the cabin.

Standing at the heavy, oak door, Tom shivered. In the centre of the door was a huge knocker, shaped like a lion's head. Twitching from one leg to the other, he couldn't make up his mind whether he should ring the bell or use the huge knocker.

He took out a ring of old-fashioned keys.

The ancient oak door had a massive black iron lock, cast in the shape of a serpent's head. He held the key in the palm of his hand for a moment, staring at the matching serpent's head.

She turned the knob, but hesitated to open the door.

She ventured a step closer to the door. Then another.

He reached out with a quaking hand, but before he could touch the handle, the door swung open of its own accord.

Turning the handle, he gave the door a cautious push, waited a few minutes and then went inside.

She eased down the handle a fraction at a time; stopped a moment and listened. The rusty hinges hadn't squeaked. She opened it a bit more, unsure of what she would discover inside.

SECTION 3 – REACTION

WORDS	

Nouns	**Tragedy**, disaster, secrets, sadness, despair
	Danger, trouble, presence, shadows, force
	Tingle, prickle
	Fear, dread, horror, terror, panic, urge
	Courage, resolve, determination
	Mind, thoughts, feeling, sense, sensation, urge, logic, imagination
	Nerves, muscles, skin, sweat
	Neck, back, spine, legs, hands, palms, fingers, nails
	Heart, veins, chest, throat, breath, mouth, lips
	Look, glance, eyes, eyebrows
	Breath, gasp, murmur, whisper, whine, groan, sob
	Shudder, shiver, goosebumps

Similes/ Metaphors	**Like an electric shock**, a tornado of thoughts and ideas
Adjectives	**Cautious**, nervous, anxious, alert
	Urgent, desperate
	Tingling, prickling, spider-like, pulsing, pounding, thumping, thudding
	Cold, ice-cold, icy, chilly, hollow, tight, aching
	Huge, yawning, deep, raw, sharp, ragged, jagged, shuddering, suffocating
	Numb, silent, muted, muffled, jumbled, incoherent
	Wide, blue, brown, grey
	Dark, dangerous, threatening, malignant, ominous, menacing
Verbs	**Tensed**, warned, urged, screamed
	Forced, willed, fought, mustered
	Moved, started, prickled, crawled, shot, tore, ran, raced, leaped, erupted, surged, filled
	Churned, pounded, thudded, hammered, slammed
	Looked, glanced, checked, strained, watched
	Swallowed, smothered, covered, clamped, silenced, breathed in, sucked, caught, held, opened, blew out, escaped
	Sank, lowered, trailed off, whispered, gasped, muttered, yelled
	Startled, jumped, jerked, reeled
	Shivered, trembled, shook, quivered, shuddered
	Shrank back, backed away, ran, fled
	Bit, gnawed
Adverbs	**Quickly**, cautiously, furtively, nervously

PHRASES – NOUNS AND ADJECTIVES

* ★ For no apparent reason
* ★ After a moment . . .
* ★ *Out of the corner of her eye . . .*
* ★ To his right . . .
* ★ *Tingling sensation*

- ☆ An eerie sensation
- ☆ A tingling sixth sense
- ☆ Distinct feeling
- ☆ Feeling of unease
- ☆ Alert to any danger
- ☆ Sadness and despair
- ☆ Sense of something ominous, menacing
- ☆ Sense of a threatening, malignant presence
- ☆ *A slow chill*
- ☆ A cold, spider-like sensation
- ☆ Ice-cold shiver
- ☆ Cold thought
- ☆ An icy dread
- ☆ *Every muscle in his body*
- ☆ Every nerve in her body
- ☆ Skin on the back of his neck
- ☆ *Surge of adrenalin*
- ☆ A trickle of sweat
- ☆ *Hollow feeling*
- ☆ Tight knot in the pit of her stomach
- ☆ Nervous swallow
- ☆ *Like a startled owl*

PHRASES – VERBS

- ☆ As night approached and the shadows lengthened . . .
- ☆ As soon as he had entered the . . .
- ☆ As if she was being pulled into something dark and dangerous
- ☆ Like an invisible thread was pulling him towards the house
- ☆ Warned him he was walking into trouble
- ☆ Screamed at him to get out
- ☆ Gripped by an urge to turn and run
- ☆ Fought an underlying sense of panic
- ☆ *Looked up at the . . . and got the weirdest feeling*
- ☆ Had the distinct feeling he was being watched
- ☆ Felt as if there were eyes everywhere
- ☆ Felt it was full of dark secrets
- ☆ Felt as if it had been destroyed by tragedy
- ☆ Trapped in its wall, cemented into the fabric of the building, locked behind its door
- ☆ *Summoned him like a dark, unblinking eye*
- ☆ Before he knew what he was doing . . .
- ☆ Willed himself to move
- ☆ Fought back the urge to flee

* Mustered up the courage and . . .
* Seemed to move of their own accord
* *Shot through her*
* Crawled down his spine
* Prickled as he approached the entrance
* *Broke out on his upper lip*
* Broke out on her palms
* Rubbed them dry on her trousers
* *Heart pounded*
* Leaped in her chest like a wild salmon
* Reeled as she stared at the door
* *Held her breath*
* Sucked in a breath
* Let out a shallow gasp
* Forced herself to breathe slowly
* *Made him look sharply backwards*
* Looked nervously round every corner
* Checked nervously over her shoulder
* Glanced round nervously as he heard . . .
* Flickered from side to side
* Scanned the windows
* Searched for any sign of movement
* *Flickered across her face*
* Betrayed her nervousness
* *Lowered her voice*
* Sank to a murmur
* (voice) trailed off as she realised what lay ahead
* Covered her mouth
* Whispered through her fingers
* Hesitated just before she reached the door

SENTENCES

A tight knot in the pit of her stomach warned Gail she was walking into trouble. Shuddering, she fought back the urge to flee.

The skin on the back of his neck prickled as he approached the entrance. The place felt evil. It was the type of place that made people quicken their step as they passed.

He sensed that something was wrong here. Very wrong. Why had he come? Was it too late to turn back?

She looked up at the dark, unblinking eyes of the Tudor mansion and she got the weirdest feeling – a feeling of unease and a sense of a threatening, malignant presence.

The skin on the back of his neck prickled as he approached the entrance. The place felt evil.

It was as if she was being pulled into something dark and dangerous by a hand she couldn't see, and couldn't stop even if she wanted to.

Something urged him on. Every nerve in his body screamed at him to get away. But before he knew what he was doing, his legs seemed to move of their own accord, and he edged towards the front door.

The broken door summoned him like a dark, unblinking eye.

Gripped by an urge to turn and run, he knew he couldn't. It was like an invisible thread was pulling him towards the house.

A cold, spider-like sensation crawled down her spine. The prickling sensation moved to her fingers. She felt a cold sweat break out above her upper lip.

As a surge of adrenalin shot through her, every nerve in Katie's body was on high alert.

Even though he knew that the building had been deserted for some time, Tom had the distinct feeling they were being watched from one of the upper windows. Sweat broke out on the palms of his hands and he had to keep rubbing them dry on his trousers.

He glanced round nervously as he heard the snap of a twig behind him. His eyes flickered from side to side and he lowered his voice.

His voice trailed off as he realised what lay ahead.

Cautiously, she reached out towards the door, her hand shaking and adrenalin surging through her veins.

5
Buildings (inside)

The staircase was dark and gloomy, and spiralled steeply upwards. Andrew was unable to see even the part that went straight up ahead of him, so there was no way of knowing what waited for him at the top.

Slowly, he started to ascend the narrow stairs, but every step Andrew took was followed by a creaking echo. **No matter how hard he tried to control the creeping terror spreading through him, his eyes widened and his body jerked at every noise. Goosebumps riddled his body** as the torchlight flickered unsteadily, casting dancing, flickering shadows in front of him. **He began to imagine something hideous in every shadow.**

Something brushed against his hand; **his heart lurched**. With his right hand, he swatted the air in front of him. His flailing hand became caught up in a curtain of cobwebs that dangled from the ceiling.

Startled, he dropped the torch, which clattered to the ground; the light flickered and died, leaving him shrouded in darkness.

SECTION 1 – SETTING

WORDS

Nouns	**Entrance**, hall, hallway, corridor, passage, galleries, landing, maze, warren
	Steps, stairs, staircase
	Room, attic, lounge, sitting room, dining room, library, study, cellar, basement, tomb, crypt, vault, chamber, archways, alcoves

Walls, shelf, wallpaper, painting, portraits, lords, eyes, tapestry, battle scene, mirror, reflection

Call-bells, speaking-tube, telephone, dinner gong

Floor, floorboards, carpet, rug, iron ring

Ceiling, rafters, beams

Fireplace, mantelpiece, furniture, dining table, bookcases, wardrobe, cupboard, chests, four-poster bed, grandfather clock, lantern clock, suits of armour, breastplates, shields, swords, bayonets, stuffed birds and animals, stag's head, antlers

Skeleton, skull, coffins

Darkness, gloom, shadows, silhouette

Shapes

Light, glow, lamps, candle, oil lamps, brazier, torch, bulbs, chandelier

Bats, spider, owl

Dust, dirt, grime, cobwebs

Silence, sound, noises, echo, whisper, rustle, creak, groan

Wind, breeze, draught, gust

Similes/ Metaphors	**Like a medieval knight's hall**, like an upturned boat, like dusty muslin curtains
Adjectives	**Narrow**, small, long, garret

Large, big, vast, huge, enormous, high, wide

Impressive, grand, magnificent, ornate, arched, intricately carved, ornamented, polished, gleaming

Stained, leaded, diamond-leaded, translucent

Winding, twisting, spiral, straight

Marble, stone, brass, gold, silver, wooden, mahogany, wood-panelled, oak, oak-panelled, oak-beamed

Wall-mounted, floor-to-ceiling, high-beamed

Old, antique, ancient

Cold, icy, bitter, draughty

Secretive, forbidding, oppressive

Weak, patchy, flecked, slanting, dim, dimly lit, gloomy, eerie, dark, black

Dusty, bare, empty, echoing, creaking, musty

Torn, broken, peeling, threadbare, rotten

Assorted, watchful, faded, long-forgotten

Verbs

Led, went, ran, stretched, faced with, passed, opened onto, ended at

Twisted, turned, curled, wound, spiralled, swept down

Dotted around, lined, filled, piled high, spread, covered, carpeted, draped

Saw, noticed, made out, picked out, looked like, stared down, gazed down, appeared

Hung, clung, dangled, swung, stood, supported, thrust

Moved, went, entered, stood, sat

Shadowed, steeped, shrouded, filtered, entered through, smeared by

Lit, glowed, poured into, pierced, glittered, shimmered

Danced, flickered, whirled, spun, swirled, rushed, billowed, leaped

Sounded, echoed, rushed, tore, rattled, creaked, squeaked, scratched, grunted, crashed, slammed

Swooped, scurried, scuffled

PHRASES – NOUNS AND ADJECTIVES

- ★ *A long night*
- ★ At first, he . . .
- ★ A moment's pause, then . . .
- ★ Minutes afterwards . . .
- ★ *Close to the house* . . .
- ★ Somewhere in the house . . .
- ★ In each of the corners . . .
- ★ In the far corner . . .
- ★ All the stairs and corners
- ★ *An impressive room*
- ★ Like going back in time to medieval England
- ★ *Beside it* . . .
- ★ By the side of the fireplace . . .
- ★ *On the top floor* . . .

* In the cellar . . .
* In the middle of the stairway . . .
* *Over her head . . .*
* Outside the room . . .
* *Arched entrances*
* Intricately carved archways
* Two rows of empty alcoves
* *A dark flight of stairs ahead*
* Stone steps
* Wooden, spiral stairs
* Narrow garret staircase
* Wide staircase
* Grand staircase
* Ornately carved, oak staircase
* Small landing
* *High ceiling*
* Ancient ceiling
* Imposing high-beamed ceiling
* *Gleaming oak panelling*
* Polished wooden floor
* Wooden floorboards
* *Small and leaded window-panes*
* Flecked, translucent leaded panes of glass
* *Narrow, gloomy hallway*
* Vast, echoing, entrance hall
* Long straight hallway
* Long corridor lined with paintings
* Narrow, oak-panelled corridor
* Two rows of small black doors
* *Low, oak-beamed room*
* High, arched room like a medieval knight's hall
* *Dark mahogany furniture*
* Antique four-poster bed
* Vast oak dining table
* Old oak chests
* Tall grandfather clock
* Ornate, wall-mounted lantern clock
* *An antique, brass speaking-tube*
* Ancient box of call-bells and wires
* Antique brass dinner gong
* Stacks of old, dusty packing cases
* Rows full of old family portraits
* Dark rectangle where a picture . . .
* Gloomy old portraits

* Watchful eyes of assorted members of . . .
* Huge tapestry of a battle
* Ornamented breastplates of a suit of armour
* Glass cases of stuffed birds and animals
* *Torn curtain*
* Threadbare carpet
* Cloud of dust
* Dead, musty smell
* Rotten with age
* Holes in the rotting boards
* *Enormously large chandelier*
* Flickering oil lamps
* *Secretive places*
* Place of shadows and whispers
* Only sign of life . . .
* Oppressive stillness of the house
* As if a black cloud . . .
* As a shaft of moonlight . . .
* In the dim light . . .
* Difficult at first to . . .
* Shadows in the room
* Dark and gloomy
* Dark and forbidding
* Thick, eerie darkness
* Just visible in the gloom was . . .
* Murky finger of light
* Only a gloomy light
* Weak and patchy light
* Dim light from the chandelier
* *Draughty corridor*
* Draughty, stone passages
* Icy breeze
* Bitter wind
* *Eerily empty and silent*
* Not even the whispering creaks and groans of a house at night
* *Creak of the stairs*
* Creaking echo
* Slight click
* More scuffling – then silence
* Like a ghostly echo behind her
* Tiptoe of a footstep in the passage
* Faint movement of the floorboards
* Like fingernails clawing at stone
* Movement at the door like a scratching mouse

⋆ Faint scratching noises inside the walls
⋆ Sound of a door . . .

⋆ *Appeared that no one had . . .*
⋆ Lived in the house for some time
⋆ *Entered a narrow hallway*
⋆ Entered a vast, entrance hall
⋆ Faced with a long, dimly-lit corridor
⋆ Stretched in front of him was . . .
⋆ Opened onto a long corridor
⋆ Found himself in a long, narrow corridor
⋆ Ran underneath the house
⋆ Wound like a maze
⋆ Ended at a low door
⋆ *Moved through chill corridors, through galleries*
⋆ Stood in the middle of the room
⋆ Had never been in that room before
⋆ *As he moved further into the room . . .*
⋆ As they stood on the top of the steps . . .
⋆ When he went through the door . . .
⋆ When he looked up . . .
⋆ As the door was shut . . .
⋆ *Waited until his eyes adjusted to the gloom*
⋆ Started to pick out . . .
⋆ Made out a few items of furniture
⋆ Noticed that there was . . .
⋆ Noticed that a few of the alcoves contained . . .
⋆ *Dotted around the room*
⋆ Filled with antique furniture
⋆ Piled high with . . .
⋆ Covered in white sheets
⋆ *Supported by a magnificent oak beam*
⋆ Dangled on long chains from the beams
⋆ Swung from side to side
⋆ *Lined the wood-panelled walls*
⋆ Lined in dark panelled wood
⋆ Covered the walls along the corridor
⋆ Covered the entire wall
⋆ Covered with floor-to-ceiling bookcases
⋆ Draped with tapestries
⋆ Lined with faded portraits of forgotten lords

- ★ Stared down at him as he passed
- ★ Gazed down on them
- ★ *Used to summon the servants*
- ★ Hanging beside it was . . .
- ★ Sat at the foot of the stairs
- ★ *Led up to the first floor*
- ★ Leading up to the attic was . . .
- ★ Led directly from the great hall
- ★ Descended into the darkness
- ★ *Twisted and turned sharply*
- ★ Swept dramatically down to the entrance hall
- ★ Curled upwards
- ★ Changed direction at every corner
- ★ Spiralled up to the top of the house
- ★ Wound around and down
- ★ Descended a wide spiral staircase of ancient stone
- ★ *Could not see what waited for her at the top*
- ★ Made it impossible to see down into the basement
- ★ *Steeped in a thick, eerie darkness*
- ★ Shrouded in darkness
- ★ Made the candle dance and flicker
- ★ Sent shadows whirling around the walls
- ★ Lit by early morning light
- ★ Lit only by two lamps in opposite corners
- ★ Dimly lit by table lamps
- ★ Pierced the gloom
- ★ Swung his torch from side to side . . .
- ★ Bathed in a strange light
- ★ Flickered as if the bulbs were coming to the end of their days
- ★ Filtered through into the room
- ★ Entered through the slanting windows in the roof
- ★ Smeared by layers of dust and grime
- ★ Covered with a layer of crawling damp and mould
- ★ Glittered above the . . .
- ★ *Covered in cobwebs*
- ★ Shimmered with cobwebs
- ★ Spun a web from a broken pane of glass
- ★ Hung from the walls
- ★ Hung across one of the upstairs windows
- ★ Draped with cobweb curtains
- ★ Hung everywhere like dusty muslin curtains
- ★ *Leaped and danced*
- ★ Billowed in the sudden breeze
- ★ Swirled in the breeze coming from the closed window

- ★ *Showed on the ceiling*
- ★ Spread from the ground
- ★ Stretched from every surface
- ★ Carpeted the floor
- ★ Covered in a carpet of dust
- ★ *Thrust a tendril to the sill*
- ★ Smelt of damp and mildew
- ★ *Gnawed great holes in the floor*
- ★ Lay the bleached bones of a rat
- ★ *Sounded above her*
- ★ Came from the hallway
- ★ . . . could be heard
- ★ Listened to . . .
- ★ Heard voices and scuffling, then grunting
- ★ Noise of the latch lifting gently and then let fall again
- ★ Tore through the draughty corridors
- ★ Rattled the windows
- ★ Followed by a creaking echo
- ★ Made hollow noises
- ★ Echoed on the floorboards
- ★ Creaked as she moved across to the window
- ★ Rattled in their frames
- ★ Shrieked in warning
- ★ *Brushed against the windows*
- ★ Swooped down from the rafters
- ★ Scurried across the wall
- ★ Rushed towards her
- ★ Hit by a flurry of wings, talons, and a curved beak

SENTENCES

The stained glass door opened out onto a vast, wood-panelled medieval hall.

As the walls in the house were all of dark oak panelling, it was difficult to spot the doors. But as she stared intently at the wall, suddenly she spotted a crack, then a handle, and then the shape of the door.

The handle turned. Slowly at first. Then with more force as the rusty lock creaked and groaned.

The wide staircase swept dramatically down to the entrance hall.

The wooden stairs spiralled their way to the rooms upstairs.

Through the door, he could just make out a flight of stairs.

The spiral stairs twisted and turned sharply, changing direction at every corner.

He climbed up the winding stairs and went through a high, arched room like a medieval knight's hall.

From there, a narrow, garret staircase led right up to the top of the house, where a low, dusty, oak-beamed room nestled under the roof. It was obvious from the dust and cobwebs that no one had been that way for a very long time.

He had entered a narrow hallway, and ahead of him was a flight of stairs leading up to the first floor.

The staircase was dark and gloomy and every step she took was followed by a creaking echo.

The staircase spiralled steeply upwards. She was unable to see even the part that went straight up ahead of her, so there was no way of knowing what waited for her at the top.

Stone steps led down into the darkness, which curved away, making it impossible for them to see right down into the basement.

The door opened onto a long, dimly-lit corridor.

The corridor ended at a low door.

The passage wound around and down.

A long corridor stretched out in front of them.

She was faced with a long corridor, steeped in a thick, eerie darkness.

A narrow corridor led to the main hall where a grand staircase curled upwards. A tall grandfather clock sat at the foot of the stairs.

The corridors were long and lined with paintings.

The passages wound like a maze, and he followed them blindly, searching desperately for the stairs.

A bitter wind tore through the draughty corridors and rattled the windows.

As they stood on the top of the steps, a cold draught rushed up to them, making the candle dance and flicker, sending shadows whirling around the walls.

The tomb was shrouded in darkness. Just visible in the gloom, stretched in front of him, were two rows of empty alcoves. As he moved further into the chamber, he noticed that a few of the alcoves contained decaying coffins. Brass plates announced the identity of the residents.

She waited in the long, narrow passage on the top floor. With its two rows of small black doors all shut, it was like a corridor in some medieval castle.

In the cellar, there was a long corridor that stretched underneath the house, off which arched entrances led to various chambers. In the dim light it was difficult at first to see what they contained.

It was dark. He waited until his eyes adjusted to the gloom. Gradually, he started to pick out a few shapes dotted around the room.

As a shaft of moonlight pierced the gloom, he made out a few items of furniture covered in white sheets.

He swung his torch from side to side as he moved through chill corridors, through galleries lined with faded portraits of forgotten lords that stared down at him as he passed.

The attic was filled with antique furniture and stacks of old, dusty packing cases and chests.

Old oak chests were dotted around the room.

An antique four-poster bed stood in the middle of the room.

On the wall was an ancient box of call-bells and wires that had been used to summon the servants.

By the side of the fireplace was an antique, brass speaking-tube.

Rows of family portraits covered the walls along the corridor, but she noticed that there was one dark rectangle where a picture had obviously once hung.

The watchful eyes of assorted members of the Stevenson family gazed down on them from the gloomy old portraits that lined the wood-panelled walls.

A huge tapestry of a battle covered the entire wall. Beside it, there was a big dinner gong, its leather stick still dangling beside it.

When she opened the door, a cold draught rushed towards her. She had never been in this room before. It was like going back in time to medieval England. The walls were draped with tapestries and the high ceiling was supported by a magnificent oak beam.

The ancient ceiling looked like an upturned boat. Flickering oil lamps dangled on long chains from the beams.

In each of the corners, glittered the ornamented breastplates of a magnificent suit of armour.

The marble shelf was piled high with glass cases of stuffed birds and animals. Mounted on the walls were enormous stag's heads.

The big house was dusty and bare. All the stairs and corners were secretive places, covered in cobwebs. A place of shadows and whispers.

The old house was dark and forbidding. The only sign of life was a torn curtain hanging across one of the upstairs windows.

It appeared that no one had lived in the house for some time. The wallpaper was torn and peeling, the carpet threadbare, the lights shimmering with cobwebs, and a cloud of dust hung over everything.

The beams were draped with cobweb curtains that billowed in the sudden breeze.

Cobwebs hung everywhere like dusty muslin curtains.

A great black spider had spun a web from a broken pane of glass, while ivy, spreading up from the ground, thrust a tendril to the sill. In the far corner lay the bleached bones of a rat.

The ladder leading up to the attic was rotten with age, and rats had gnawed great holes in the floor.

Bats swooped down from the rafters. Cobwebs clung to his mouth and nose. A huge black spider scurried across the wall.

The stillness of the house was oppressive, as if a black cloud had descended over the building.

Not even the whispering creaks and groans of a house at night could be heard.

The floor made hollow noises and had jagged holes in it where the boards had rotted.

The wooden floorboards creaked as she moved across to the window, but like a ghostly echo, seconds after she trod on them.

A slight click came from the hallway, and when he looked up, the cellar door opened by itself.

The window-panes were small and leaded, and rattled in their frames.

Distantly, an owl called once, then again.

A bat brushed against the windows, and close to the house an owl shrieked in warning.

The room was dark, lit only by two lamps in opposite corners.

The dim light from the chandelier flickered as if the bulbs were coming to the end of their days.

The light that entered through the slanting windows in the roof was weak and patchy. Over the years, the windows in the roof of the attic had been smeared by layers of dust and grime.

SECTION 2 – INTERACTION

WORDS	
Nouns	**Staircase**, stairwell, stairs, steps, floorboards
	Corridor, passage, galleries, hall, hallway, room
	Portraits, bells

	Light, torch, candle, shadows, darkness
	Chest, knees, legs, feet, chest, arms, hands, ears, balance
Similes/ Metaphors	**Like a metal detector**, as if to ward off the cold
Adjectives	**Corpse-like**, frozen, motionless
	Careful, cautious, stealthy
	Fast, quick, swift
Verbs	**Found**, located
	Stood, waited, paused, hesitated, hovered, leaned
	Paralysed, rooted
	Sat, crouched, huddled
	Pulled, drew, hugged
	Peered, peeked, craned, looked, watched, searched
	Listened, strained, heard, clicked, hissed, swished, squeaked, rattled, thumped, crashed, slammed
	Moved, entered, followed, crossed
	Stepped, trod, walked, edged, inched, slipped, crept, crawled, scrambled, ducked, dived, flattened
	Climbed, ascended, descended
	Avoided, evaded
	Eased, pushed, opened, lifted, turned, swung, jammed
	Felt, spread, waved, swatted, pressed, jerked, yanked, hammered, pounded
	Ran, raced, darted, bolted
	Skidded, stumbled, fell, dropped, flew, tumbled, smashed, clattered

PHRASES – NOUNS AND ADJECTIVES

★ Just to her left
★ To the side . . .
★ Above the door . . .
★ *With his right hand, he . . .*
★ With a shaking hand . . .

- ✭ Flailing hand
- ✭ *In the darkness ...*
- ✭ Pitch black beyond
- ✭ Flickering light in the darkness
- ✭ Hidden by the staircase
- ✭ *To the front door*
- ✭ Towards the room from which the light ...
- ✭ Down chilly corridors
- ✭ Through galleries lined with ...
- ✭ Over the ground in front of her
- ✭ *Nearly at the top of the stairs when ...*
- ✭ *Faded portraits of forgotten lords*
- ✭ Chorus of clanging bells

PHRASES – VERBS

- ✭ As quietly as she could ...
- ✭ *Without being seen*
- ✭ *Waited on the stairs*
- ✭ Paused at the top of the stairs
- ✭ Sat down on the steps
- ✭ Huddled in the darkness underneath the stairs
- ✭ Couldn't move from the bottom of the stairs
- ✭ Rooted to the spot
- ✭ Sat, corpse-like, frozen and motionless
- ✭ Couldn't move – her feet were glued to the floor
- ✭ *Drew her knees up against her chest*
- ✭ Hugged her knees against her chest as if to ward off the cold
- ✭ *Peered down*
- ✭ Peered through the open doors
- ✭ Watched the hall below
- ✭ *Listened at each of the doors*
- ✭ Listened for any sound that might reveal its location
- ✭ *Crawled under the first flight of steps*
- ✭ Crept stealthily forwards
- ✭ Crept out into the passage
- ✭ Stumbled towards the light
- ✭ Crept down the dark, icy passage
- ✭ Trod carefully down the corridor
- ✭ Moved cautiously down the ...
- ✭ Started to ascend the stairs slowly
- ✭ Avoided the creaky floorboards
- ✭ Counted every step as she descended slowly

- *Put his foot on the first rung*
- Took his weight
- Climbed the ladder until he was level with the attic
- *Moved slowly across the hall*
- Inched his way to the corner of the landing
- Edged closer to the door
- *Shifted the pile of crates*
- Revealed an ancient-looking door set in the wall
- *Turned and walked up to a wooden door*
- Leaned closer and put his ear to the door
- Put his eye to the crack
- Put her eye to the narrow gap between the hinges
- Craned their necks to see what was inside
- *Stood poised at the handle*
- Before he could touch the handle . . .
- Just in time to see her bedroom door . . .
- Reached out towards the door, hand shaking
- Turned the knob
- Tugged on the handle
- Eased down the handle, a fraction at a time
- Took hold of the handle, paused
- Turned the handle swiftly and entered the room
- *Gave the door a cautious push*
- Eased the door open a crack
- Eased the door ajar
- Let the door drift open slowly
- Opened the door a couple of centimetres . . . opened it a bit more
- *Stepped through the door*
- Slipped through the door into the darkness
- Moved fast and dashed inside
- Ducked sideways through the door
- *Jammed a piece of paper in the hinge*
- Prevented the door closing fully
- *Used his torch to guide him*
- Flew out of his hand
- Clattered on the ground
- Flickered and died
- Left him shrouded in darkness
- *Spread her arms*
- Thrust his arm out in front of him
- Used their outstretched hands to guide them
- Ran it along the wall until he located the light switch
- Felt for the next step
- Felt for the wood of the bottom stair

- As she turned . . .
- Waved her arms like a metal detector
- Moved his hands wildly in front of him
- Swatted the air in front of him
- *Pulled the door shut*
- Hammered on all the doors
- *Skidded on the wooden floor*
- Lost his balance
- Fell backwards
- Tumbled backwards
- Managed to keep his feet for a couple of steps
- Smashed against the bottom step
- *Ran in a blind panic*
- Scrambled to her feet
- Found her legs again and ran
- Crossed the hall quickly
- Darted down the corridor
- Raced down the corridor
- Took the stairs two at a time

SENTENCES

She waited on the stairs, sitting down carefully, drawing her knees up against her chest so she could watch the hall below without being seen.

She sat down on the steps, hugging her knees against her chest as if to ward off the cold.

He huddled in the darkness, listening for any sound that might reveal where it was.

She couldn't move. It was as if someone had glued her feet to the floor.

She paused at the top of the stairs, peering down, trying to control the creeping terror that was spreading through her.

He put his foot on the first rung of the rickety, wooden ladder. It held his weight. Carefully, he tested the next rung. It creaked but didn't break. Rung by rung, he ascended the ladder, testing each one as he went until he was level with the entrance to the attic.

She crept out into the passage and approached the door cautiously.

She crept down the dark, icy passage and listened at each of the doors.

Using his torch to guide him, he moved cautiously down the chilly corridors, through galleries lined with faded portraits of forgotten lords.

She crawled behind the curtains so that she was hidden from sight.

She crept stealthily forwards, her hands clenched into tight fists.

Treading carefully down the corridor, avoiding the creaky floorboards, hardly daring to breathe, she peered into the rooms through the open doors.

She counted every step as she descended slowly, feeling her way for the next step in the dark.

Slowly, he started to ascend the stairs. His heart lurched as something brushed against his hand. With his right hand, he swatted the air in front of him.

As she turned, the darkness seemed to envelop the stairs, and she had to spread her arms and feel for the wood of the bottom stair, crouching and waving her arms like a metal detector over the ground in front of her.

He was nearly at the top of the stairs. Suddenly, he fell backwards, managed to keep his feet for a couple of steps, but eventually lost his balance and tumbled backwards, smashing against the bottom step.

She stumbled towards the light, the passage leading her on and on.

She was determined not to let her unease get the better of her, so she raced across the hall and up the staircase towards the room from which the light had been shining.

Trembling, she pressed an ear to the smooth wood.

She paused outside the door, put her ear to the door, listening for a moment. Nothing. Then, with a shaking hand, she reached for the doorknob.

Leaning closer, Katie put her ear to the door. Nothing. She tugged on the handle and slipped through the door into the room.

He thrust his hand out in front of him, and ran it along the wall until he located the light switch.

Tom jammed a piece of paper into the hinge to stop the door closing fully.

He was so startled that the torch flew out of his hand and clattered to the ground. The light flickered and died, leaving him shrouded in darkness.

SECTION 3 – REACTION

WORDS

Nouns	**Mind**, thoughts, logic, imagination, anticipation
	Feeling, sense, sensation, awareness, certainty
	Questions, reason, answers
	Tension, unease, dread, fear, terror, horror, foreboding, premonition

Evil, danger, warning

Presence

Body, bones, limbs, spine, back, nerves, skin, hair, scalp, roots

Sweat, shiver, chill, tingle, goosebumps, shudder

Head, forehead, neck, face, eyes, eyebrows, nose, throat, mouth, tongue, lips

Heart, veins, pulse, blood, breath, chest, ribs

Legs, feet, toes, hands, palms, fists, fingers, nails

Gasp, whine, groan, sob, scream, shriek, howl, yell

Similes/ Metaphors	**Like an electric current**, bolts of electricity, tornado of thoughts and ideas, like a tidal wave of terror, like a cold skeletal hand, like a wintry breeze, vaporous tentacles, as cold as the freezing air
Adjectives	**Cold**, chilly, icy, bitter, aching
	Hideous, repulsive, ghastly, monstrous, grotesque, gruesome, grisly
	Rigid, tense, stiff, frozen, stock-still
	Terrified, petrified, fearful, panic-stricken, horror-struck
	Deep, raw, sharp, jagged, ragged, shuddering, suffocating
	Numb, muted, muffled, silent
	Pulsing, pounding, thudding, thumping
	Unsteady, shaky, unstable, wobbly
	Desperate, agitated, feverish
	Huge, yawning, high-pitched, piercing, sharp, shrill
	Jumbled, incoherent
	Wide, blue, brown, grey
Verbs	**Felt**, was aware, sensed, warned, urged, screamed
	Knew, expected, prepared, steeled
	Waited, hesitated, paused, stopped, paralysed
	Buzzed, pulsed, stirred, broke out, crept, pinched, trickled, prickled, tingled
	Clawed, gripped, thudded, pounded, hammered, slammed, spread, raced, riddled

Heard, woke

Startled, jumped, leapt, jerked, reeled, shook, trembled, shivered, shuddered, quivered, quaked

Shut, squeezed, clamped, flew open, snapped open

Looked, gazed, glanced, peered, swept, scanned, searched, watched, settled, stared, glued

Breathed in, sucked in, took, caught, held, silenced

Blew out, escaped, gasped, muttered, murmured, whispered, sobbed, cried, yelled, screamed

Bit, chewed, gnawed, rubbed, clenched, clutched

Flailed, floundered, waved, swatted

PHRASES – NOUNS AND ADJECTIVES

- *Out of the corner of her eye . . .*
- *Through the gap in the door . . .*
- Just outside the door . . .
- To his right . . .
- Open door to the basement
- Creak of the stairs
- Faint movement of the floorboards
- *For no apparent reason . . .*
- No obvious reason for his fear
- Fear of the long, dark corridor to his room
- *Strange sensation*
- An odd feeling
- Sense of foreboding
- Growing awareness of impending evil
- Quivering dread of a grisly presence
- *An icy dread*
- Cold thought
- Chilly feeling
- Cold sweat
- An aching cold
- Like a cold, skeletal hand
- *Every nerve in her body*
- Hairs on the back of his arms
- Bolts of electricity
- Like a tidal wave of terror
- Pulsing, pounding tornado of thoughts and fears
- More afraid than she had ever been in her life

* Rigid with tension
* *Wide, blue eyes*
* Wide with horror
* *Muted whine of terror*

PHRASES – VERBS

* Imagination had got the better of her logic
* Premonition that something bad was about to happen
* *Determined not to let her unease get the better of her*
* Tried to ignore the fear he had never felt before
* Tried to control the creeping terror spreading through her
* *Steeled herself*
* Tried to calm his jagged nerves
* Tried to calm her thumping heart
* Shook his numb senses to life
* Needed to clear his head – needed to think clearly
* Prepared to descend the stairs to the cellar
* *Warned him not to climb the stairs*
* Urged him to run
* Screamed at her to get out of the house
* *Could feel the hair stirring on his scalp*
* Tingling with anticipation
* Broke out at the roots of his hair
* Shot up her spine
* Ran down her body
* Sweating despite the chilly air in the passage
* Felt an icy chill crawl up her spine
* Erupted from her skin
* Filled with iced water
* Started at his toes and fingers
* Moved up into his chest and throat
* Prickled as a light breeze drifted through the door
* *Started to shiver*
* Aware that his hand was shaking
* Riddled her body
* *Jumped when she heard …*
* Jumped out of her skin
* Jumped at the slightest sound
* Drowning in her fear
* Startled him like an electric shock
* Couldn't have turned if she had wanted to
* Didn't want to know what was behind her

- ★ Jumped every time the stairs creaked under her feet
- ★ Expected to see something hideous in every shadow
- ★ Unsure of what she would discover inside
- ★ *Hammered in her chest*
- ★ Started to thud in her chest
- ★ Pounded in her ears
- ★ Thudded against his ribs
- ★ Reeled as he stared at the door
- ★ Slammed in his chest
- ★ Surged through her veins
- ★ Felt his blood had turned to liquid lead
- ★ Before he had climbed more than a few stairs . . .
- ★ As she reached the bend in the stairs
- ★ When he looked up . . .
- ★ *Glanced to the left and saw . . .*
- ★ Gazed up the narrow stairway
- ★ Saw only as far as the bend
- ★ Glanced around fearfully
- ★ Darted to and fro, searching for any movement
- ★ Kept their eyes glued to the door
- ★ Scanned the windows
- ★ Squeezed her eyes shut
- ★ Afraid to look
- ★ Too terrified to look back
- ★ *Afraid to look behind her*
- ★ Realised that his eyes were clamped shut
- ★ Stole into her eyes as she huddled behind the door
- ★ Snapped his eyes open
- ★ *Bit her lip*
- ★ Knitted her eyebrows together, listening for the sound of . . .
- ★ *Took deep breaths*
- ★ Held their breath
- ★ Sucked in a breath
- ★ Took a sharp intake of breath
- ★ Too scared to make a noise
- ★ Hardly dared to breathe
- ★ Silenced her screams
- ★ Clutched his hand to his mouth to stop himself screaming out
- ★ Gaped open in a silent scream
- ★ Opened her mouth to shout, but nothing would come out
- ★ Escaped in tiny, suffocating gasps
- ★ Escaped his throat
- ★ Caught his breath in a sob
- ★ Muttered incoherently to himself

- ☆ Managed to stammer in a high-pitched squeak
- ☆ Shrieked as something brushed her face
- ☆ *Paralysed by fear*
- ☆ Crouched in the shadows of the stairwell
- ☆ Made her body jerk at every noise
- ☆ Felt her legs begin to quiver
- ☆ Shook as he held onto the door
- ☆ Lurched as something brushed against his head
- ☆ Flailed wildly in front of her
- ☆ Dug her nails into her palms to stop them shaking
- ☆ Clenched into tight fists
- ☆ Hesitated just before she reached the open door

SENTENCES

- ☆ Foreboding buzzed along his limbs like an electric current pulsing just beneath the skin.

- ☆ She had a strange feeling – a premonition that something bad was about to happen.

- ☆ He felt a sudden shiver. He tried to shake off his tension, but in vain. He began to have a growing awareness of impending evil.

- ☆ A sense of foreboding crept through her, and sweat trickled down her forehead. Something wasn't right!

- ☆ His heart was thudding in his chest. He didn't know why. There was no obvious reason for his fear.

- ☆ There was no one else there. She knew that. But something was urging her to run.

- ☆ As soon as he had stepped into the hotel, an eerie sensation had enveloped him and would not go away. At night, in particular, he felt very uneasy. The feeling was getting stronger by the day. It was like the hotel was watching, waiting, biding its time.

- ☆ As soon as he had entered the castle, he'd been fighting an underlying sense of panic and as night approached and the shadows lengthened, the castle suddenly felt full of dark secrets.

- ☆ The church felt as if it had been destroyed by tragedy. Sadness and despair were trapped in its walls, cemented into the fabric of the building, locked behind its doors.

- ☆ Something was very wrong. He could feel it. A tingling sixth sense of danger lurking in the shadows.

- ☆ Something terrible had happened here – she could feel it – sense something ominous, menacing . . . wanted to get away, to run from whatever waited for her.

★ *He felt as if he was being watched. But when he scanned the hall, there was no one there.*

★ For a brief second, she thought the light caught someone, lurking behind the curtains. She opened her mouth to cry out, but when she looked again . . . there was no one there.

★ An uneasy feeling of being watched settled over her. There was no one there. It didn't make sense!

★ It was a long night and at first he jumped at the slightest sound – a creak of the stairs or a faint movement of the floorboards.

★ *He didn't understand why the open doorway should make him feel so uneasy.*

★ The first creak of the door startled him like an electric shock.

★ The hairs on her arms prickled as a light breeze drifted through the door.

★ The hairs on the back of his arms prickled as a chilly breeze wafted down from the end of the corridor.

★ She felt an icy chill crawl up her spine. Paralysed by fear, her imagination worked with feverish haste.

★ Goosebumps riddled her body as the torchlight flickered unsteadily, casting dancing, shuddering shadows in front of her.

★ Every nerve in his body warned him not to climb the stairs.

★ He tried to ignore the fear he had never felt before – the fear of walking down the long, dark corridor to his room.

★ He could feel the hair stirring on his scalp and then sweat broke out at the roots of his hair. Before he had climbed more than a few stairs, a chilly feeling crept up his spine.

★ He was sweating despite the chilly air in the passage. His skin was tingling with anticipation.

★ She felt a cold chill crawl up her spine. Her imagination had got the better of her logic. For no apparent reason, she was paralysed by fear. Her mind whirled, making her body jerk at every noise.

★ *She bit her lip and dug her nails into her palms to stop them shaking.*

★ As he edged towards the door, he was aware that his hand was shaking.

★ A shudder ran down her body and she felt her legs begin to quiver.

★ *He held his breath and gazed up at the narrow stairway, seeing only as far as the bend; the rest was steeped in shadow.*

- ✶ She steeled herself and prepared to descend the stairs to the cellar.

- ✶ Her heart started to thud in her chest as she crouched in the shadows of the stairwell.

- ✶ His heart lurched as something brushed against his hand.

- ✶ He jumped when he heard a sound behind the door, his heart hammering in his chest.

- ✶ She jumped when she heard the creaking sound behind her, her heart missing a beat.

- ✶ She glanced to the left and saw an open door leading down to the basement. Every nerve in her body screamed at her to get out of the house.

- ✶ His heart hammered in his chest, his mind reeling as he stared at the door.

- ✶ Her mind was a whirlwind – a pulsing, pounding, surging tornado of thoughts and fears.

- ✶ In the silence, the only sound was the roar of her blood pounding in her ears.

- ✶ *His whole body was rigid with tension.*

- ✶ She hesitated just before she reached the open door, suddenly more afraid than she had ever been in her life.

- ✶ Frozen to the spot, unable to breathe, the darkness swirled around her as she reached the bend in the stairs.

- ✶ *Her eyes widened and her body jerked at every noise.*

- ✶ She glanced around fearfully, expecting to see something hideous in every shadow.

- ✶ Her eyes darted to and fro, searching for any movement.

- ✶ *She shrieked as something brushed her face. As her hands flailed wildly in front of her, they were caught up in a curtain of cobwebs that dangled from the ceiling.*

- ✶ His hands were clenched into tight fists and he could only manage to stammer in a high-pitched squeak.

- ✶ He clutched his hand to his mouth to stop himself screaming out, but as his hand brushed against something in the dark, he threw back his head and yelled at the top of his voice.

6

Secret passages and tunnels

THE S/C-I-R STRUCTURE

He tapped, pushed, pulled at bits of the heavy carved panelling near the fireplace. Eventually, one of the wooden leaves turned in his hand. **His eyes widened and he gasped.** A section of the wooden panel had clicked open like a flap to reveal a hidden passage – a low, dark tunnel leading deep underground.

Where water had leaked in from the rocks, the walls and floor glistened with damp. They edged down the glistening, stone stairs – slipping and sliding on the moss-covered steps. A **piercing scream echoed** around the tunnel as her foot skidded from under her. She made a grab for Tom's arm. But she was too late.

Suddenly, millions of bats, like a black plume of smoke, fluttered from every corner. **Her eyes wide with terror**, she flapped her hands madly in front of her. The passage rang with the **echoes of her shrieking**.

His heart hammered in his chest as the torch flickered and died, and he was left floundering around in the dark, feeling his way with his outstretched hands against the tunnel walls.

SECTION 1 – SECRET PASSAGES

Setting

WORDS

Nouns	**Tunnels**, labyrinth, maze
	Hall, passage, room, study, lounge
	Basement, cellar, vault
	Door, floor, wall, panel, panelling, fireplace, mantelpiece
	Corner, section
	Trapdoor, manhole cover, opening, board
	Handle, ring, chain, hinge
	Flight, stairs, stairway, steps
	Darkness, shadows, candles, candle-holders, torchlight, torches
	Noise, whisper
	Touch, cobwebs, mould, dust
	Glow, gleam
	Air, breeze, waft, smell, stench, reek
Adjectives	**Narrow**, tiny, wide, large, steep, spiral, endless
	Wooden, stone, metal, iron, brass, silver
	Hidden, secret, gaping, sliding, shut
	Triangular, round, door-shaped, odd, misshapen
	Rusting, rickety
	Clammy, stale, cold, icy, freezing
	Black, red, flaming, inky, blank
	Billowing, flickering, dying, dim
Verbs	**Concealed**, disguised
	Built, fitted, poked, jutted
	Moved, appeared, rose, dropped, opened
	Vanished, disappeared

Turned, swung, revolved, pivoted

Revealed, glimpsed, filtered, filled

Carved, hewn

Felt, prickled, brushed

Heard, clicked, creaked

PHRASES – NOUNS AND ADJECTIVES

- ★ Just below his eye-line
- ★ *A secret bolt-hole*
- ★ Priest hole
- ★ *Extra door in the lounge*
- ★ Rickety door in the furthest corner
- ★ In the upper part of the door
- ★ *A tiny section of the wooden panel*
- ★ Heavy carved panelling near the fireplace
- ★ Blank wall
- ★ A mass of stone
- ★ Block of stone on a hinge
- ★ A triangular block of stone
- ★ The section of the wall to the right of the fireplace
- ★ Door-shaped opening in the corner of the room
- ★ *Ring of black iron*
- ★ Iron ring handle of the studded door
- ★ Dangling chain in the corner
- ★ Creaking rope on its rusty hinges
- ★ *A sliding trapdoor*
- ★ A large round board like a wooden manhole cover
- ★ *Until at last it . . .*
- ★ Very slowly, the great stone . . .
- ★ *A large opening in the wall*
- ★ Opening wide enough to . . .
- ★ Gaping hole in the woodblock floor
- ★ *Secret door*
- ★ Metal doors
- ★ Vault door
- ★ Wooden trapdoor
- ★ Dark hole
- ★ *Narrow flight of steps*
- ★ A small metal rung
- ★ Hidden staircase
- ★ Little stairway

- Set of narrow stone stairs
- Flight of rickety wooden steps
- Steep, narrow flight of stairs
- Steep natural stairway
- Flight of spiral steps
- Endless flight of crumbling moss-covered steps
- *Carpet of dust*
- A current of cold air

PHRASES – VERBS

- *When it was shut, the stone was . . .*
- *Concealed behind the tapestry*
- Disguised as a bookcase
- Appeared solid and unbroken
- Built into a huge stone pillar
- Built into the floor
- Poked out of the floor
- Sunk into the boards
- Set inside the buttress
- Fitted so that it was impossible to find it inside the room
- Glimpsed the edge of a curved slab of wood
- Moved by a lever and a rope
- *Swung aside to reveal*
- Pivoted ponderously
- Pivoted on a central axis
- Began to slide backwards
- Clicked open like a flap
- Rose slowly from the floor
- Slid up into the stonework
- Creaked up out of the stone
- Rose until it vanished altogether
- Vanished into the rock above
- Clicked open a door
- Opened to unsuspecting intruders
- *Revealed a trapdoor*
- Must lead somewhere
- Lead down to . . .
- Opened into . . .
- Widened into another room
- Went off in all directions
- Dropped deeper underground
- Led down into a black void

* Led down at a steep angle
* Disappeared inside the cliff
* Twisted steeply to the tunnel below
* Corkscrewed up through the building
* Stretched unseen into the unfathomable darkness
* *Grew accustomed to the light*
* Could just make out . . .
* Caught a glimpse of . . .
* Disappeared out of sight
* Grew darker
* Peered into the inky blackness
* Made it appear that the shadows were reaching out to him
* Drove out the light
* *Prickled his bare arms*
* Brushed her back
* Swung closed behind them
* *Had set foot in there for centuries*
* Saw . . . carved into the passage wall
* *Heard a whisper of sound*
* Could hear footsteps ringing out
* Filtered through the grille in the wall
* Hewn from the stone

SENTENCES

A section of the wooden panel clicked open like a flap to reveal a hidden passage.

A large opening in the wall revealed a set of stairs that twisted steeply to the tunnel below.

Tom noticed that one of the stones jutted out more than the others. As he pressed the stone, a section of the wall to his right moved, sending a current of cold air brushing against his bare arms.

Suddenly, she heard the muffled sound of a locking mechanism releasing within the stonework. Then, part of the wall pivoted and swung aside to reveal a spiral flight of stairs.

Gail noticed a rickety door in the furthest corner, hidden in the shadows. When she got close to the door, she noticed that it was studded with black nails, and one of the panels was carved with ancient symbols.

Poking out of the floor was a rusting iron ring. A trapdoor had been built into the floor.

Interaction

WORDS

Nouns	**Panel**, panelling, fireplace, mantelpiece, door
	Trapdoor, stones, stonework
	Ring, chain, hinge, disc, wooden leaves, locking mechanism
	Head, hand, palm
	Flight, stairs, stairway, steps
Adjectives	**Hidden**, secret
	Iron, stone
	Small, round
	Crumbling, moss-covered
	Carved
Verbs	**Felt**, thrust, pressed, grasped, pushed, pulled, tugged, heaved
	Twisted, turned, tapped, slid
	Stood, descended
	Peered, gazed
	Released, swung, revolved

PHRASES – NOUNS AND ADJECTIVES

- ★ Huge fireplace
- ★ Handle of a hidden door
- ★ Rusting iron ring
- ★ Block of stone on a hinge
- ★ Bits of the heavy carved panelling near the fireplace
- ★ One of the wooden leaves
- ★ Small, round disc
- ★ Crumbling, moss-covered steps

PHRASES – VERBS

- ★ Thrust her head into . . .
- ★ Felt around the inside

- ✶ Felt around for a door
- ✶ Grasped a chain dangling in the furthest corner
- ✶ *Tugged the chain*
- ✶ Tapped, pushed at . . .
- ✶ Pressed the mantelpiece
- ✶ Pushed it hard with his palm
- ✶ Twisted it anti-clockwise
- ✶ Pushed at the central panel
- ✶ Pushed aside a pile of stones
- ✶ *Turned in his hand*
- ✶ Released a locking mechanism in the stonework
- ✶ Slid back
- ✶ Heaved back the . . .
- ✶ Swung the door open
- ✶ *Stood on the top step*
- ✶ Tumbled through the opening
- ✶ Disappeared in the blink of an eye
- ✶ Revolved again and he was back in the room
- ✶ Pulled the trapdoor behind them
- ✶ Descended an endless flight of . . .

SENTENCES

Tapping and pushing at bits of the heavy carved panelling near the fireplace, he eventually found one of the wooden leaves that turned in his hand.

He felt around the block of stone until he found a small, round disc.

He removed the top stones from the cairn, and then moved the rest aside until he glimpsed the edge of a curved slab of wood.

He tugged at the wooden cover and revealed a hidden staircase that corkscrewed underground.

Thrusting her head into the great fireplace, Katie felt around the inside. Her hand suddenly grasped a chain dangling in the furthest corner.

When she tugged on the chain, a section of the wooden panelling to the side of the fireplace slid open like a door, revealing a set of narrow stone stairs that corkscrewed up through the building.

Quickly, he descended an endless flight of crumbling, moss-covered steps.

SECTION 2 – TUNNELS

Setting

WORDS

Nouns	**Maze**, labyrinth, crypt, vault
	Passages, passageways, path, stairs, walls, niches
	Light, lamp, torch, beam
	Stone, rock
	Stench, dust, water, bats, skulls
Adjectives	**Long**, low, narrow, twisting, steep
	Huge, small
	Dark, black, inky, gloomy, dim, shadowy, ghostly, eerie, green, red
	Slippery, dangerous
	Cold, damp, glistening
	Putrid, sickly
	Rough, smooth
	Gushing, crashing
	Burning
Verbs	**Bent**, curved, wound, twisted, turned, coiled, snaked
	Led, stretched, opened, enclosed, branched
	Sloped, climbed, ascended, dropped, descended
	Squeezed, crawled
	Lit, illuminated, pierced
	Revealed, glimpsed
	Heard, boomed, crackled, crunched, dripped, echoed
	Sculpted, carved
	Polished, glistened
	Startled, disturbed, flew, fluttered
	Burned, sputtered, flickered

PHRASES – NOUNS AND ADJECTIVES

- ★ Low, dark tunnels
- ★ Long, twisting path
- ★ Narrow tunnel
- ★ Labyrinth with an endless puzzle of staircases and tunnels
- ★ Inky black maze of dangerous, slippery paths
- ★ Labyrinthine set of passageways and niches
- ★ Barely enough headroom to stand up
- ★ *Niches in the walls*
- ★ A hole in the rock the size of a small door
- ★ *Clammy, cold, icy to the touch*
- ★ As cold as a crypt
- ★ Cold air all around them. Icy cold
- ★ Like a cold, dry mouth
- ★ *Light of one dim candle*
- ★ Silver gleam
- ★ Brass candleholders on the wall
- ★ Odd, misshapen shadows
- ★ Inky blackness
- ★ By the flaming torchlight
- ★ Billowing torches
- ★ Flickering light of a flaming torch
- ★ A dim glow
- ★ Torch in the niche
- ★ Burning torches
- ★ Ghostly light
- ★ Beam of the torch
- ★ Beam of light
- ★ White light
- ★ A huge shadow
- ★ Dark space between each dim lamp
- ★ *Somewhere in the distance*
- ★ Rattling noise like a chain being dropped into a coffin
- ★ Dying echo in the freezing passage
- ★ Humming sound
- ★ Crashing wave
- ★ Dripping water
- ★ Gushing water
- ★ *Putrid, sickly stench*
- ★ Waft of stale air
- ★ Cobwebs and mould

PHRASES – VERBS

- ⋆ *Wound underground*
- ⋆ Twisted and turned like a maze
- ⋆ Began to bend to the right
- ⋆ Curved so far she could no longer see the opening
- ⋆ Dropped off at a sharp angle
- ⋆ Stretched back deep into the cliff
- ⋆ Led off in different directions
- ⋆ Branched into several tunnels
- ⋆ Opened out into an underground chamber
- ⋆ Sloped downhill
- ⋆ *Pointed the beam of the torch ahead*
- ⋆ Marked flickering pathways
- ⋆ Crackled down the passage like a camera flash
- ⋆ Had a dim light to guide his steps
- ⋆ Pierced the shadows
- ⋆ Lit only by the narrow beam of light from the torch
- ⋆ Lit at long intervals
- ⋆ Lit by the green glow of an emergency light
- ⋆ Illuminated a steep, natural stairway
- ⋆ *Glimpsed a shelf of grinning skulls*
- ⋆ Revealed glimpses of . . .
- ⋆ Covered in pictures of . . .
- ⋆ Carved into the rock
- ⋆ Glistened with damp
- ⋆ *Heard echoes*
- ⋆ Filled the tunnel
- ⋆ Crunched on the broken shells and bones
- ⋆ Echoed and crashed back at him
- ⋆ Heard a shout echoing through the caves
- ⋆ Rang with the echoes of his scream
- ⋆ Dripped from the ceiling and echoed around the walls
- ⋆ Boomed like a clap of thunder
- ⋆ Burned down and sputtered
- ⋆ *Felt cold under his hands*
- ⋆ Struck the wall beneath her and sprayed upwards
- ⋆ Polished into dangerous, slippery paths
- ⋆ Sculpted into jagged blades
- ⋆ *Disturbed a number of squadrons of bats*
- ⋆ Came towards them, flying in close formation
- ⋆ Fluttered from every corner
- ⋆ Flew out through . . .

SENTENCES

The cave was a winding, underground maze of low, dark tunnels.

Where water had leaked in from the rocks, the walls and floor glistened with damp.

It began to bend to the right and soon it had curved so far that looking back they could no longer see the opening.

As they climbed down the steep, stone stairway, a blast of cold air crashed into them. The tunnel was as cold as a crypt and dark as night.

The air was cold all around him. Icy cold. As he continued down, a waft of stale air drifted towards him. In the flickering light it looked like the odd, misshapen shadows were reaching out to him. The corridor grew darker, the air got staler. Peering into the inky blackness, he caught a glimpse of movement.

Interaction

WORDS

Nouns	**Cavern**, opening, hole, slope, path, walls, niches
	Bats, skulls
	Light, lamp, torch, beam
	Smoke, plume
	Echoes
Adjectives	**Long**, narrow, twisting, steep, precipitous
	Damp, dangerous
	Black, smoky, sputtering
Verbs	**Ventured**, emerged, followed, crossed
	Squeezed, edged, descended
	Slipped, slid, skidded
	Glimpsed, fluttered, flapped
	Rang, echoed

PHRASES – NOUNS AND ADJECTIVES

* ★ A huge cavern
* ★ Steep slope

* Precipitous path
* Damp and dangerous
* Niches in the walls
* Millions of bats, like a black plume of smoke

PHRASES – VERBS

* Ventured further in
* Squeezed through the hole
* Edged down the . . .
* *Emerged into an opening*
* Led off in all different directions
* Followed the long, twisting path
* Moved through the tunnel
* Crossed a narrow ledge
* Edged down the stone steps
* Squeezed along a murky corridor
* Pulled her deeper into the blackness
* Squeezed through a hole carved out of the rocky wall
* Descended a precipitous path into a huge cavern
* Emerged from the passage into . . .
* *Used the light from their torch to guide their steps*
* Followed the smoky light of the sputtering torch
* Glimpsed a shelf of grinning skulls
* Stopped to search . . .
* *Fluttered from every corner*
* Flapped his hands in front of him
* Rang with the echoes of his scream
* Crunched on the broken shells and bones
* *Dripped from the roof*
* Carved out of the rocky wall

SENTENCES

They followed the long, twisting path using the light from their torch to guide their steps.

Squeezing through the hole that had been carved out of the rocky wall, they descended a precipitous path into a huge cavern.

Following the smoky light of the sputtering torch, they moved cautiously through the tunnel, stopping to search the niches in the walls. Suddenly, to their left, they glimpsed a shelf of grinning skulls.

They edged down the glistening, stone steps – slipping and sliding on the damp steps. She grabbed his arm to steady herself as her foot skidded from under her.

Suddenly, millions of bats, like a black plume of smoke, fluttered from every corner and the passage rang with the echoes of his scream as he flapped his hands in front of him.

He ducked as a swish of wings rushed through the air and bats brushed his head with their furry bodies.

SECTION 3 – REACTION (SECRET PASSAGES AND TUNNELS)

WORDS

Nouns	**Brain**, heart, throat, chest, breath, neck, hands
	Instinct, sensation, panic
	Sound, footsteps, scream
Adjectives	**Dry**, ice-cold, tingling, lingering
	Fast, feverish
	Outstretched
	Echoing
Verbs	**Knew**, realised, remembered
	Stopped, tensed, fought
	Banged, clenched, stopped, squeezed
	Moved, edged, slithered
	Glanced, flickered
	Swallowed, gulped, gasped, screamed
	Felt, groped, floundered

PHRASES – NOUNS AND ADJECTIVES

- ★ Ice-cold needles into the back of his neck
- ★ Throat suddenly dry
- ★ Painful gasps
- ★ With his outstretched hands against the tunnel walls

- ★ Way out of the maze of tunnels
- ★ Echoing footsteps

PHRASES – VERBS

- ★ Had a tingling sensation that he wasn't alone
- ★ Tensed, fighting her body's natural instinct to run
- ★ Knew he had to think of something fast
- ★ Had to fight hard to . . .
- ★ Had a lingering chill
- ★ Tried desperately to remember the way they had come
- ★ Getting closer by the minute
- ★ *Heart almost stopped*
- ★ Clenched in panic
- ★ Banged against his ribs
- ★ Swallowed, his throat suddenly dry
- ★ Coated her forehead
- ★ *Glanced behind him*
- ★ Glanced back over her shoulder
- ★ *Felt his way*
- ★ Floundered around in the dark
- ★ *Slithered to a halt*

SENTENCES

She tensed, fighting her body's natural instinct to run, and she was having to fight hard to do so.

He had a lingering chill, as if someone was pushing ice-cold needles into the back of his neck.

His stomach clenched in panic and he knew he had to think of something fast. The sound of echoing footsteps was getting closer by the minute.

His heart banging against his ribs, he squeezed through the hole and swung the trapdoor shut behind him.

He swallowed, his throat suddenly dry.

He slithered to a halt, his breath coming in painful gasps.

As the torch flickered and died, he was left floundering around in the dark, feeling his way with his outstretched hands against the tunnel walls.

Her mind was working with feverish haste as she tried desperately to remember the way out of the maze of tunnels.

Part 2
Creating suspense

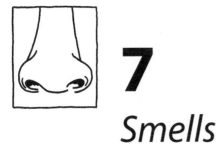

7

Smells

Choose the smells that would best represent the character of the ghost and the reason for its haunting presence. For example:

- ★ If it seeks revenge, the smells are likely to be nasty, unpleasant.
- ★ If it is there to pass on a message or recover an object, the smells are likely to be more pleasant.
- ★ The ghost may have to decide whether the main character is a threat or accomplice, and the lingering scent will depend on this decision.

THE S/C-I-R STRUCTURE

The hairs on her arms prickled as a light breeze brought the smell of lavender drifting through the door. Kitty was crouched behind the curtain and hadn't moved a muscle for five minutes. Ever since she had first been aware of the smell, **she had been feeling very uneasy**. She waited – still did not move. Cautiously, she leaned forward so that she could peer through the gap.

Someone had walked into his room when he was asleep. He had been woken when the door had opened, and a cold draught had rushed towards him, bringing with it stale, dank air like a cellar that had been locked up for centuries. He sat bolt upright, **his eyes darting frantically from side to side, around the room. Every nerve in his body screamed at him that it was still there.**

SECTION 1 – SETTING

A. Pleasant smells

WORDS	

Nouns	**Smell**, scent, aroma, fragrance, perfume
	Jasmine, juniper, cinnamon, ginger, pine needles, apple blossom, cherry blossom, orange, lemon, almond, rosemary, geranium, honeysuckle, lavender, sandalwood, myrrh, peach, lilac, lily, eucalyptus, camphor, rose, spearmint, peppermint, aniseed
	Soap, washing powder, polish, boot polish, leather
Adjectives	**Sweet**, clean, fresh, heavy, fragrant, perfumed, aromatic
Verbs	**Scented**, wafted, drifted, smelt, mingled, blended, lingered

PHRASES – NOUNS AND ADJECTIVES

* Thick with the scent of . . .
* Roses and cherry blossom
* Scent of honeysuckle
* Lavender and lilac perfume
* Smell of pine needles and cinnamon
* Scents of Christmas
* Smell of boot polish
* As if all the flowers and spices of the world . . .
* Heavy in the air

PHRASES – VERBS

* Scented with . . .
* Blended and mingled together
* Lingered in the air
* Wafted in the air
* Drifted towards her
* Tossed in the air
* Overcome by the smell of . . .

SENTENCES

The air was thick with the scent of honeysuckle.

The summer house was scented with roses and cherry blossom, even though the autumn winds had stolen their flowers.

The air in the attic was heavy with the scent of lavender and lilac.

Opening the old oak chest, it was as if all the flowers and spices of the world had been blended together and tossed in the air.

She took a deep breath as the smell of boot polish wafted through the room.

As they flicked through the photos in the ancient, battered tin, the smell of pine needles and cinnamon filled the room with the scents of Christmas.

B. Unpleasant smells

WORDS

Nouns	**Smell**, stink, stench, reek
	Graveyard, cellar, basement, attic, chest, box, bookcase
	Clothes, dress, gown, uniform, bandages
	Damp, mildew, mould, water, sea, seaweed
	Dust, soot, smoke, fumes, paraffin
	Ground, earth, plants, weeds
	Pain, death, decay, flesh, corpse, meat, blood
	Nose, nostrils, breath, throat, cough, vomit
Adjectives	**Thick**, heavy, warm, dusty, musty, cloying
	Salty, bitter, acidic, damp, dank, stagnant
	Pungent, odorous, burnt, scorched
	Rotten, decaying, rancid, diseased, revolting, stinking, putrefying, corrupt, fetid, decomposing, festering
Verbs	**Smelt**, reeked
	Rose, drifted, wafted, seeped, released
	Rushed, surged, filled, dogged, lingered
	Brought, gave off

Covered, cupped, clutched, caught, attacked

Stung, choked, coughed, churned, clenched, retched, vomited

Left, shut out

PHRASES – NOUNS AND ADJECTIVES

* ☆ Cold draught
* ☆ *Musty clothes*
* ☆ Dust and mould
* ☆ Dank, musty smell
* ☆ *Stink of seaweed*
* ☆ Stagnant water and damp earth
* ☆ Stinking stench of dead water and bitter decay
* ☆ *Choking acrid smoke*
* ☆ Curtain of rancid fumes
* ☆ Thick, rancid smell of paraffin
* ☆ *Diseased breath*
* ☆ Musty smell of decay
* ☆ Smell of pain and death
* ☆ Decaying flesh
* ☆ Putrefying smell of rotting meat
* ☆ Revolting smell of burnt flesh
* ☆ Corrupt, diseased breath
* ☆ Heavy smell of decay, of the dead
* ☆ *Stench of graveyards and rotting corpses*

PHRASES – VERBS

* ☆ Like a cellar that had been locked up for centuries
* ☆ Could smell the musty lace of her gown
* ☆ Reeked of rotten meat, damp and decay
* ☆ Gave off a smell of rot and graveyards
* ☆ Smelt its corrupt, diseased breath
* ☆ *Was released into the cold air*
* ☆ Hidden behind a curtain of rancid fumes
* ☆ Rose from his clothing
* ☆ Rose from the shadows
* ☆ Wafted towards her
* ☆ Wafted up from the darkness
* ☆ Drifted towards her
* ☆ Seeped from behind the bookcase
* ☆ Rushed towards her

* *Lingered in the room*
* Dogged the air
* Brought with it stale, dank air

SENTENCES

As she drew closer, Tom could smell the musty lace of her gown.

The thick, rancid smell of paraffin dogged the air and caught in the back of their throats.

They covered their noses and mouths to block out the putrefying smell of rotting meat.

As he opened the trunk, a dank, musty smell was released into the cold air and surged up her nostrils.

The room reeked of rotten meat, damp and decay. Even the plants seemed to give off a smell of rot and graveyards.

She needed to leave the room to escape the smell of dust and mould, the heavy smell of decay – the dead.

A stinking stench of dead water and bitter decay rose from the shadows.

When she opened the door a cold draught rushed towards her, bringing with it stale, dank air like a cellar that had been locked up for centuries.

SECTION 2 – INTERACTION

WORDS

Nouns	**Smell**, sign, source, direction
	Passage, door, lever, handle, bookcase
	Nose, nostrils, breath, throat, mouth, face, eyes, hand, fingers
	Senses, muscles
	Cough, vomit
	Shudder, shiver
Adjectives	**Nervous**, cautious, furtive
	Quick, swift, desperate, frantic
Verbs	**Covered**, cupped, clutched, gripped

Tickled, stung, caught, surged, attacked, seeped

Held, took, tasted

Choked, coughed, churned, clenched, retched, vomited

Waited, crouched, moved, stumbled, ran, darted, quickened

Whirled, spun, turned, recoiled

Looked, peered, peeped, flicked, flickered, searched, scanned

Whispered, groaned, moaned

Left, shut out, pushed, slammed, sealed

PHRASES – NOUNS AND ADJECTIVES

* As the stench of graveyards and rotting corpses . . .
* *Still no sign of her*
* Nothing there
* Even though the smell of lavender . . .
* Scent of honeysuckle
* *Revolting smell of burnt flesh*
* Stench of graveyards and decay
* Musty smell of decay

PHRASES – VERBS

* *Where was the smell coming from?*
* *Tickled her nostrils*
* Stung his nostrils and eyes
* Surged up her nostrils and down the back of her throat
* Caught in the back of her throat
* Attacked their senses
* Attacked their nostrils and throats
* *Cupped her hand over her nose and mouth*
* Clutched her hand to her mouth
* Seeped through her fingers
* Held their breath
* Took deep breaths
* Tasted decay
* Recoiled as . . . blew onto her face
* *Clenched and churned*
* Hit the back of her throat
* Coughed and retched

* Bent over and retched violently
* *Needed to leave the room to escape the smell of ...*
* Shut out the musty smell of decay
* Slammed the door shut
* As she turned the door handle ...
* *Waited a moment and then followed*
* Waited – still did not move
* Hadn't moved a muscle for five minutes
* Crouched behind the curtain
* Leaned forward so that she could peer through the gap
* Stumbled towards the light
* Shivered and quickened his pace
* Whirled around
* Turned on her heel
* *Darted around the room*
* Peeped around the corner of the door
* Looked around furtively
* Looked frantically back over his shoulder
* Searched for the source of the scent
* *Gripped the handle tighter*
* Pushed the lever to seal the passage
* *Shut out the musty smell of decay*
* Sealed the passage
* Seeped from behind the bookcase
* *Aware that her hand was shaking*
* Whispered through her fingers

SENTENCES

She stumbled towards the light, the smell drifting towards her and leading her further down the passage.

She whirled around, her eyes darting around the room, searching for the source of the scent.

Tom waited for a moment and then followed. He peeped around the corner of the door. There was nothing there. So where was that smell coming from?

She looked round furtively, covered her mouth and whispered through her fingers.

As she turned the door handle, the scent of honeysuckle seeped under the door and tickled her nostrils. She gripped the handle tighter, aware that her hand was shaking.

Kitty was crouched behind the curtain and hadn't moved a muscle for five minutes. She waited – still did not move. Still there was no sign of her, even though the smell of lavender filled the room. Cautiously, she leaned forward so that she could peer through the gap.

Holding their breath, they pushed the lever to seal the passage and shut out the musty smell of decay, which was seeping from behind the bookcase and attacking their nostrils and throats.

Kitty cupped her fingers around her nose and mouth, but the stench of graveyards and decay wafting up from the darkness seeped through her fingers and made her retch.

She recoiled as his diseased breath blew onto her face.

Her stomach churned as the revolting smell of burnt flesh drifted towards her. Clutching her hand to her mouth, she bent over and retched violently.

Vomit hit the back of her throat as she turned on her heel and slammed the door shut.

As the stench of graveyards and rotting corpses rose from the shadows, he shivered and quickened his pace, looking frantically back over his shoulder.

SECTION 3 – REACTION

WORDS	
Nouns	**Scent**, smell, sound, sign, presence, someone
	Sense, feeling, sensation, doom, dread, premonition, foreboding
	Fear, terror
	Tension, nerves, trance
	Body, bones, muscles, nerves, skin, hair, roots
	Head, temples, eyes, arms, hands
	Heart, veins, blood, pulse, chest, ribs
	Mouth, tongue, throat, windpipe, lips
	Whisper, gasp, moan, groan, sob, scream
Adjectives	**Close**, nearby, impending
	Hidden, invisible, unknown
	Strange, uneasy, faint, nauseous
	Alert, drawn, anxious, nervous, bewildered

Tense, rigid, frozen, still, motionless

Terrified, fearful

Sharp, urgent, desperate, rasping, ragged

Bad, evil, dangerous, threatening, ominous, menacing, hideous

Wide, staring, bulging, startled, strained

Silent, quiet, trembling, quivering

Cold, icy, chilly, shuddering

Verbs   **Felt**, prickled, tingled, stirred, broke out, crept, stole, snaked

Ran, surged, erupted, spread, strained, stretched

Knew, sensed, felt, imagined, expected

Warned, urged, screamed

Fought, dampened

Seized, gripped, choked, squeezed

Chewed, bit, gnawed

Drew, held, gasped, swallowed, blew out

Trembled, shook, shivered, shuddered, quivered

Folded, hugged, grabbed, gripped, clutched

Paced, moved, walked

PHRASES – NOUNS AND ADJECTIVES

- ☆ As the scent of . . . .
- ☆ *Every nerve in his body*
- ☆ Every bone in his body
- ☆ Hairs on her arms
- ☆ *A tingling sixth sense*
- ☆ Cold, icy dread
- ☆ Chilly feeling
- ☆ Needles of icy fear
- ☆ *Quivering dread of an invisible presence*
- ☆ *Utterly alert*
- ☆ Rigid with tension
- ☆ *Wide, staring eyes*
- ☆ Alert and strained
- ☆ As if in a trance

* *Silent scream*
* For a while neither of them . . .
* *Drawn and anxious as she . . .*

PHRASES – VERBS

* *Certain there was someone in the room*
* Any sign that it was still there
* Certain now it was somewhere nearby
* Presence was nearer, but still invisible
* Fear of when it would appear again, what would happen next
* *At any moment the smell would be followed by . . .*
* No time to think, no time to do anything
* As he turned his head . . .
* As she walked into the room . . .
* Before he had climbed more than a few stairs . . .
* As the blood pounded in his temples . . .
* *Made her feel uneasy*
* Gave her a strange feeling
* Felt her body tense and her senses sharpen
* *Prickled her neck*
* Tingled at the back of his neck
* Prickled as a light breeze brought the scent of . . .
* Could feel the hair stirring on his scalp
* Broke out at the roots of his hair
* Crept over him
* Ran through his body
* *Warned him not to go any further*
* Premonition that something bad was about to happen
* Warned him to be alert
* Urged him to move
* *Fought to remain calm*
* Tried to dampen the sense of impending doom
* *Could smell it coming closer*
* Could smell it when she walked into the room
* Could smell it . . . the scent of eucalyptus
* Could not see, but knew was there because he could smell it
* Seeped under the wooden door, which was all that separated them
* *Knew then what it was*
* Had to get out of there and fast
* Knew that he had only seconds before it arrived
* Would soon be near enough to touch her
* Standing right outside the door

* Walked into her room when she was asleep and woken her
* Screamed at her that it was still there
* *Erupted inside his head*
* Seized his senses
* Choked his breath
* Gripped him, snaked around his windpipe
* Missed a beat
* Spread into his chest
* Squeezed like a vice
* *Stole into his stomach*
* Felt nauseous and faint
* Felt a sickness in his stomach, as though he had eaten something bad
* Dipped and swayed beneath her
* *Expected to see something hideous in every shadow*
* Strained to breaking point
* *Ran his tongue nervously over his lips*
* Chewed nervously on her tongue
* *Watched with bated breath*
* Blew out her cheeks
* Dropped to an urgent whisper
* Swallowed, his throat suddenly dry
* Drew a rasping breath
* Lowered his voice
* Shrank into silence
* Voice froze in her throat
* Opened her mouth wide in a silent scream
* Words came in gasps
* Spoke in a rush
* Opened his mouth to speak, but closed it again
* *Glanced rapidly round*
* Glanced fearfully around
* Strained to pierce the darkness
* Flicked from the door to the window
* Darted back and forth uncertainly
* Darted wildly from side to side
* Peered into the shadows
* Squeezed his eyes shut, afraid to look
* Searched the darkness for any other sign, any sound that it was still there
* *Aware that his hand was shaking*
* Shivered, suddenly aware of the sound of her heart pounding loudly
* *Grabbed a chair*
* Folded her arms across her chest
* Gripping it tightly, while . . .
* *Paced backwards and forwards across the room*
* Tried to find the source of the smell

For some reason, ever since she had first been aware of the scent of rose blossom in the room, she had been feeling very uneasy.

The hairs on her arms prickled as a light breeze brought the scent of peppermint drifting through the door.

Every nerve of her body was on edge.

Before he had climbed more than a few stairs, the smell of leather drifted towards him and a chilly feeling crept up his spine.

It was a quivering dread of a presence he could not see, but knew was there . . . he could smell it.

As she walked into the room, she could smell it. She searched the darkness for any other sign, any sound that it was still there.

The presence was nearer, still invisible but she could smell its breath . . . coming closer. She shuddered as she realised that soon it would be near enough to touch her.

Her face was expressionless, but inwardly she was fighting to remain calm.

Her face was drawn and anxious as she paced backwards and forwards across the room trying to find the source of the smell.

He ran his tongue nervously over his lips.

He swallowed, his throat suddenly dry.

She folded her arms across her chest and chewed nervously on her tongue.

Her whole body was rigid with tension.

He was aware that his hand was shaking.

A shudder ran through his body.

She shivered, suddenly aware of the sound of her heart pounding loudly.

She felt her body tense and her senses sharpen as she waited with bated breath.

As the blood pounded in his temples, his brain quickened and all his senses were alert.

Glancing rapidly round, his eyes flicked from the door to the window.

His eyes darted back and forth uncertainly and he opened his mouth to speak, but closed it again.

Her voice dropped to an urgent whisper.

For a while neither of them spoke.

Her heart missed a beat. Blowing out her cheeks, she drew a rasping breath and tried to dampen the sense of impending doom as the dank, musty smell filled the room.

Every nerve in his body warned him not to go any further.

He was utterly alert. Every nerve in his body was straining to breaking point.

As the stench filled the room, every bone in his body was tensed and the skin tingled at the back of his neck, warning him to be alert.

Katie was stabbed by a splinter of fear, fear of when it would appear again, what would happen next.

The stench of a diseased breath lingered in the room. It gave her a strange feeling – a premonition that something bad was about to happen.

He knew then what it was, and knew that he had only seconds before it arrived. He had to get out of there – and fast.

There was no time to think, no time to do anything.

As the scent of old leather drifted towards him, a tingling sixth sense made him look up. As he turned his head, he froze. It was standing right above him.

Panic gripped him, snaking around his windpipe, choking his breath.

Needles of icy fear prickled her neck.

He could feel the hair stirring on his scalp and then sweat broke out at the roots of his hair.

A cold, icy dread stole into his stomach, spread into his chest and squeezed like a vice.

Kitty was shaking with terror and dread that at any moment the smell would be followed by the chorus of clanging bells.

His wide eyes strained to pierce the darkness and darted wildly from side to side, certain there was someone in the room.

Her eyes darted frantically from side to side, around the room, certain now it was somewhere nearby.

She glanced fearfully around, expecting to see something hideous in every shadow.

As lavender perfume wafted in front of him, he squeezed his eyes shut, afraid to look.

She felt nauseous and faint. Grabbing a chair, she gripped it tightly, while the ground dipped and swayed beneath her. She was terrified and bewildered.

He felt a sickness in his stomach, as though he had eaten something bad. It was standing right outside the door. He could smell it. The thick, rancid smell of petrol seeped under the wooden door. It was all that separated them.

Someone had walked into her room when she was asleep. That's why she had woken. The reek of acrid smoke rushed towards her. Every nerve in her body screamed at her that it was still there.

As panic seized his senses, a silent scream erupted inside his head, urging him to move.

8
Temperature

The presence of a ghost is often hinted at or preceded by a dramatic drop in temperature. Adding this element to your description increases atmosphere and suspense as it hints to the reader that something is about to happen – that the ghost is present!

THE S/C-I-R STRUCTURE

Exactly as the church clock chimed the last stroke of midnight, she **woke with a start, afraid and rigid**. An icy chill had swept into the room. She **shivered** as it whipped around her shoulders. It was deathly cold and lasted for a brief few seconds. She **lay motionless, ears straining for any sound, eyes peering into the shadows**.

Foreboding buzzed along her limbs like an electric current pulsing just beneath the skin. She had a creeping certainty that there was something, someone in the room with her; breathing on her; resting icy cold fingers on her pillow. Clutching the bedsheets, she pulled them tight under her chin. She **felt icy fingers close around her heart** as cold as the ice tomb that had surrounded her. **Her stomach tightened and twisted as a single word roared in her head. It came out as a rasping whisper.** The ghost!

SECTION 1 – SETTING

WORDS

Nouns	**Breath**, air, mist, clouds, wind, draught, breeze, gust, gale
	Bones, skin, shoulders, legs, ankles, toes, arms, hand, fingers
	Goosebumps, shiver, shudder
Similes/ Metaphors	**Icy fingers**, like the jaws of a vice, like acid, like a swirling white mist, whisper of cold air, like a cat, like a cold blanket
Adjectives	**Chilly**, icy, bitter, freezing, deathly, deadly, savage, ferocious bone-crushing, intense
	Brief, swirling
Verbs	**Dropped**, dipped, plummeted
	Brushed, rubbed, swirled, clung, draped, rushed, swept
	Tingled, gripped, pierced, whipped, gnawed, sunk, burned, scalded
	Shivered, shuddered, trembled, quivered
	Whispered, moaned, howled, shrieked, screeched

PHRASES – NOUNS AND ADJECTIVES

- ⋆ Cold for no apparent reason
- ⋆ No warmth from the flames
- ⋆ From some cold, deadly place
- ⋆ Icy cold draught outside the door
- ⋆ *Whisper of cold air*
- ⋆ Cold breath of air
- ⋆ Icy fingers
- ⋆ Bitter wind
- ⋆ Savage cold
- ⋆ Intense, deathly cold
- ⋆ Savage, bone-crushing cold
- ⋆ Like the jaws of a vice
- ⋆ *Breath in icy clouds around them*
- ⋆ Breath like a swirling white mist
- ⋆ *Goosebumps on their arms*
- ⋆ Freezing from the inside
- ⋆ Feeling of deathly cold

PHRASES – VERBS

* ★ Woke in the middle of the night
* ★ Lasted for a few brief seconds
* ★ *Closer they got to the . . .*
* ★ Closed in on him
* ★ Swept the room
* ★ Rushed out to meet them
* ★ Plummeted until her breath rose in icy clouds
* ★ *Clung to him*
* ★ Rubbed against her ankles like a cat
* ★ Draped over her like a cold blanket
* ★ Whipped around her shoulders
* ★ Sunk its teeth into his bones
* ★ Scalded their skin like acid
* ★ Gnawed away from the inside
* ★ *Took their breath away*
* ★ Smoked in the freezing air
* ★ Pierced by a cold shudder
* ★ Gripped by cold and shivering
* ★ Trembled in her hand

SENTENCES

In the freezing air, their breath was in clouds around them.

She woke in the middle of the night, shivering. The chilly air draped around her like an icy blanket.

Suddenly, an icy chill seemed to sweep into the room. It was deathly cold and lasted for a few brief seconds.

She recoiled as the cold air rushed out to meet her.

A blast of freezing air slammed into him.

The cold clung to him as it whipped around his shoulders.

The closer they got to the attic, the colder they felt. The torch shook as her hands froze.

The temperature suddenly dropped for no apparent reason.

The cold from the open door closed in on him; a savage, bone-crushing cold that sunk its teeth into his bones.

The ferocity of the intense cold took their breath away. It was a deathly breath that scalded their skin like acid.

Closing in on her like the jaws of a vice, the cold gnawed away from the inside, and even though the fire was still lit there was no warmth from the flames.

SECTION 2 – INTERACTION

WORDS	
Nouns	**Clock**, midnight, dark, shadows
	Fear, unease
	Passage, room, window, door, curtains, shutters, chair, bed, bedclothes, duvet, bedsheets, blanket, dressing gown, coat
	Breath, air, wind, puff, draught, breeze, gust
	Sweat, chill, cold, shiver
	Muscles, skin
	Shoulders, arms, hands, fingers, elbows, chest, neck, chin, legs, knees, feet
	Breath, voice, croak
Adjectives	**Slow**, cautious, still, motionless
	Alert, upright
	Cold, icy, freezing, bitter, deathly, savage
Verbs	**Felt**, tickled, tingled, trickled, erupted
	Brushed, rubbed, swirled, draped, rushed, swept
	Fluttered, billowed
	Woke, lay, sat
	Shivered, shuddered, trembled, quivered
	Pulled, drew, folded, hugged, gripped, clutched
	Moved, jerked, lurched, whirled, spun
	Hovered, ducked, crept, moved, stepped, continued
	Listened, strained
	Looked, peered, scanned
	Spoke, lowered, gulped, gasped
Adverbs	**Tightly**, quickly, wildly, frantically, desperately
	Slowly, nervously, cautiously

PHRASES – NOUNS AND ADJECTIVES

* ★ Slowly, cautiously, she . . .
* ★ Tight, frozen muscles
* ★ Every sense in her body
* ★ *Cold sweat*
* ★ Cold shiver
* ★ Icy chill
* ★ Deathly cold
* ★ Freezing air
* ★ Bitter cold in the room
* ★ Savage, deathly cold
* ★ Dark, icy passage
* ★ *Croak of fear*

PHRASES – VERBS

* ★ Exactly as the church clock chimed the last stroke of midnight
* ★ Felt a puff of cold air
* ★ Fluttered in the sudden breeze
* ★ Rushed out to meet him
* ★ Swept into the room
* ★ Draped over her like an icy blanket
* ★ *Woke with a start*
* ★ Lay motionless
* ★ Sat bolt upright in bed
* ★ *Trickled down his back*
* ★ Erupted on her arms
* ★ *Brushed his hand*
* ★ Rubbed her arms
* ★ Jerked his hands back
* ★ Moved his fingers wildly in front of him
* ★ Clutched the bedsheets
* ★ Pulled them tight under her chin
* ★ Folded tightly across her chest and her neck
* ★ Disappeared into his hunched shoulders
* ★ Drew her dressing gown around her to block out the cold
* ★ Elbows jutted out as he hugged himself
* ★ Hugged her knees against her chest
* ★ Leant forward in his chair
* ★ *Peered into the shadows*
* ★ Peered warily into the room
* ★ Looked around cautiously before he spoke

- Scanned the dark
- *Hovered at the door*
- Forced her feet to move
- Determined not to let her unease get the better of her
- Sat down on the steps
- Backed away
- Ducked as a savage, deathly cold . . .
- *Crept down the dark, icy passage*
- Towards the room from which the screaming had been coming
- Took a step into the room
- Stepped forward
- Moved towards the . . .
- Continued down the passage
- Whirled round to face the door
- Put some distance between herself and the . . .
- *Listened at each of the doors*
- Strained for any sound
- *Lowered his voice*
- Took his breath away
- Gulped quick breaths
- Opened her mouth to speak, but only a croak of fear emerged

SENTENCES

Exactly as the church clock chimed the last stroke of midnight, he woke with a start, sat bolt upright in bed, his eyes scanning the dark. An icy chill had swept into the room.

He lay motionless, his ears straining for any sound, his eyes peering into the shadows.

She clutched the bedsheets, pulling them tight under her chin.

A cold shiver made her rub her arms. Goosebumps had erupted on her arms.

She sat down on the steps, hugging her knees against her chest.

His heart lurched as the billowing curtains fluttered in the sudden breeze and brushed his hand. Moving his fingers wildly in front of him, he suddenly felt a puff of cold air. He jerked his hands back. The window was closed. Cold sweat trickled down his back.

She shuddered, her elbows jutting out as she hugged herself.

Her arms were folded tightly across her chest and her neck disappeared into her hunched shoulders.

She sat bolt upright, gulping quick breaths, and drew her dressing gown around her to block out the cold.

Her muscles tightened. She stopped. Unable to move.

Forcing her feet to move, she stepped forward.

She crept down the dark, icy passage and listened at each of the doors.

She hovered at the door and peered warily into the room.

Slowly, cautiously, she took a step into the room. Then another. It was empty. The bitter cold in the room draped over her like an icy blanket.

She was determined not to let her unease get the better of her, and continued down the passage despite the freezing air that sunk its teeth into her bones.

He ducked as a savage, deathly gust of cold air rushed out to meet him, taking his breath away.

She backed away, putting some distance between herself and the door, adrenalin making every sense in her body alert.

He lowered his voice, leant forward in his chair, and looked around cautiously before he spoke.

She stiffened . . . opened her mouth to speak but only a croak of fear emerged.

SECTION 3 – REACTION

WORDS

Nouns	**Reason**, imagination, sensation
	Tension, dread, shock
	Danger, darkness, silence
	House, floor, room, door
	Air, chill, cold, draught, breeze, gust
	Heat, warmth, fire, flames
	Touch, goosebumps, shivers, sweat
	Body, bones, spine, limbs, skin, hair
	Neck, face, cheeks, jaw, throat, lips, teeth
	Arms, hands, fingers, palms, nails, feet, toes
	Heart, chest, veins, blood
	Noise, breath, whisper, murmur
	Look, glance

Similes/ Metaphors	**Ice tomb**, icy fingers, like a cold, skeletal hand pinching his nerves, like ice-cold needles into the back of his neck, as if turned to iced water, like castanets, like a dark fog, like an electric current, leaped like a wild salmon in his chest
Adjectives	**Icy**, cold, prickly, chilly, aching, savage
	Strange, disturbing
	Trembling, shaking, shivering, shuddering
	Deathly pale, rigid, numb
	Nervous, rasping, ragged
Verbs	**Awoke**, warned
	Dropped, plummeted
	Breathed on, rested, met with, wafted, rushed
	Felt, brought, started, sent, buzzed, pulsed, crept, slithered, waved
	Moved, closed, squeezed, tightened, twisted
	Gripped, penetrated, riddled
	Froze, rooted, cowered, shivered
	Pushed, lifted, dug, buried, jerked, reached
	Gnashed, clenched, gnawed, bit, chattered
	Sank, lowered, whispered, murmured, shrieked, roared
	Strained, darted

PHRASES – NOUNS AND ADJECTIVES

* *Strange sensation*
* Icy dread
* *As if someone . . .*
* Something strange and deeply disturbing
* Something, someone in the room with her
* *Cold for no apparent reason*
* Suddenly chilled
* Icy cold to her touch
* An aching cold that . . .
* Icy and prickly
* As cold as an ice tomb
* No warmth from the flames

- *As the cold and shock . . .*
- Sweating and drenched in sweat
- *Wide eyes*
- Deathly pale face
- *Sound of his own breathing*
- Almost deafening in the silence
- *Every bone in his body*
- Trembling hands
- Hairs on his arms
- Like a cold, skeletal hand

PHRASES – VERBS

- As the clock struck midnight . . .
- Whenever she entered the top floor . . .
- *Certain there was something in the room with him*
- *Awoke afraid and rigid*
- Warned him to be alert
- Warned him that danger was near
- Paralysed by fear
- Rooted to the spot
- Hesitated just before she reached the open door
- Imagination whirled
- Jerked at every noise
- *Met with a gust of savage cold air*
- Wafted down from the end of the corridor
- Had a creeping certainty that there was . . .
- Breathing on her
- Resting icy cold fingers on her pillow
- *Began to feel cold*
- Temperature plummeted
- Turned icy
- Prickled as a chilly breeze . . .
- Brought a chill that gradually crept over her
- Broke out in a shiver of goosebumps
- Felt icy fingers close around her heart
- Brought a lingering, damp chill
- Felt an icy, cold chill crawl up her spine
- Felt numb with cold
- Chilled to the core with fear
- Pushed ice-cold needles into the back of his neck
- Sweating despite the cold
- No amount of heat could drive away

- *Tingled at the back of his neck*
- Buzzed along his limbs like an electric current
- Pulsed just beneath the skin
- Prickled with anticipation
- Had returned to tickle her bare arms
- Prickled his neck as . . .
- Gripped the back of his neck
- Sent a shiver down his spine
- Gradually crept over her
- Reached around her spine
- Waved up and down all through him
- Riddled her body
- Penetrated her entire body
- *Started to shiver*
- Shivered violently
- Gnawed at his bones
- Started at his toes and fingers
- Moved up into his chest and throat
- *Settled on her like a dark fog*
- Leaped like a wild salmon in his chest
- Tightened and twisted as a single word roared in her head
- More afraid than she had ever been in her life
- *Lifted a hand to feel her face and shuddered*
- Buried her head in her hands and sobbed
- Dug her nails into her palms to stop them shaking
- *Exchanged a nervous look*
- Flickered briefly to Robert's face
- Strained to pierce the darkness
- Darted wildly from side to side
- *Gnashed against each other inside her cheeks*
- Clenched her teeth so hard her jaw ached
- Bit her lip
- Chattered like castanets
- Too scared to make a noise
- *Forced him to take a shuddering breath*
- Could hardly breathe, could hardly stand
- Struggled to control her ragged breaths
- Sank to a murmur
- Came out as a rasping whisper
- Shrieked as the cold air brushed her face

SENTENCES

She awoke afraid and rigid.

She was rooted to the spot, hands trembling and her face deathly pale.

She hesitated just before she reached the open door, suddenly more afraid than she had ever been in her life.

Something strange was happening in the house. Something strange and deeply disturbing. Whenever she entered the top floor, she was met with a gust of savage cold air.

The hairs on his arms prickled as a chilly breeze wafted down from the end of the corridor.

His skin broke out in a shiver of goosebumps as the cold and shock struck.

She felt an icy chill crawl up her spine. Paralysed by fear, her imagination worked with feverish haste.

Foreboding buzzed along his limbs like an electric current pulsing just beneath the skin.

He began to feel cold. Icy dread prickled his neck as the clock struck midnight, and the temperature plummeted, warning him that danger was near.

A strange sensation had gripped the back of his neck, like a cold, skeletal hand pinching his nerves, sending a shiver down his spine.

He had a creeping certainty that there was something, someone in the room with him; breathing on him; resting icy cold fingers on his pillow.

Every bone in his body was tensed and the skin tingled at the back of his neck, warning him to be alert. His wide eyes strained to pierce the darkness and darted wildly from side to side, certain there was something in the room with him.

She had a lingering chill, as if someone was pushing ice-cold needles into the back of her neck.

He was sweating despite the cold. His skin prickled with anticipation.

She started to shiver. It was an aching cold that gnawed at her bones, starting at her toes and fingers, and moving up into her chest and throat.

The blood in her veins felt as if it had turned to ice water, she was so cold.

She felt a cold chill crawl up her spine. Paralysed by fear, her imagination whirled and her body jerked at every noise.

She woke, feeling numb with cold and chilled to the core with fear.

She lifted a hand to feel her face and shuddered; it was icy cold to her touch. She shivered more violently. She buried her head in her hands and sobbed.

The air was icy and prickly and the tension so great he could hardly breathe, could hardly stand, his heart nearly bursting through his chest.

His heart leaped like a wild salmon in his chest and forced him to take a shuddering breath.

Fear slithered around her like a dark fog, bringing a damp chill that gradually crept over her, even though she was sweating and drenched in sweat.

Her teeth gnashed against each other inside her cheeks.

She clenched her teeth so hard her jaw ached.

His jaw was trembling, his teeth chattering like castanets and no matter how hard he bit his lips, he couldn't control either.

She was too scared to make a noise.

The sound of his own breathing was almost deafening in the silence.

His voice sank to a murmur.

She shrieked as the cold air brushed her face.

He felt icy fingers close around his heart as cold as the ice tomb that surrounded him. His stomach tightened and twisted as a single word roared in his head. It came out as a rasping whisper. Ghost!

She bit her lip and dug her nails into her palms to stop them shaking.

Kitty's eyes flickered briefly to Robert's face and they exchanged a nervous look.

9
Sounds

She shouted frantically down the phone, trying to make herself heard above the crackling on the line.

All of a sudden the line went dead; the lights flickered and went out. **A shivering wave of terror charged down her spine.** Had she heard something? Was there someone in the corridor? These questions **cascaded through her mind** as she stood in the dark, rooted to the spot, her **eyes squinting through the shadows for the slightest movement, expecting to see something hideous in every shadow.**

Trembling, she pressed her ear to the door. Something was coming closer. **She could feel its presence. She was suddenly more afraid than she had ever been in her life.**

SECTION 1 – SETTING

WORDS

Nouns	**House**, castle, yard, passage, corridor, hall, room, stairs, basement
	Wall, floorboards, door, lock, window, shutter, glass, curtains
	Light, chandelier, plumbing, pipes, rocking-chair, bookcase, bed, wardrobe, phone, dress, silk
	Footsteps, feet, boot, heel, shuffle
	Chains, axe, sword
	Air, wind, draught, breeze, gale

Rustle, scrape, flutter, swish, tap, click, patter, creak, crackle

Knock, thud, bang, crash, blast, slam, echo

Breath, voice, whisper, murmur, mutter, sigh, hiss, moan, groan, grunt

Rattle, wheeze, cough

Laugh, laughter, giggle, snort, cackle, snicker, gurgle

Cry, sob, howl, scream, shriek, screech, roar

Venom, menace

Similes/ Metaphors

Like the shriek of a seagull, like a drill, like a wrapper

Adjectives

Old, ancient, rusty

Buzzing, crackling, splintering

Quick, swift, hurried, scrambling, shuffling

Small, weak, faint, quiet, calm

Low, low-pitched, deep, smooth, soft

Dull, misty, muffled, distant, hollow

Loud, booming, thunderous, deafening

Sharp, shrill, piercing, ear-splitting, bone-wrenching, juddering, grinding

Deep, dry, rough, hoarse, croaky, scratchy, throaty, guttural, rasping, hissing, gasping, racking, wheezing

Cold, icy, frosty, clipped

Harsh, cruel, threatening, venomous

Sad, sorrowful, mournful, grief-stricken, tortured

Angry, teasing, mocking, snickering, chortling, sneering, demonic, malignant, fiendish

Odd, strange, peculiar, mysterious, eerie

Frantic, desperate

Verbs

Scratched, scraped, rustled, swished, creaked, clicked, clinked, crackled, clanked, clanged, crashed, splintered, smashed

Rattled, banged, boomed, slammed, crashed, thudded, juddered, vibrated, jarred, pierced

Scuttled, scurried, stomped, shuffled

Whipped, shattered, shredded

Sighed, whispered, hummed, buzzed, whined, sucked, moaned, groaned

Cried, sobbed, wailed, howled, screamed, shrieked, screeched

Laughed, giggled, cackled, gurgled, snickered, chortled, sneered, snorted, jeered

Cracked, rasped

Spoke, whistled

PHRASES – NOUNS AND ADJECTIVES

* In the passage ahead of him
* From far off in the house
* From somewhere inside
* From up the stairs
* From behind the wooden panelling
* In the corridor
* Outside the door
* Outside the window
* Deep in the basement
* Behind his bed
* Rustle behind him
* Not far away
* *Close to his shoulder*
* Near his ear
* *Swish of silk*
* Soft thud
* Clink of a chandelier
* Creak of a rocking-chair
* Flapping curtain
* *Scratching sound*
* Humming pipes
* Strange buzzing noise
* *Footsteps on the stairs*
* Slow shuffle
* Shuffling footsteps
* Scuffling run
* Swift patter of footsteps
* Squeak of a boot heel
* Thump and thud of his feet
* *Splintering sound*
* Shattering of breaking glass

* Juddering crash
* Piercing blast
* Crashing sounds, slamming noises
* Thudding of an axe
* Clanking of chains
* Clink, clang of a sword
* *Prickly murmur*
* Rasping hiss
* Soft, misty voice
* Dry rattle
* Throaty wheeze
* Rasping breath
* Husky murmur
* Ghostly whisper
* Muffled voice
* Croaky voice
* Loud, rasping rattle
* Faint wheezing from the back of the room
* Cracked, old voice
* *Low snickering*
* Shrill whisper
* Squeaky, rasping voice
* Rasping hiss
* Threatening hiss
* Venomous hiss
* *Stifled snort*
* Scornful giggle
* Snickering cackle
* Chortling cackles
* Throaty cackle
* Malignant cackle
* Half screech, half laughter
* Manic laughter
* Loud demonic laugh
* Shrill and harsh like the shriek of a seagull
* *Frosty voice*
* Cold and cruel
* Ice-cold venom
* Low, cold and full of menace
* *Tortured screams*
* Frantic cry
* Howls and shrieks of a misty presence
* Bone-wrenching scream
* Blood-curdling scream

★ Eerie, ear-splitting shriek
★ *Thunderous voice*
★ Guttural roar

PHRASES – VERBS

★ Announced the ghost's presence
★ *Kept him awake*
★ Echoed in his head
★ Bored into him like a drill
★ Echoed through the castle
★ Echoed around the room
★ Echoed off the shadowy walls
★ Died away in their own echoes
★ *Came out of the shadows*
★ Flapped in the wind
★ Vibrated through the wall
★ Scraped on the cobbled yard
★ Boomed along the corridor walls
★ Moved back and forth across the wooden floorboards
★ Rattled the windows as it wailed by
★ *Moved closer to his room*
★ Rumbled closer until it filled her ears
★ *Spoke directly into her ear*
★ Whispered her name
★ Sighed in her ear
★ *Drifted through the door*
★ Blew into the room
★ Scuttled across the floor
★ Darted across the room
★ *Creaked open*
★ Thud and click as the lock turned
★ Rustled like a wrapper
★ Crackled on the line
★ Muffled by the fog
★ *Ripped through the silence*
★ Shattered the silence
★ Calm shattered by . . .
★ Slashed through the air
★ Sliced the air in the room
★ Slammed open
★ Boomed ominously

Her heart hammered in her chest as the eerie silence was broken by the flapping of the curtain, which blew into the room.

The chandelier clinked in the draught from the window.

She held her breath as the floorboards creaked and something moved closer to her hiding place.

Suddenly, she heard a rustle behind her. She was afraid to move, terrified of what was waiting for her in the shadows.

The noises seemed to be closing in on them – the gurgle of the pipes, rustle of the curtains, creak of the floorboards, shuffling footsteps down the corridor.

She froze. The sound was right behind her in the room.

She sensed a movement. Something was behind her.

That night she woke from a deep sleep a little after midnight and lay a minute listening intently, trying to place the source of the sounds outside the door.

He became aware of faint, muffled sounds of movement.

Then he heard a sound – the quiet, stealthy sound of someone or something moving.

A flicker of sound from the darkness alerted her to the presence.

The nightly whispers had returned, riding on the wind through a gap under the door.

A cracked, old voice rasped and rattled somewhere near her ear.

The dry, hoarse voice wheezed from behind the bookcase as it tilted and the books flew off the shelves to make a pile in the middle of the room.

A scratching sound vibrated the floor as a faint whispering drifted through the air from the back of the room.

It was as if something was sucking air through its teeth, then letting it out in a rasping hiss.

Half screech, half laughter slashed the air.

It was a monstrous voice that visited her nightly – a whisper of ice-cold venom, a freezing breath on her cheek.

A laugh like a screeching seagull echoed down the corridor.

A piercing, spine-chilling scream ripped through the air and sent her scuttling to the safety of the bathroom.

A brief, desperate howl of pain echoed through the building. Then silence. Moments later, the howling started again.

A faint grating sounded deep within the wall, followed by the sound of muffled footsteps.

He whirled round in terror. There was nothing there. But he knew he had heard footsteps.

They stiffened as the sound of footsteps behind them echoed in the silence. Someone was following them.

She heard the slow shuffle as someone moved around the room upstairs, and then came an eerie, spine-tingling noise.

The footsteps outside in the passage sounded awkward, clumsy scrapes which shattered the silence with their echoes.

Something huge was moving towards him. Its slow, shuffling feet were getting closer with every step.

The silence was suddenly broken by the squeak of a boot heel and the clanking of a chain being dragged across the tiled floor.

The shattering crash of breaking glass and splintering woodwork echoed through the tower.

He crouched behind the door as the thud, thud of an axe pounded down the corridor outside his room; the portraits of long forgotten relatives ripped and torn from the walls.

As the scream of an owl sliced through the air, something scuttled down the passage, and he had a fleeting glimpse of a swooping shadow.

His voice broke up as the crackling on the line became louder and more insistent. Then all of a sudden the line went dead. Down the corridor a door slammed shut.

He heard voices and scuffling and grunting. More scuffling. Then silence.

Somewhere in the house, a door crashed.

Faint scratching noises, like fingernails clawing at stone, came from inside the walls.

He listened nervously to the boots echoing on the floorboards, the sound of a door shutting, and shivered as silence descended on the room again.

There was the tiptoe of a footstep in the passage, the noise of the latch lifting gently and then let fall again, as the door was fastened. A moment's pause, then the footsteps tiptoed away again.

She turned away – just in time to see her bedroom door slowly swinging open.

As she woke, she became aware of the door creaking and swinging open behind her.

Before he could touch the handle, the door swung open, and he found himself looking at . . .

The door closed behind him with a thud as a sudden gust of wind rushed through the room.

Something was coming closer. She could feel its presence.

The footsteps were louder. Another creak, another shuffle just down the corridor. Only seconds away.

The clanging of chains was getting closer. Whoever it was had almost reached the top of the stairs. In seconds, they would be close enough for him to see.

The shuffling footsteps edged nearer. Soon they would be on the landing and heading straight for her room.

The footsteps were growing louder and getting closer. He could hear the creak of boot leather and then, one foot dragging along the floor.

SECTION 2 – INTERACTION

WORDS

Nouns	**Path**, house, corner, gap
	Room, door, hinges, stairs, window, chests
	Sound, noises, footsteps, shoe, steps
	Sense, hearing, breathing, adrenalin
	Body, muscle, head, eyes, ears, arms, hands, fingers, feet
	Whisper, rustle, shuffle, creak, scream, shriek
Pronouns	**Whatever**, something, somebody
Adjectives	**Close**, next, approaching
	Harsh, hideous
	Certain, unsure, cautious, afraid, terrified
	Shaking, still, motionless, paralysed, cross-legged
Verbs	**Began**, started
	Shuddered, slammed, rang, creaked, crashed
	Opened, shut, closed
	Expected, discovered
	Alarmed, startled, galvanised
	Listened, strained, heard, blocked

Touched, felt, pressed, ran, pushed, slapped, thrust, y a n k e d, wrenched

Rammed, jammed, clapped

Lifted, raised, turned, whirled, whipped

Looked, saw, glimpsed, glanced, peered, stared, scanned, searched

Sat, crouched, huddled

Stopped, halted, waited, stayed, paused, hesitated, lingered

Glued, rooted, froze, tensed

Backed away, retreated

Stood, moved, approached, ventured, emerged

Crept, crawled, drew closer

Trod, stepped, edged, inched, hugged, skirted, flattened

Leaped, jumped, shot upwards, sprang, dived

Darted, raced, bolted

Adverbs   **Silently**, slowly, nervously, anxiously, furtively

Quickly

Ominously

PHRASES – NOUNS AND ADJECTIVES

* As the sound of footsteps . . .
* *With a shaking hand . . .*
* With trembling hands
* *One of the smaller rooms*
* In the corner of the room
* In the shadows
* *Down the path, away from the house*
* Through the gap between the huge oak chests
* *With every sense alert . . .*
* Every muscle in his body . . .
* Huge wave of adrenalin
* Taut muscles
* With heightened hearing . . .
* Ready to . . .
* Motionless, alert
* As fast as possible

* *Approaching feet*
* Ominously close
* *Rusty hinges*
* Harsh, hideous shriek from within

PHRASES – VERBS

* *Certain he had heard a sound*
* Unsure of what she would discover inside
* It was like somebody had . . .
* As he stood and listened . . .
* While she scanned the corridor . . .
* Before going inside . . .
* About to go back to her room when . . .
* The next thing he knew was . . .
* *As the whispering started again . . .*
* As the steps moved closer . . .
* As he heard the sound of . . . behind him . . .
* As the lightning flashed . . .
* As the door in front of him shuddered and slammed shut . . .
* With her arms pressed over her ears . . .
* As she touched the door . . .
* As she screwed her eyes shut . . .
* Fully expecting whatever was out there to . . .
* Until he reached the safety of his room
* *Creaked under her feet*
* Slammed behind her
* Sent it crashing open
* Closed in on him
* Lost in the shriek of the gale
* *Listened for a moment*
* Listened for a moment. Nothing. Then . . .
* Listened nervously for the sound of . . .
* Listened until there was another sound to guide him
* *Put an ear to the . . .*
* Trembled as she pressed an ear to the wood
* Couldn't tell where the noise was coming from
* *Filled her head*
* Ears rang with a scream
* Clapped her hands over her ears to block out the noise
* Rammed her fingers into her ears
* Blocked out the chorus of clanging bells
* *Lay in bed in the darkness*

- ★ Shot upright
- ★ Shot upwards into a sitting position
- ★ Pushed himself upright in bed
- ★ Leaped out of her bed
- ★ Terrified of raising her head
- ★ Jumped every time . . .
- ★ Tried to control the creeping terror that was spreading through her
- ★ Galvanised by her panic
- ★ *Froze and tensed*
- ★ *Afraid to move*
- ★ *Paralysed by fear*
- ★ Stopped dead in his tracks
- ★ Couldn't move
- ★ Glued her feet to the floor
- ★ Sat cross-legged on the floor
- ★ Sat motionless for several minutes
- ★ Stood behind the door
- ★ *Waited a few moments*
- ★ Paused at the top of the stairs
- ★ Paused outside the door
- ★ Paused again to listen for the sound of . . .
- ★ Hesitated at the foot of the stairs
- ★ Hesitated and then went into the . . .
- ★ Halted at every rustle, shuffle, creak
- ★ *Ducked behind a cabinet*
- ★ Ducked back into . . .
- ★ Crouched behind . . .
- ★ *Backed away from the locked door*
- ★ Slipped further into the shadows
- ★ Lingered in the shadows
- ★ Huddled in the darkness
- ★ Flattened himself against the wall
- ★ *Opened his eyes as he heard*
- ★ Glanced around the room
- ★ Kept glancing behind him
- ★ Peered down the stairs
- ★ Peered furtively around the corners
- ★ Peeked through the open doors
- ★ Lifted her head enough to . . .
- ★ Whipped her head around
- ★ Glanced anxiously over her shoulder
- ★ Looked over the curve of her shoulder to see if anyone was there
- ★ Stared at the locked door
- ★ Scanned the room

* Searched the shadows, the dusty corners
* Caught a brief glimpse of . . .
* *Turned around*
* Whirled round to face . . .
* *Crept out into the passage*
* Crept down the dark, icy cold passage
* Drew closer
* Moved towards the sound
* Moved closer to the room
* Crawled towards the noises
* Crept forward and scanned the room
* Approached the closed door
* Ventured a step closer to the door . . . then another
* Moved silently into the adjoining room
* Managed to start moving again
* Emerged in a low, dark room
* Stayed close to the walls
* Skirted the suits of armour
* Hugged the shadows
* Trod carefully down the corridor
* Avoided creaky floorboards
* Edged down the corridor, paused . . . nothing stirred
* *Felt along the wall for the light switch*
* Ran it along the wall until he located the light switch
* Slapped on the main bedroom light switch on the wall next to it
* Thrust his hand out in front of him
* Reached out a hand to try the door
* Reached for the doorknob
* Yanked on the handle . . . wouldn't budge . . . locked
* Turned the handle
* Eased the handle down a fraction at a time
* Opened it a bit more
* Gave the door a cautious push
* Turned the door handle and stepped inside
* Wrenched the door open
* *Dived into his room*
* Quickened his pace
* Sprang up and darted to the door
* Raced down the corridor
* Darted around the room
* Sprinted across the passage
* Changed direction
* Ran to the next corner
* Raced down the passage

- ★ Darted up the stairs
- ★ Saw a door ahead and raced towards it
- ★ Ran out of the heavy front door
- ★ Bolted outside
- ★ *Caught against something*
- ★ Stumbled and crashed to the floor
- ★ *Hardly dared to breathe*
- ★ Took a deep breath

SENTENCES

The next thing he knew, he was sitting bolt upright, his ears ringing with manic laughter like the shriek of a seagull.

She shot upright and glanced around the room.

Shooting upwards into a sitting position, she clutched the duvet to her face.

He pushed himself upright in bed, turned around, his eyes darting around the room, searching the shadows, the dusty corners.

Lying in bed in the darkness, her sense of hearing heightened, a huge wave of adrenalin swept through her body.

Galvanised by her panic, she leaped out of her bed and ran to the door, slapping on the main bedroom light switch on the wall next to it.

She couldn't move. It was like somebody had glued her feet to the floor.

He froze, certain he had heard a sound. Every sense was alert and his muscles taut as he stood and listened.

Kitty sat motionless for several minutes while she scanned the corridor. Then as the whispering started again, she sprang up and darted to the door.

He stopped dead in his tracks as he heard the sound of footsteps behind him. Quickly, he changed direction, raced down the passage, and ducked behind a cabinet in the corner of the room.

She paused at the top of the stairs, peering down, trying to control the creeping terror that was spreading through her.

He spun round, ready to run as the door in front of him shuddered and slammed shut.

She straightened. Listened. Peered towards the open window.

She crouched on the ground. She was afraid to move. Terrified of raising her head.

She sat cross-legged on the floor in the shadows, and listened nervously for the sound of splintering glass.

She was about to go back to her room when she heard a sound. She froze and tensed. Taking a deep breath, she whirled round to face the door.

She paused outside the door, listening for a moment, then, with a shaking hand, she reached for the doorknob.

Slowly, he moved towards the flapping curtain.

She crept out into the passage and approached the closed door.

As the sound of footsteps drew closer, she ducked back into one of the smaller rooms and stood there, behind the door, hardly daring to breathe.

She ventured a step closer to the door. Then another. Trembling, she pressed an ear to the wood.

She backed away from the locked door, staring at it, fully expecting whatever was using the axe to send the door crashing open.

She crept forward and scanned the room. It was empty. She moved silently into the adjoining room.

She crept down the dark, icy cold passage and listened at each of the doors.

She ventured a step closer to the door. Then another.

The noise had suddenly stopped. She paused outside, put an ear to the door, listening for a moment. Nothing. Then, with a shaking hand, she reached for the doorknob.

Writhing and twisting, Katie crawled through the gap between the huge oak chests towards the noises and emerged in a low, dark room.

Katie skirted the suits of armour, hugging the shadows, peering furtively around the corners.

He kept glancing behind him, listening for the venomous hiss, every muscle in his body tensed.

Her shoe caught against something and she stumbled and crashed to the floor.

Treading carefully, avoiding creaky floorboards, hardly daring to breathe, she peered through the open doors.

Her legs wobbled, threatening to give way.

Whipping her head round, she scanned the room. It was empty.

She felt along the wall for the light switch.

He thrust his hand out in front of him, and ran it along the wall until he located the light switch.

She reached out a hand to try the door. As she touched it, there was a harsh, hideous shriek from within.

She eased the handle down a fraction at a time; stopped a moment and listened. She opened it a bit more, unsure of what she would discover inside.

The demonic laughter filled her head. She clapped her hands over her ears to block it out.

Her face was pinched with terror as she screwed her eyes shut and rammed her fingers into her ears to block out the creak of the rocking-chair.

He ran to the next corner, waited a moment and peered round.

He glanced anxiously over his shoulder as the steps moved closer. Darting up the stairs, he saw a door ahead and raced towards it. He yanked on the handle; wrenched the door open; dived inside.

She raced down the corridor with her arms pressed over her ears to block out the chorus of clanging bells and ran out, the heavy front door slamming behind her. She bolted outside, down the path, away from the house as fast as she could.

He couldn't tell where the noise was coming from. He quickened his pace, but the ground was uneven and he stumbled, crashing to the ground.

SECTION 3 – REACTION

WORDS	
Nouns	**Mind**, senses, feeling, dream, nightmare, premonition, foreboding
	Presence, visitor
	Silence, sound, footsteps, shuffle, rustle
	Voice, sigh, whisper, shouts, sob, wail
	Pain, misery
	Movement, shadow
	Body, bone, spine, ribs, hair, sweat
	Heart, blood, chest, throat
	Head, neck, ears, eyes
	Feet, hands, palms, nails
	Expression
	Breath, breathing
	Urgency, panic

Similes/ Metaphors	**Pale mask in the moonlight**, like an electric shock, shivering wave of terror, seized him in its jaws
Adjectives	**Tense**, rigid, afraid, terrified
	Wide, staring, alert
	Pale, troubled, urgent, desperate
	Strange, eerie
	Cold, chilling
	Muffled, faint, raspy
	Loud, deafening
	Skeletal, shrivelled, grisly, hideous
Verbs	**Woke**, awoke
	Listened, strained, heard, squeaked, thundered
	Tensed, jumped, shook, shivered, shuddered
	Knew, expected
	Fought, forced, ordered, commanded, found
	Felt, tingled, ran, bubbled, curdled, prickled, buzzed
	Seized, clenched, writhed, twisted, thudded, hammered, pounded
	Descended, intensified
	Settled on, knitted, bit, gnawed
	Clutched, clung, covered
	Lay, crouched, rooted
	Squeezed shut, clamped shut, flew open, snapped open, saw, glanced
	Held, dropped, trailed off, caught

PHRASES – NOUNS AND ADJECTIVES

- ★ A long night
- ★ In the middle of the night . . .
- ★ *At first he . . .*
- ★ With bated breath . . .
- ★ *Something deep in her mind*
- ★ Not a dream
- ★ Inwardly she . . .

- *Just outside the door*
- Wide awake
- Every bone in his body
- A prickle at the bottom of her spine
- Up into his hair and down to his feet
- *A troubled expression*
- Face was expressionless
- Face a pale mask in the moonlight
- *Not alone in the house*
- First creak of the door
- Creak of the stairs
- Rustle behind her
- Muffled shuffling on the wooden floor
- Very slow footsteps, one at a time, with long pauses in between
- Faint movement of the floorboards
- Skeletal hand on the door handle
- Scrape of shrivelled bone
- Wailing full of human misery and pain
- Something in the desperate urgency of the shouts
- Deafening sound of his own breathing
- Almost deafening in the silence
- *At any moment...*
- Ominously close
- Closer by the minute

PHRASES – VERBS

- Something was very wrong
- Premonition that something bad was about to happen
- Whatever was on the other side of the door . . .
- All that separated them was . . .
- *As if time had stopped*
- As she listened to the sounds . . .
- As she strained for the sound of . . .
- As the footsteps came closer and closer . . .
- *All her senses were on high alert*
- Woke in a cold sweat
- Awoke, afraid and rigid
- Paralysed with fear
- Had a strange feeling
- Had she heard something?
- Could she really hear raspy breathing outside the door?
- Was there someone in the corridor?

- ★ Tumbled frantically through her head
- ★ Told her it was no ordinary visitor outside her door
- ★ Could hear it . . . didn't want to see it
- ★ Knew that whatever had been whispering in the passage was now . . .
- ★ Expected to see something hideous in every shadow
- ★ *Felt her body tense and her senses sharpen*
- ★ Tingled at the back of her neck
- ★ Ran the length of his body
- ★ Started to prickle as her ears buzzed with the sound of . . .
- ★ Jumped when she heard a sound behind the . . .
- ★ Jerked at every new noise, at the slightest sound
- ★ Jumped every time a sound carried down the corridor
- ★ Shivered as the silence descended on the room again
- ★ Refused to stop shaking
- ★ *Could feel the panic*
- ★ Like something cold creeping over him
- ★ Had a chilling effect
- ★ More afraid than she had ever been in her life
- ★ Only bit of him that was moving was his heart
- ★ Made the blood curdle
- ★ Seized him in its jaws
- ★ Bubbled in her throat
- ★ Intensified when the sigh changed into . . .
- ★ Started to thud in her chest
- ★ Hammered inside her chest
- ★ Clenched in panic
- ★ Thudded in the hollow of her throat
- ★ Pounded so hard it seemed about to break his ribs
- ★ Writhed and twisted in her stomach
- ★ Startled her like an electric shock
- ★ Sent a shivering wave of terror down his spine
- ★ Charged down his spine like an electric shock
- ★ Shuddered and went rigid, as if rooted to the spot
- ★ *Had to force herself to*
- ★ Fought to remain calm
- ★ Pushed through her fear
- ★ Commanded her body to stop trembling
- ★ Knew he had to think of something fast
- ★ Found the courage to put one foot in front of the other
- ★ Knew she had to do whatever she needed to get out of there
- ★ *Settled on her face*
- ★ Bit her lips
- ★ Knitted her eyebrows together
- ★ *Had begun again*

- ☆ Could hear the whispering getting closer
- ☆ Heard from a little way off
- ☆ Heard the footsteps thudding up the stairs
- ☆ Squeaked on the wooden floor
- ☆ Waited for the thunder of boots on the stairs
- ☆ Filled her head until it felt like it would split apart
- ☆ Shook her head from left to right to get rid of the noise
- ☆ *Held their breath*
- ☆ Too tense to breathe
- ☆ Dropped to an urgent whisper
- ☆ Trailed off as the noises started again
- ☆ Caught his breath in a sob
- ☆ *Flew open in the darkness*
- ☆ Snapped her eyes open
- ☆ Glanced around fearfully
- ☆ Saw it at the end of the corridor
- ☆ Afraid to look
- ☆ Squeezed her eyes shut
- ☆ Realised that her eyes were clamped shut
- ☆ *Clutched the duvet about her head*
- ☆ Dug her nails into her palms
- ☆ Covered her ears with the palms of her hands
- ☆ *Lay in his bed*
- ☆ Crouched in the dark
- ☆ Felt her legs begin to quiver
- ☆ Shuddered and went rigid, as if rooted to the spot
- ☆ Wanted to get up and run, but she knew she couldn't
- ☆ Hesitated before she reached the open door
- ☆ Waited, frozen to the spot
- ☆ Waited for the noises to stop

SENTENCES

She awoke, afraid and rigid.

It was a long night and at first he jumped at the slightest sound – a creak of the stairs or a faint movement of the floorboards.

She woke in a cold sweat in the middle of the night.

She had a strange feeling – a premonition that something bad was about to happen.

Had she heard something? Was there someone in the corridor? These questions tumbled frantically through her mind as she clutched the duvet above her head.

Something deep in her mind told her that it was no ordinary visitor outside her door.

He lay in his bed, his face a pale mask in the moonlight. Occasionally, a tremor would run the length of his body.

Every bone in his body was tensed, his senses sharpened. The skin tingled at the back of his neck as he waited with bated breath for the noises to start again.

All her senses were on high alert as she strained for the sound of the shuffling footsteps.

He could hear the whispering getting closer. A shiver charged down his spine like an electric shock.

He shivered as the silence descended on the room again.

As she listened to the sounds, a troubled expression settled on her face.

Her face was expressionless, but inwardly she was fighting to remain calm.

He knew that whatever had been whispering in the passage was now standing outside the door, listening.

Could she really hear the raspy breathing outside the door?

Whatever lay on the other side of the door, she didn't want to see it.

It was standing right outside the door. She could hear it. All that separated them was a wooden door. She shivered as the image of a skeletal hand on the door handle – the scrape of shrivelled bone – rushed through her head.

Coldness writhed and twisted in her stomach. Something was very wrong.

She felt her legs begin to quiver.

Her heart started to thud in her chest as she crouched in the dark.

She jumped when she heard a creaking sound behind her, her heart hammering inside her chest.

Kitty was shaking with terror and dread that at any moment the noises would start again.

There was something in the desperate urgency of the shouts that sent a shivering wave of terror down his spine.

His stomach clenched in panic and he knew he had to think of something fast. The sound of echoing footsteps was getting closer by the minute.

She could feel the panic as a prickle at the bottom of her spine. Terrified, she had to force herself to find the courage to put one foot in front of the other.

Panic bubbled in her throat as suddenly she saw it at the end of the corridor.

Her heart hammered in her chest as the footsteps came closer and closer, squeaking on the wooden floor.

The first creak of the door startled him like an electric shock.

She jumped when she heard a sound behind the door, her heart thudding against her ribs.

It had a chilling effect, like something cold creeping over him, up into his hair and down to his feet. The terror intensified when the sigh changed into a wailing full of human misery and pain that made the blood curdle.

She hesitated just before she reached the open door, suddenly more afraid than she had ever been in her life.

The only bit of him that was moving was his heart, which pounded so hard it seemed about to break his ribs.

It was as if time had stopped. She shuddered and went rigid, as if rooted to the spot.

She was paralysed with fear and jumped every time a sound carried down the corridor.

She wanted to get up and run, but she knew she couldn't. She had heard the footsteps thudding up the stairs.

His voice trailed off as the noises started again.

Her voice dropped to an urgent whisper.

He caught his breath in a sob; the footsteps had begun again.

The sound of his own breathing was almost deafening in the silence.

The voice filled her head until it felt it would split apart.

Her ears began to buzz and she shook her head from left to right to get rid of the noise.

She had to squeeze her eyes shut and cover her ears with the palms of her hands, all the time begging for the noises to stop.

She squeezed her eyes shut, afraid to look.

She realised that her eyes were clamped shut and she snapped them open.

Her eyes widened and her body jerked at every new noise.

She glanced around fearfully, expecting to see something hideous in every shadow.

Her eyes flew open in the darkness. She was wide awake now, and too tense to breathe. This was no dream. She was not alone in the house.

She knitted her eyebrows together, listening for the sound, and there it was, a muffled shuffling on the wooden floor just outside the door.

Desperately, she commanded her body to stop trembling. It refused. Ignored her pleas to get away as far as possible from the noises. But she knew she had to do whatever it took to get out of there. She bit her lip and dug her nails into her palms. She pushed through her fear, her pulse thudding in the hollow of her throat, and eventually started to move.

10
Touch

Kitty was woken in the middle of the night. A hot panting breath had touched the back of her neck . . . as if there was somebody in the room, close to the bed, leaning over her. **Every nerve in her body warned Kitty not to move.**

    Drenched in sweat, heart racing, Kitty kept her eyes squeezed shut, **too terrified to look to see who had woken her.**

    As she lay motionless in the bed, another puff of hot air brushed her cheek. **Every nerve in her body screamed out in terror.** In the end, Kitty **could do nothing to prevent the muted sob that escaped her throat.**

SECTION 1 – SETTING

WORDS	

Nouns	**Body**, back, spine, bones, arms, hands, fist, fingers, legs, feet, ankles, shoe
	Head, neck, face, skin, hair, nerves, cheek, ears, nose, nostrils
	Breath, air, dust, wind, heat, cold, ice, acid
	Hallway, room
	Curtains, shutters, light, shadows
	Edges, points
	Touch, grip, grasp
Similes/ Metaphors	**Like rippling silk**, like a feather, like a dead fish, like a damp towel, as if touched by acid, with icy fingers
Adjectives	**Round**, hollow

Rough, coarse, bristly, hairy, furry

Dry, stale, crusty, cracked, brittle, dead, wrinkled, shrivelled, withered

Cold, chill, icy, freezing, glacial, bitter, frosty, savage, bone-crushing

Hot, fiery, boiling, searing, scorching, scalding, burning, blistering, sizzling

Sharp, spiky, prickly, jagged, pointed, thorny, needle-sharp, claw-like

Wet, damp, slippery, mouldy, sticky, slimy, soggy, squelchy, oily, greasy, waxy, sleek

Verbs

Felt, touched, tickled, brushed, caressed

Rippled, flickered, fluttered, swished, slithered

Pushed, pulled, tugged, grabbed, gripped, clutched

Hit, moved, nudged, bashed

Tore, scratched, pricked, stung, tangled

Rushed, surged, wrapped, enveloped

Bent, ducked, lowered, kicked

PHRASES – NOUNS AND ADJECTIVES

* As if somebody . . .
* At the same time . . .
* *On the back of his neck*
* Above his head
* *Slight tickle on her neck*
* Warm breath
* Hot breath of someone close to her
* Like rippling silk
* Like a feather over their faces
* *Sleek and slimy*
* Slimy, like a dead fish
* *Needle-sharp points*
* Jagged edges
* *Chill air*
* Puff of cold air
* Icy breath on the back of his neck
* Savage, bone-crushing cold

- Bitter icy air
- Gust of fiery wind
- Billowing curtains

PHRASES – VERBS

- *Felt somebody very near her*
- Bent over her head
- Could feel the hot breath
- Felt a hot panting breath on her cheek
- Surged past her cheek
- Felt a heavy pressure on his back
- *Tickled his ear*
- Caressed her cheek
- Flickered over their faces
- Brushed against his face
- Brushed his head with its icy fingers
- *Slithered over his shoe*
- Plucked at his ankle
- Pricked his fingers
- *Rushed through the air*
- Fluttered towards the light
- Wrapped tightly around her
- Enveloped the room
- Hit him as he entered the attic
- *Stung her face*
- As if he had been touched by acid
- Tangled in his hair
- Scratched at his skin
- Tore at his face and hands
- Ran down his spine
- Felt icy fingers grab him
- Clutched him in its claw-like grasp
- Tried to pull him back into the room
- *Felt as if she was freezing from the inside*
- Gripped him like a clenched fist
- *Burnt her nostrils*
- Hurt her nose
- *Ducked as something dark . . .*
- Cowered away from the icy chill
- *Tugged at the duvet on his bed*
- Bashed against her legs
- Ran straight past her into the hallway

★ *Kicked something round, hollow*
★ Rolled away into the shadows

SENTENCES

Something soft brushed her face as if somebody had just touched it very gently.

She felt a hot breath on the back of her neck as if there was somebody very near her, bending over her head.

A breath of wind tickled his ear like rippling silk.

The warm breath caressed them like a feather flickering over their faces.

Suddenly she felt a puff of cold air as though the breath of someone leaning over her had caressed her cheek.

He ducked as something dark rushed through the air and brushed his head with its icy fingers.

The billowing curtains fluttered towards the light and brushed against his face like rippling silk.

Something sleek and sticky slithered over his shoe and plucked at his ankle.

His hand touched something above his head; something slimy, like a dead fish.

Robert could feel a breeze on the back of his neck. Shivers ran down his spine as if he had been touched by acid.

He felt icy fingers grab him and try to pull him back into the room.

She felt as if she was freezing from the inside.

The cold that enveloped the room gripped him like a strong, clenched fist.

He cowered away from the icy chill that hit him as he entered the attic.

She had been dozing and suddenly felt a heavy pressure on her back. At the same time, she felt a hot panting breath on her cheek.

The dry air hurt her nose and burnt her nostrils as she inhaled.

Her foot kicked something round, hollow, something which rolled away into the shadows.

SECTION 2 – INTERACTION

WORDS

Nouns	**Passage**, corridor, room, wall, corner, ground, stairs, step, doorway, door, handle, knob, furniture, bed, pillow

Bats, wings

Body, back, shoulder, leg, knees, foot, ankle, boot, hand, arms, fingers, eyes, mouth

Heart, chest, ribs, pulse

Darkness, torch, light

Echoes, scream

Similes/ Metaphors	**Like a black plume of smoke**, waved her arms like a metal detector
Adjectives	**Alarmed**, startled, shocked, terrified
	Breathless, shaking, trembling, shuddering
	Bare, furry, hairy
	Outstretched, flailing
Verbs	**Reached**, felt, touched, swept, fumbled, groped, grasped, grabbed, clutched, twisted, turned
	Glued, rooted
	Lifted, raised, twisted, spun, whirled
	Crept, inched, edged, hugged, shuffled, scrambled
	Stumbled, skidded, slipped, fell, sunk
	Backed, jerked, cringed, recoiled, struggled
	Ducked, dived, rushed, dashed, darted, bolted, hurtled
	Slammed, leaned, pressed
	Looked, shot, scanned
	Thudded, pounded, hammered
	Dropped, flew out of, fell, clattered, shattered, flickered, died
	Fluttered, swished
	Screamed, yelled, shrieked
Adverbs	**Sharply**, desperately, violently, manically, tightly
	Slowly, gingerly
	Headlong, sideways, backwards, forwards

PHRASES – NOUNS AND ADJECTIVES

- ★ With her right hand . . .
- ★ *In front of him*
- ★ In the doorway
- ★ Over the ground in front of her
- ★ With her back against the wall . . .
- ★ Bare foot
- ★ Flailing hand
- ★ Hundreds of bats, like a black plume of smoke
- ★ *Breathless and shaking*
- ★ So startled that he . . .

PHRASES – VERBS

- ★ Whatever was on the other side . . .
- ★ As she turned . . .
- ★ As she moved her leg . . .
- ★ As the torch flickered and died . . .
- ★ As his hand waved manically . . .
- ★ Woken in the middle of the night
- ★ *Touched something*
- ★ Grasped the handle
- ★ Grabbed the knob
- ★ Clutched the handle with both hands
- ★ Tried to prevent it turning
- ★ Twisted violently back and forth in her fingers
- ★ *Felt gingerly along the wall*
- ★ Felt the way with her outstretched hand
- ★ Felt her way for the next step in the dark
- ★ Had to spread her arms and feel for the wood on the stairs
- ★ Waved her arms like a metal detector
- ★ Clutched at the furniture
- ★ Groped for something to break her fall
- ★ *Fumbled through her pocket for her torch*
- ★ Tried desperately to feel for the torch
- ★ Swept her fingers over the ground
- ★ Threw her arm out
- ★ Flung her hand out in front of her
- ★ Swatted the air in front of him
- ★ Flailed in front of her as she searched for the door
- ★ Floundered with his outstretched hands
- ★ Flapped his hands in front of him

- ★ *Couldn't move*
- ★ *Glued to the . . .*
- ★ *Jerked backwards*
- ★ Raised her head from the pillow
- ★ Twisted round sharply
- ★ Spun round
- ★ Whirled round and found herself face-to-face with . . .
- ★ *Crept close to the wall*
- ★ Inched her way to the door
- ★ Hugged the wall with her back
- ★ Shuffled sideways, one foot crossing the other
- ★ Scrambled on his hands and knees
- ★ Scrambled to her feet
- ★ *Bolted down the corridor*
- ★ Dived through the door
- ★ Didn't stop to look back
- ★ *Slipped on . . .*
- ★ Caught his boot on something
- ★ Caught on something behind her
- ★ Coiled around her ankle
- ★ Never saw the thing that seized hold of her
- ★ *Stumbled, falling forwards*
- ★ Fell headlong down the stairs
- ★ Sunk into the mud
- ★ Skidded onto his knees
- ★ Thrashed against its grip
- ★ *Backed away from the door*
- ★ Backed into the room
- ★ Pressed her back against the door
- ★ Slammed the door shut behind her
- ★ Cringed backwards quickly
- ★ Recoiled from the door in terror
- ★ Struggled to get away
- ★ *Shot a look over her shoulder*
- ★ Looked frantically from side to side and over her shoulders
- ★ *Thudded against her ribs*
- ★ Pounded in her chest
- ★ *Clutched his hand to his mouth*
- ★ Stopped himself screaming out
- ★ Rung with the echoes of his scream
- ★ *Dropped his torch*
- ★ Flew out of his hand
- ★ Clattered, shattering on the ground
- ★ Flickered and went out

- ★ *Fluttered from every corner*
- ★ *Ducked as a swish of wings rushed through the air*
- ★ *Brushed his head with their furry bodies*

SENTENCES

He was woken in the middle of the night. As he moved his leg, Tom's bare foot touched something. He raised his head from the pillow and twisted round sharply.

Katie fumbled through her pocket for her torch.

He was so startled that the torch flew out of his hand and clattered, shattering on the ground. The light flickered and went out.

He had to scramble on his hands and knees in the doorway to find it, hoping that it still worked.

He caught his boot on something, skidded onto his knees and dropped his torch. Desperately sweeping his fingers over the ground, he searched for the torch.

His arms flailed in front of him as he searched for the door.

She stumbled and flung her hand out in front of her, groping for something to break her fall.

As the torch flickered and died, he was left floundering with his outstretched hands clutching at the furniture.

With his right hand he swatted the air in front of him.

Throwing her arm out, she felt gingerly along the wall.

She crept close to the wall as all light deserted her. With her back pressed against the wall, she inched her way to the door, feeling the way with her outstretched hand.

As she turned, the darkness seemed to blanket the stairs, and spreading her arms to feel her way, Kitty crouched and waved her arms like a metal detector over the ground in front of her.

She counted every step as she descended slowly, feeling her way for the next step in the dark.

Hugging the wall with her back, she shuffled sideways, one foot crossing the other, until she reached the door.

She spun round, her heart pounding in her chest.

She whirled around, but never saw the thing that seized hold of her.

She jerked backwards and bolted down the corridor.

She backed away from the door, breathless and shaking.

Alarmed, she backed into the room, slamming the door shut behind her, and pressed her back against it.

She recoiled from the door in terror. She grabbed the knob, clutching it tightly with both hands, and trying to prevent it turning.

She looked frantically from side to side and over her shoulders.

Her flailing hand grasped the handle and she dived through the door.

She scrambled to her feet and bolted down the hall, her heart thudding against her ribs. She didn't stop to look back.

He clutched his hand to his mouth to stop himself screaming out.

Her foot caught on something behind her. She shot a look over her shoulder as something coiled around her ankle. She thrashed against its grip and screamed.

Suddenly, hundreds of bats, like a black plume of smoke, fluttered from every corner and the passage rang with the echoes of his scream as he flapped his hands in front of him. He ducked as a swish of wings rushed through the air and bats brushed his head with their furry bodies.

SECTION 3 – REACTION

WORDS

Nouns	**Certainty**, terror, horror
	Body, spine, neck, arms, hands, fingers
	Chest, ribs, heart, veins, pulse, blood, nerves, fibre, hairs
	Head, face, eyes
	Mouth, throat, windpipe, tongue, lips
	Skin, goosebumps, shivers, sweat, pins and needles
	Breath, voice, sob, cry, whine, howl, scream
Pronouns	**Something**, someone, whatever
Adjectives	**Wide**, staring
	Pale, ashen
	Terrified, frozen, paralysed
	Creeping, shaking
	Tight, thin, high-pitched, shrill

Verbs	**Felt**, prickled, rushed, shot
	Squeezed, twisted, coiled, gripped, wrenched, choked, lodged
	Throbbed, pounded, racked
	Froze, stopped, stood still, rooted
	Touched, recoiled, flailed
	Lifted, raised, fixed, strained, stared, scanned
	Drew, sucked, held, silenced
	Uttered, escaped, whimpered, screamed, yelled, echoed

PHRASES – NOUNS AND ADJECTIVES

- ★ Something inside her
- ★ Creeping certainty that . . .
- ★ Something, someone in the room with him
- ★ *Every nerve in his body . . .*
- ★ Every fibre in his body . . .
- ★ Entire body
- ★ Beads of sweat
- ★ *Too terrified to . . .*
- ★ An electric bolt of alarm
- ★ Bolts of electricity
- ★ *Trembling hands*
- ★ Pins and needles
- ★ Outstretched arm was paralysed
- ★ *Frozen tongue*
- ★ Not a sound from . . .
- ★ *Wide eyes*
- ★ Wide, staring eyes
- ★ Narrowed eyes
- ★ Ashen face

PHRASES – VERBS

- ★ Unsure of what had just happened
- ★ Felt the hairs go up on the back of her neck
- ★ Broke out in a shiver of goosebumps as . . .
- ★ Warned him not to move
- ★ Pulse stopped, her heart stood still
- ★ Blood was suddenly chilled
- ★ *Pounded in her temples*

- ⋆ Squeezed tight
- ⋆ Missed a beat
- ⋆ Leaped like a wild salmon in his chest
- ⋆ Drenched in sweat and heart racing
- ⋆ Felt the terror like a red throb in her head
- ⋆ Gripped him like a snake coiling around his throat
- ⋆ Choking his windpipe
- ⋆ Lodged as a hard lump in her throat
- ⋆ Twisted inside her chest
- ⋆ Shot up her spine
- ⋆ Shot through her heart
- ⋆ Racked her body
- ⋆ Felt like one giant, throbbing heart
- ⋆ Like a sponge being wrung dry
- ⋆ *Felt her body tremble*
- ⋆ Even though his arm was shaking . . .
- ⋆ Prickled painfully in his ankle
- ⋆ Rooted to the spot
- ⋆ Recoiled in horror
- ⋆ *Wiped her brow and upper lip*
- ⋆ Stopped, her arms in the air, her mouth opened
- ⋆ Flailed wildly in front of her
- ⋆ *Raised her eyes*
- ⋆ Scanned the room
- ⋆ Strained to pierce the darkness
- ⋆ Darted to and fro
- ⋆ Darted wildly from side to side
- ⋆ Couldn't look up at whatever had touched her
- ⋆ Kept her narrowed eyes fixed to the floor
- ⋆ *Drew in a deep breath*
- ⋆ Sucked in her breath as . . .
- ⋆ Forced him to take a shuddering breath
- ⋆ Silenced her screams
- ⋆ Twisted in a scream that never came
- ⋆ Blew it out hard to stop herself howling
- ⋆ Uttered a silent, desperate cry
- ⋆ Uttered a thin, high-pitched scream
- ⋆ Couldn't help the muted whine of terror that escaped his throat
- ⋆ Whimpered and covered her face with her hands
- ⋆ Screamed out in terror
- ⋆ Shrieked as something brushed her face
- ⋆ Threw back his head and yelled at the top of his voice
- ⋆ Wrenched its way out of her chest
- ⋆ *Breathing on him*

☆ Brushed against something in the dark
   ☆ Resting icy cold fingers on his pillow

SENTENCES

She felt the hairs go up on the back of her neck.

Something inside him squeezed tight, like a sponge being wrung dry.

He had a creeping certainty that there was something, someone in the room with him; breathing on him; resting icy cold fingers on his pillow.

His entire body felt like one giant, throbbing heart.

Every fibre in his body was screaming out in terror.

An electric bolt of alarm shot through her heart.

Her pulse stopped, her heart stood still, her outstretched arm was paralysed.

Every nerve in his body warned him not to move, even though his arm was shaking and pins and needles prickled painfully in his ankle.

She felt the terror like a red throb in her head, the blood pounding in her temples.

Horror gripped him like a snake coiling around his throat and choking his windpipe.

She was rooted to the spot, hands trembling and her face ashen and drenched in sweat.

Her heart was pounding. Drawing in a deep breath, she blew it out hard to stop herself howling.

She sucked in her breath as shivers racked her body.

His heart leaped like a wild salmon in his chest and forced him to take a shuddering breath.

The terror rushed through her veins and lodged as a hard lump in her throat, silencing her screams.

No sound came from his frozen tongue.

She sucked in her breath as shivers racked her body.

He couldn't help the muted whine of terror that escaped his throat.

A sob wrenched its way out of her chest.

She stopped, her arms in the air, her mouth open, and uttered a silent, desperate cry.

She shrieked as something brushed her face.

She uttered a thin, high-pitched scream, which echoed through the house.

He clutched his hand to his mouth to stop himself screaming out, but as his hand brushed against something in the dark, he threw back his head and yelled at the top of his voice.

His wide eyes strained to pierce the darkness and darted wildly from side to side.

Drenched in sweat and heart racing, Kitty kept her narrowed eyes fixed to the floor, too terrified to look up at whatever had touched her.

He froze, unsure of what had just happened.

Her hands flailed wildly in front of her.

She wiped her brow and upper lip, but the beads of sweat erupted again.

11
Eerie presence

Behind her reflection in the mirror was a taller, dark silhouette, standing very still. Watching.

Her heart thudding in her chest, she whirled round and was blinded by a ghastly, glinting light flashing onto the wall.

With her wide eyes fixed on the strange shimmering shape, she backed out of the room, slamming the door shut behind her, and bolted down the stairs, taking them two at a time, not daring to look back until she was outside the house.

She turned to look at the house . . . **took a sharp intake of breath**. A face . . . a flickering shadow stared down at her from the first floor window. **Her legs shook uncontrollably, sweat beaded her forehead and gathered on her upper lip. Every nerve in her body screamed at her to get away from the house.**

SECTION 1 – SETTING

WORDS	
Nouns	**Path**, house, ruins, corridor, passage, hall, attic, basement, floor, wall, door, window, curtain
	Suits of armour, portraits
	Mirror, reflection, shadows, shape, silhouette
	Light, switch, button, torchlight, candles
	Sign, movement
	Breath, air, haze, mist, fog, shimmer, vapour, space, vacuum
Similes/ Metaphors	**Slinky, grey arms**, like a misty serpent, like an icy breath, like a padded quilt, like a dark blanket

Adjectives	**Heavy**, thick, hot, suffocating
	Icy, chilly, wet, damp
	Dark, grey, gloomy, white, yellow, luminous
	Flickering, swirling, billowing
	Glinting, shimmering
	Brief, fleeting, lingering
	Ugly, ghostly, eerie, brooding, monstrous, hideous, grotesque
Verbs	**Hung**, floated, spread, descended
	Rose, crept, flicked, slid, slipped, slithered, prowled, drifted, twisted, swirled
	Spread, covered, draped, filled, blanketed
	Burst, flooded, blinded
	Muffled, smothered, suffocated
	Saw, glimpsed, caught sight of
	Shimmered, flashed, shadowed
	Lurked, watched, waited, trapped

PHRASES – NOUNS AND ADJECTIVES

- ★ In the passage ahead of him . . .
- ★ From far off in the house . . .
- ★ Through a gap in the open door
- ★ Over the ruins . . .
- ★ In front of her . . .
- ★ In front of the door
- ★ Close up behind her
- ★ Just ahead . . .
- ★ Onto the opposite wall
- ★ In the flickering torchlight . . .
- ★ *Blanket of grey mist*
- ★ Coils of mist
- ★ Slinky, grey arms
- ★ Like a misty serpent
- ★ Like an icy breath
- ★ Veil of icy mist
- ★ Brooding mist
- ★ Swirling mist
- ★ Billowing grey mist

* Like a padded quilt
* *Like a dark blanket*
* Full of shadows
* Wind-blown candles
* *Strange light in the room*
* Damp, yellow fog
* Eerie luminous yellow
* Ghastly, glinting light
* *Misty haze*
* Space in the air
* Shimmering vacuum
* White shape
* Another taller silhouette close behind her
* *Only silence and utter stillness*
* Lingering stench of . . .
* Hint of dried blood
* Heavy, hot and suffocating

PHRASES – VERBS

* *As the air shimmered in front of him . . .*
* As she moved before the mirror . . .
* As she glanced in the mirror . . .
* As she backed into the room . . .
* Silence. Something was going to happen
* Appeared from nowhere
* *Hung over the ruins*
* Crept up on the house
* Slid along the window
* Crept along the gravel path
* Floated above the grass outside the window
* Shadowed by a dark and terrible brooding cloud
* *Floated above the table*
* Hung above the bed
* Hung like a stilled breath on everything that it touched
* *Crept along the hall floor*
* Descended from the top of the stairs
* Drifted up from the basement
* Crept low through the attic
* Flicked its tongue into every gap of the corridor
* Prowled around them
* Slithered over their feet
* *Rose and spread*

* Drifted through the air
* Filled the air with its slinky, grey arms
* Flooded the attic, momentarily blinding him
* Draped over the room
* Smothered all sound and light
* Blanketed everything like a padded quilt
* *Twisted the furniture into monstrous shapes*
* Burst out at him as it parted
* Waited a moment and then slipped back along the passage
* *Glanced at her reflection*
* Saw a fleeting movement
* Caught a fleeting glimpse of . . .
* Glimpsed something dark
* Trapped behind a misty curtain
* Flashed in the mirror
* Shuddered as she stood there
* Shimmered in front of them
* *Became more distinct*
* Stood very still in the shadows
* Lurking. Watching. Waiting.
* Moved with her
* Swished out of sight
* Seemed to take another step towards him
* Played hide and seek with the shadows
* Couldn't see it, but knew it was there

SENTENCES

A billowing grey mist appeared from nowhere, floating above the grass outside the window. It rose and spread, and filled the air with its slinky, grey arms.

As the scent of lavender drifted through the air, a mist like an icy breath descended from the stairs.

A swirling mist had crept along the hall floor, making the stairs, suits of armour and portraits suddenly burst out at him as it parted.

A brooding mist crept low through the attic, prowling around them, slithering over their feet.

It was a clear day, but a damp, yellow fog hung over the ruins and twisted the trees into monstrous shapes.

As he opened the chest, a light flooded the attic, momentarily blinding him.

The ghost was trapped behind a misty curtain, but slowly became more distinct.

Turning towards a space in the air, he saw a sort of shimmering vacuum in front of the door.

A ghastly, glinting light flashed in the mirror onto the opposite wall.

As the air shimmered in front of them, it became heavy, hot and suffocating as if a dark blanket had been draped over the room.

It was like the air had been sucked out of the room, smothering all sound and light until only silence and utter stillness remained. In front of her was a sort of misty haze.

In the flickering torchlight she caught a fleeting glimpse of a white shape just ahead. Standing very still in the shadows. Lurking. Watching. Waiting.

The light in the room was strange; an eerie luminous yellow. The wind was quiet. Silence. Something was going to happen. He could feel it in the air.

Wind-blown candles played hide and seek with the shadows. When another candle went out, the eerie shadows seemed to take another step towards him.

She searched the darkness for any sign, any sound. There was nothing. Just the lingering stench of cigar smoke.

The mirror shuddered as he stood before it.

She glanced at her reflection in the mirror and was sure there was another taller silhouette close up behind her.

As she backed into the room, something moved with her. She couldn't see it, but she knew it was there. The hint of dried blood hung in the air.

Something caught her eye. A face . . . a flickering shadow in the first-floor window.

Out of the corner of her eye she could see something dark swish out of sight.

As she glanced in the mirror, she thought she saw a fleeting movement through a gap in the open door.

SECTION 2 – INTERACTION

WORDS	
Nouns	**House**, ruins, tracks, garden, hedge, ground, wall
	Corridor, room, bedroom, stairs, banister
	Window, curtain, condensation, bed, covers, door, key
	Light, lamp, switch
	Clock, stroke, midnight

Head, shoulder, side, neck, hand, palm, fingers, feet, muscle, eyes, mouth, breath

Mist, shadow, shape, silhouette, reflection

Movement

Similes/ Metaphors

Like a rabbit caught in the headlights

Adjectives

Alarmed, startled, nervous, anxious, frightened, scared, terrified

Certain, unsure

Frozen, numb, clumsy

Creeping

Verbs

Chimed

Woke, shot upright

Spread, shivered, trembled, quaked

Steadied, controlled

Waited, paused, stopped, halted, rooted, glued

Dropped, rolled, crouched, huddled

Moved, edged, inched, manoeuvred

Shuffled, scrambled, stumbled

Clambered, leaped

Fell back, pulled away, backed away, retreated

Shut, slammed, jammed, locked, leaned against, pressed

Lifted, raised, strained, looked back, glanced

Watched, stared, squinted, scanned, searched, probed

Darted, flickered, peered, peeked

Spotted, saw, glimpsed, caught sight of

Felt, reached, thrust, groped, picked up, pulled, grasped, clutched, clung

Held, gritted, clenched, gasped, screamed

PHRASES – NOUNS AND ADJECTIVES

★ *Too frightened to . . .*
★ Not sure which way

- ★ Like a rabbit in the headlights
- ★ *With the palm of his hand . . .*
- ★ *Towards the window*
- ★ Just beyond the corner of the house

PHRASES – VERBS

- ★ As the clock chimed the last stroke of midnight . . .
- ★ With his eyes fixed on the shape in front of him . . .
- ★ *Woke with a start*
- ★ Shot upright
- ★ Sat bolt upright in bed
- ★ Edged out of her bed
- ★ Clambered out of bed
- ★ Leaped out of bed
- ★ *Galvanised by her panic*
- ★ Tried to control the creeping terror that was spreading through her
- ★ *Shivered with fear*
- ★ Certain that she didn't want to stay there
- ★ Didn't know which way to run
- ★ *Couldn't move*
- ★ Stopped dead in his tracks
- ★ Steadied herself against the wall
- ★ Glued to . . .
- ★ Rooted to the ground
- ★ Hadn't moved a muscle for five minutes
- ★ Waited, watched . . . still did not move
- ★ Paused at the end of the corridor
- ★ *Shuffled his feet nervously*
- ★ Scrambled to his feet
- ★ Rolled onto her side
- ★ Dropped to his knees
- ★ Crouched on all fours
- ★ Crouched behind the curtain
- ★ Clung to each other
- ★ *Began to move*
- ★ Edged towards the window
- ★ Made her way slowly towards . . .
- ★ Groped her way towards the main light
- ★ Manoeuvred around her bedroom
- ★ Stumbled towards the light
- ★ *Fell back slowly*
- ★ Backed into the room

- ★ Pulled back through the strange shadows to her bed
- ★ Slammed the door shut behind her
- ★ Pressed her back against the door
- ★ Pressed closer to the window until his nose was touching the glass
- ★ *Peered down the corridor*
- ★ Squinted his eyes
- ★ Squinted through the mist
- ★ Stared straight ahead
- ★ Peered outside
- ★ Stared through the window
- ★ Peered out from behind the curtain
- ★ Peeked through the posts of the banister
- ★ Peered through the hedge at the house
- ★ Glanced round the room
- ★ Spotted a silhouette
- ★ Caught sight of a shadow
- ★ Scanned the shadows
- ★ Probed the garden for a flicker of movement
- ★ Stared upwards
- ★ Darted left and right
- ★ Looked again
- ★ Searched the darkness for any sign, any sound
- ★ *Lifted her head above the sill*
- ★ Strained her neck upwards
- ★ Dared a peek around the side of the wall
- ★ Kept looking back over his shoulder
- ★ Glanced over her shoulder again
- ★ *Thrust his hand out in front of him*
- ★ Clutched his hand to his mouth
- ★ Pulled the covers up as high as they would go
- ★ Reached across to switch on the lamp beside her bed
- ★ Felt along the wall for the light switch
- ★ Ran it along the wall until he located the light switch
- ★ Pressed the button – nothing happened
- ★ Flipped on the outdoor light
- ★ Slapped on the main bedroom light switch
- ★ Cleared the condensation from the window
- ★ *Tried to pick up the key*
- ★ So scared his fingers felt frozen, numb, clumsy
- ★ Grasped the key and twisted it
- ★ Locked herself in
- ★ *Held his breath*
- ★ Gritted her teeth
- ★ Stopped himself screaming out

SENTENCES

She stopped dead in her tracks, staring upwards.

He couldn't move. His eyes were glued to the reflection in the mirror.

He stood rooted to the spot like a rabbit caught in the headlights. He didn't know which way to run.

She was crouched behind the curtain. She hadn't moved a muscle for five minutes. She waited, watched . . . still did not move.

They clung to each other, too frightened to move.

As her curtain billowed into the room, she shot upright and glanced at the window.

As the clock chimed the last stroke of midnight, he woke with a start, sat bolt upright in bed, his eyes scanning the shadows.

She felt along the wall for the light switch.

He thrust his hand out in front of him, and ran it along the wall until he located the light switch.

Robert reached out to switch on the bedside lamp. It was dead. He clambered out of bed, gritting his teeth and made his way towards the door.

It was dark and the room was full of shadows. She reached across to switch on the lamp beside her bed, but as she pressed the button nothing happened. Gingerly, she edged out of her bed and groped her way towards the main light. She pressed the switch. Nothing.

Galvanised by his panic, he leaped out of bed and ran to the door, slapping on the main bedroom light switch on the wall next to it.

Shivering with fear, she edged towards the window.

Crouching on all fours, Kitty manoeuvred around her bedroom towards the window. Slowly, she lifted her head above the sill and peered out from behind the curtain.

Quickly rolling onto her side, Katie strained her neck upwards to peer through the window.

She cupped her hands against the glass of the door and peered outside, her eyes scanning, squinting through the dark. She flipped on the outdoor light and spotted a white shape just beyond the corner of the house.

He pressed closer to the window until his nose was touching the glass. His breath misted the thin glass barrier between himself and the storm.

Using the palm of his hand, he quickly cleared the condensation from the window and, holding his breath, squinting his eyes, he looked again.

He watched and waited. Slowly, he peered out and squinted into the darkness. His eyes darted left and right, probing the garden for a flicker of movement.

Dropping to her knees, she peered through the hedge at the ruins.

She paused at the end of the corridor, peering down through the mist, trying to control the creeping terror that was spreading through her.

She scrambled to her feet, and began to move, not sure which way to go, only certain that she didn't want to stay there.

With his eyes fixed on the strange shadowy shape by the door, he backed away to his bed, and pulled the covers up as high as they would go.

Alarmed, she backed into the room, slamming the door shut behind her, and pressed her back against it.

He tried to pick up the key, but he was so scared his fingers felt frozen, numb, clumsy.

She grasped the key and twisted it, locking herself in.

He clutched his hand to his mouth to stop himself screaming out.

SECTION 3 – REACTION

WORDS	
Nouns	**Passage**, corridor, hall, stairs
	Gap, corner, edge, background, direction
	Room, walls, door, window, curtains, bed
	Torch, brightness, darkness, shadow
	Sign, events, instincts, senses, sensation
	Fear, horror, dread, courage
	Body, nerves, skin
	Head, forehead, eyes, blink
	Heart, chest, stomach, neck
	Mouth, cheeks, jaw, breath, lips, teeth, tongue
	Arms, hands, fingers, legs, feet
	Noise, stammer, murmur, squeak, shout
Similes/ Metaphors	**Like an electric current pulsing beneath the skin**, like a coiled spring, like crashing waves pounding the shore, like castanets, phantom flickers of light

Adjectives	**Sure**, certain, alert, wide awake
	Approaching, imminent, impending, forthcoming
	Strange, difficult, baffling, mystifying, mysterious
	Sudden, unexpected
	Intense, fierce, strong, powerful
	Dark, gloomy, shadowy, misty
	Afraid, scared, desperate, frantic, panic-stricken
	Cold, icy, tingling, prickling, spider-like
	Wide, staring, bulging, narrowed
	High-pitched, shrill, sharp, piercing
	Outstretched
Verbs	**Warned**, urged, screamed
	Felt, buzzed, tingled, prickled, pulsed, beaded, crawled, heaved, ran, erupted, slammed, gathered, enveloped
	Looked, fixed, stared, glued, darted, scanned, searched, strained, squinted, peered, squeezed, blinked
	Jerked, jolted, recoiled, flinched, lurched, floundered
	Opened, closed, held, blew out, clenched, chewed, gnashed
	Faltered, murmured, stammered, screamed, shrieked, screeched, yelled
Adverbs	**Nervously**, uncertainly, unsteadily, painfully
	Quickly, frantically, wildly

PHRASES – NOUNS AND ADJECTIVES

- ★ Frantic with horror of the approaching darkness
- ★ Fear of the long, dark corridor down to his room
- ★ Sudden intense brightness
- ★ *All his instincts*
- ★ Every nerve in his body
- ★ Every bone in his body
- ★ Like an electric current beneath the skin
- ★ Chest was heaving
- ★ *Out of the corner of her eye*
- ★ To his left

- Through a gap in the . . .
- Against the passage walls
- *Wide eyes*
- Wide, staring eyes
- Wide with horror
- *Shaking hands*
- *Frozen to the spot*
- Frozen in horror

PHRASES – VERBS

- Strange events had been happening lately
- Certain there was someone in the room
- As his eyes fell on the shadow prowling in the background . . .
- As the truth dawned on her . . .
- *As the torch flickered and died . . .*
- As she peered over the top of the bed . . .
- When the shadow shifted . . .
- When she stared out of the window . . .
- Still holding on to the door
- Warned him to be alert
- Warned him not to climb the stairs
- Urged him not to go any further
- Screamed at him to get away
- Nerves buzzed
- *Buzzed along his limbs*
- Tingled at the back of his neck
- Felt a cold, spider-like sensation
- Could feel the panic as a prickle in her neck
- Crawled down his back
- Ran down her body
- *Beaded her forehead*
- Erupted from her skin
- Trickled down the side of his nose into his eyes
- Collected on his forehead
- Gathered on her upper lip
- *Beat painfully fast*
- Slammed against her ribs
- Slammed in his chest as . . .
- Twisted inside her chest
- More afraid than she had ever been in her life
- Enveloped by a sense of dread
- Could feel the fear like a coiled spring in the pit of her stomach

- Slammed through her body like crashing waves pounding the shore
- *Forced herself to find the courage to . . .*
- Tried to make sense of what she had just seen
- Tried to dampen the sense of impending doom
- Tried to ignore the fear he had never felt before
- Put one foot in front of the other
- Fought her natural instinct to flee
- Knew she had to get to the bottom of . . .
- *Folded her arms across her chest*
- Felt his way with his outstretched hands
- Left floundering around in the dark
- Shook uncontrollably
- *Clenched his jaw*
- Chewed nervously on her tongue
- Bit her lip to stop her teeth chattering like castanets
- Gnashed his teeth against each other
- *Held his breath*
- Unable to breathe
- Took a sharp intake of breath
- Drew a rasping, jagged breath
- Blew out her cheeks
- Faltered and took a deep breath
- *Too scared to make a noise*
- Opened his mouth as if he was about to speak, but closed it again
- Nothing would come out however hard she tried
- Sank to a murmur
- Managed to stammer in a high-pitched squeak
- *Squeezed them shut*
- Found it difficult to look
- Made her blink
- Blinked rapidly
- *Darted to and fro*
- Darted wildly from side to side
- Darted back and forth uncertainly
- *Scanned the windows*
- Kept their eyes glued to the window
- Kept his head down and his eyes fixed to the floor
- Strained to pierce the shadows
- Searched for any sign of movement
- *Gazed up at the narrow stairway*
- Peered into the darkness of the shadowy hall
- Saw only as far as the bend
- Saw something move
- Could see the dark corridor was filled with phantom flickers of light

⋆ *Turned to look in the direction of . . .*
⋆ Recoiled . . . he saw it too

SENTENCES

When she stared out of the window, her heart twisted inside her chest.

As the shadow shifted once more, her nerves buzzed like an electric pulse beneath her skin.

Every bone in his body was tensed and the skin tingled at the back of his neck, warning him to be alert.

She was frozen to the spot, unable to breathe, the mist swirling around her.

As she peered over the top of the bed, goosebumps erupted from her skin. Through the gap in the door, she could see the dark corridor was filled with phantom flickers of light.

Out of the corner of her eye, she saw something move. She took a sharp intake of breath. Someone was standing in the doorway, staring at her.

All his instincts screamed at him to get away.

Every nerve in his body warned him not to go any further.

Every bone in his body warned him not to climb the stairs.

Blowing out her cheeks, she drew a rasping, jagged breath and tried to dampen the sense of impending doom.

She was suddenly more afraid than she had ever been in her life.

Her heart was beating painfully fast and thudded against her ribs.

Emotions slammed through her body like crashing waves pounding the shore.

She could feel the panic as a prickle in her neck. Terrified, she forced herself to find the courage to put one foot in front of the other.

She could feel the fear like a coiled spring in the pit of her stomach.

Robert felt a cold, spider-like sensation crawl down his back.

His chest was heaving, his hands, one still holding on to the door, were shaking, and his eyes were wide with horror.

A shudder ran down her body and she felt her legs begin to quiver.

He tried to ignore the fear he had never felt before – the fear of walking down the long, dark corridor to his room.

She folded her arms across her chest and chewed nervously on her tongue.

She opened her mouth to shout but nothing would come out, however hard she tried.

She faltered and took a deep breath.

Her voice sank to a murmur.

She managed to stammer in a high-pitched squeak.

As his eyes fell on the shadow prowling in the background, his smile faded. Clenching his jaw, he gnashed his teeth against each other. He was too scared to make a noise.

He found it difficult to look and kept his head down and his eyes fixed to the floor.

His eyes darted back and forth uncertainly.

Sweat had collected on his forehead and was trickling down the side of his nose into his eyes. He squeezed them shut and blinked rapidly.

The sudden intense brightness made her blink.

They kept their eyes glued to the window, searching for any sign of movement.

Her wide, staring eyes scanned the windows.

He turned to look in the direction in which she was staring. He peered into the darkness of the shadowy hall and recoiled . . . now he saw it too.

She tensed, fighting her natural instinct to flee. She knew she had to get to the bottom of these strange events that had been happening lately.

She tried to make sense of what she had seen. And as the truth dawned on her, a sense of dread enveloped her. Her legs shook uncontrollably, sweat beaded her forehead and gathered on her upper lip.

12

Strange events

As she flicked through the recent photos of the hotel, **a tingling sixth sense made her look closer at one particular photo**. Her hand froze on the mouse. Standing on the step by the front door was a strange misty silhouette.

Intrigued, she zoomed in to enlarge the image, but just as it came into focus, the computer suddenly crackled and filled with a grey, flickering mist. **A sense of foreboding crept through her. Something strange was happening in this hotel. From the moment they had arrived, she had sensed something – some kind of eerie presence lurking in the background. After seeing that photo, she was now determined to get to the bottom of it.**

The silence was broken by a sudden creak behind him. Glancing around, he saw the latch of the door was rising; the door slowly creaking open. **Bolts of electricity shot down his spine.** He was alone in the house!

Cautiously, he edged towards the door, peered round the corner, and scanned the dark corridor, his eyes squinting into the shadows, searching for any movement. There was no one there.

As he turned back into his room, the door slammed shut behind him. **He felt the hairs shoot up on the back of his neck. Beads of sweat trickled down his forehead**.

He looked at the window and for a brief second thought the light had caught someone, lurking behind the curtains. **A splinter of fear stabbed his chest.** He looked again . . . there was no one there. And the window was shut! There was no draught. It was as if the door had been pushed by an invisible force. **Heart racing**, he lunged at the door. It was locked.

SECTION 1 – SETTING

WORDS	

Nouns   **Cellar**, basement, dungeons, tunnel, attic, hall, hallway, corridor, passage, room

Wall, window, door, latch, knob, hinges, crack, gap

Table, chair, bed, bookshelves, books, paintings, portraits, suits of armour, mirror, reflection

Computer screen, television, mobile phone, photos, images, alarm, clock

Hand, fingers, grip, eye

Force, movement

Air, draught, breeze

Crash, explosion

Night, mist, moonlight, shadow, silhouette

Adjectives   **Blank**, invisible, unseen

Brief, fleeting, flickering

Dark, grey, shadowy, misty

Loud, deafening, almighty

Splintering, crashing

Sure, certain

Recent

Verbs   **Thought**, knew

Looked, glanced, saw, noticed, caught sight of

Filled, disappeared

Moved, pushed, tugged, yanked, tore, ripped, pulled, dragged

Opened, shut, closed, banged, slammed

Shuddered, leapt, sprang, fell, toppled

Rattled, crashed, shattered, exploded

Flickered, crackled

PHRASES – NOUNS AND ADJECTIVES

- ★ In the dead of night . . .
- ★ When the clock struck twelve . . .
- ★ In the middle of the room . . .
- ★ In the first-floor window
- ★ *Out of the corner of her eye . . .*
- ★ Through a gap in the open door
- ★ *Latch of the door*
- ★ Door knob
- ★ Blank screen
- ★ Recent photos of the house
- ★ *With an almighty crash . . .*
- ★ An explosion of splintering wood
- ★ No one outside . . . no draught
- ★ An unseen force
- ★ *Fleeting movement*
- ★ Strange, misty silhouette

PHRASES – VERBS

- ★ *As she backed into the room*
- ★ Thought she saw . . .
- ★ *Rattled violently*
- ★ Opened and slammed shut again
- ★ Opened and closed by themselves
- ★ Before her fingers had . . .
- ★ Pushed by an unseen force
- ★ Swung open as if of its own accord
- ★ Swung shut in her face
- ★ Banged shut behind her
- ★ Ripped out of her grip
- ★ Ripped from its hinges
- ★ Dragged by an invisible hand
- ★ *Shuddered and fell off the wall*
- ★ Leapt from the shelves
- ★ Sprang into life
- ★ *Filled with a grey mist*
- ★ Flickered and crackled
- ★ Went blank – his game had disappeared
- ★ *Shuddered as he stood before it*
- ★ Toppled onto the desk and smashed
- ★ Landed in a heap

* *Caught her eye*
* Glanced at her reflection in the mirror
* Noticed that in the right-hand corner of . . .
* Zoomed in to enlarge the image and gasped

SENTENCES

The latch of the door rose; the door opened and slammed shut again.

The window and door opened and closed by themselves. No one was outside. There was no draught!

Before her finger touched the door, it swung open as if of its own accord.

The door rattled so violently she was sure it would be ripped from its hinges with an explosion of splintering wood.

The door swung shut in her face, pushed by an unseen force.

The door knob was ripped out of her grip, banging shut behind her.

The chair suddenly moved across the floor as if dragged by an invisible hand.

The bookshelves sprang into life and books leapt from the shelves, landing in a heap in the middle of the room.

The computer screen flickered and crackled. The screen was blank, his game had disappeared.

The screen filled with a grey mist. With an almighty crash, it toppled over and crashed to the floor.

Suddenly, she noticed that in the right-hand corner of the recent photos she had taken of the house, there was a strange, misty silhouette. She zoomed in to enlarge the image, and gasped.

SECTION 2 – INTERACTION

WORDS

Nouns	**Image**, scene, devastation
	Table, couch, chair, window, curtain, wall, mirror, television, books
	Door, bolt, lock, key, knob, handle
	Pieces, fragments
	Anxiety, shock, despair, desperation

Head, eyes, nose, mouth, lips

Back, shoulders, legs, knees, feet, muscle

Hands, arms, fingers, knuckles, fists

Tone, whisper, cry, howl, scream, yell

Similes/ Metaphors	**Like a statue**, as if trapped in a block of cement, shut like a tomb
Adjectives	**Rigid**, tense, cautious, silent, motionless
	Low, thin, faltering, strangled, ragged, sharp, shrill, high-pitched, piercing
	Visible
	Quick, swift, urgent, desperate, frantic, violent
Verbs	**Knew**, wanted, warned, urged
	Froze, rooted, remained, waited
	Dropped, ducked, slumped, curled, crouched
	Wrapped, covered, hugged, clung
	Jerked, placed, threw, picked up, bit, rubbed
	Groped, clutched, gripped, grasped, yanked, tugged, turned, twisted
	Locked, sealed, trapped
	Beat, banged, knocked, hammered, kicked
	Ventured, shuffled
	Leapt up, stood, scrambled, ran, bolted, dashed, darted, lunged
	Backed, shrank, recoiled, reeled, distanced
	Pressed, jammed
	Shivered, shuddered
	Let out, blew, escaped, gasped
	Raised, peered, looked, stared, glued, fixed, scanned, swept

PHRASES – NOUNS AND ADJECTIVES

★ *In the passage ahead of him . . .*
★ Not sure which way
★ No way of escape

- *Fragments of the television*
- Pile of books
- *With her arms*
- Mouth and nose hidden behind her knees
- Only her eyes visible
- *Not strong enough*
- *Low moan of despair*
- Strangled whisper
- Note of anxiety in her voice
- Faltering tone
- Thin, high-pitched howl
- High, piercing scream
- Piercing yell

PHRASES – VERBS

- As if time had stopped
- Knew that she couldn't stay there
- *Couldn't move*
- Sat silent and motionless
- Wanted to run but . . .
- Froze like a statue
- Urged her legs and feet to move
- Hadn't moved a muscle for five minutes
- Waited – nothing happened . . . still did not move
- Shuddered and went rigid, as if rooted to the spot
- Remained locked in place as if trapped in a block of cement
- *Dropped to her knees*
- Slumped to the floor
- Curled herself into a ball
- Ducked behind the couch
- Crouched behind the curtain
- *Hugged the wall with her back*
- Ventured a step closer to the door . . . then another
- Shuffled sideways, one foot crossing the other, until she reached the . . .
- *Groped for the bolt*
- So scared his fingers felt frozen, numb, clumsy
- Clutched the side of the knob
- Yanked at the handle . . . pulled . . . pushed
- Gripped it tightly with both hands
- Tried to prevent it turning
- Twisted violently back and forth in her fingers
- *Grasped the key and twisted it*

- ☆ Locked herself in
- ☆ Felt it slide home
- ☆ *Tried to open the door*
- ☆ Frantically twisted it back and forth . . . it wouldn't budge
- ☆ Sealed shut like a tomb
- ☆ *Backed away from the door*
- ☆ Recoiled from the door in terror
- ☆ *Jerked his hands back*
- ☆ Placed her hands in front of her for support
- ☆ Clung to each other, too frightened to move
- ☆ *Tried to pick up the key*
- ☆ Wrapped around her legs
- ☆ Covered her head with her hands
- ☆ Gripped the edge of the table so hard his knuckles turned white
- ☆ Beat her fists against the locked door
- ☆ *Knocked her chair flying*
- ☆ Kicked the door shut
- ☆ Threw herself against the door
- ☆ Pressed her back against the door
- ☆ Jammed her feet into the ground as she leant into the door
- ☆ *Leapt to her feet*
- ☆ Stood quickly
- ☆ Scrambled to her feet and began to move
- ☆ Bolted for the door
- ☆ Lunged at the door
- ☆ Dashed to the window
- ☆ Put some distance between herself and the . . .
- ☆ *Raised her head cautiously*
- ☆ Peered over the top at the . . .
- ☆ Peered over the chair
- ☆ Raised his eyes in desperation above the . . .
- ☆ *Glued to the mirror*
- ☆ Darted to and fro
- ☆ Scanned the room
- ☆ Stared at the door
- ☆ Looked from side to side and over her shoulders
- ☆ Swept over the scene of devastation in front of her
- ☆ *Let out a ragged cry*
- ☆ Escaped her lips
- ☆ Shrank into silence
- ☆ Bit her tongue so as not to cry out with the pain
- ☆ *Shivered violently*
- ☆ Reeled with shock
- ☆ Shuddered and rubbed his eyes

★ Tried to clear the image of what he had just seen
★ Struck her leg on the sharp corner of the table

SENTENCES

It was as if time had stopped. She shuddered and went rigid, as if rooted to the spot.

She couldn't move. Her eyes were glued to the mirror.

They clung to each other, too frightened to move.

She wanted to run. But she couldn't move. She froze like a statue. She urged her legs and feet to move, but they remained locked in place, as if trapped in a block of cement.

She dropped to her knees, placing her hands in front of her for support.

Her eyes darted to and fro, sweeping the scene of devastation in front of her. A low moan of despair escaped her lips. She slumped to the floor and shrank into silence.

He sat silent and motionless, scanning the room.

She was crouched behind the curtain. She hadn't moved a muscle for five minutes. She waited – nothing happened. Still did not move. The fragments of the television lay shattered on the floor.

She curled herself into a ball, shivering violently, and covered her head with her hands.

With her arms wrapped around her legs, she stared at the door, her mouth and nose hidden behind her knees, only her eyes visible.

He shuddered and rubbed his eyes, as if trying to clear the image of what he had just seen.

Raising her head cautiously, she peered over the chair.

He raised his eyes in desperation above the chair, peering over the top at the heap of books.

Looking from side to side and over her shoulders, she ducked behind the couch.

He jerked his hands back, cold sweat trickling down his back.

He gripped the edge of the table so hard his knuckles turned white.

He tried to pick up the key, but he was so scared his fingers felt frozen, numb, clumsy.

She backed away from the door, breathless and shaking.

She backed away, putting some distance between herself and the door, adrenalin making every sense in her body alert.

She ventured a step closer to the door. Then another.

Hugging the wall with her back, she shuffled sideways, one foot crossing the other, until she reached the door.

She kicked the door shut and threw herself against it, groping for the bolt and breathing a sigh of relief as she felt it slide home.

She grasped the key and twisted it, locking herself in.

Clutching the side of the knob, gripping it tightly with both hands, she tried to prevent it turning, but she was not strong enough and it twisted violently back and forth in her fingers.

She pressed her back against the door. She felt it move slightly. Gasping, she jammed her feet into the ground as she leant into the door.

She lunged at the door. It was locked. She was trapped.

Quickly, she dashed to the window, yanked at the handle. She pulled. She pushed. It was also locked. There was no way of escape.

She tried to open the door, frantically twisting it back and forth. But it wouldn't budge. The house was sealed shut like a tomb. She let out a ragged cry and beat her fists against the locked door.

She scrambled to her feet and began to move, not sure which way to go, only knowing that she couldn't stay there.

Standing quickly, she struck her leg on the sharp corner of the table and bit her tongue so as not to cry out with the pain.

She was reeling with shock. Screaming, she leapt to her feet, knocking her chair flying, and bolted for the door.

SECTION 3 – REACTION

WORDS

Nouns	**Presence**
	Dread, fear, terror, foreboding, anticipation, premonition
	Feeling, sense, mind, nerve, panic
	Body, spine, bone, hair, blood
	Head, forehead, temples, neck, eyes, jaw, throat, windpipe, teeth

	Hands, fingers, feet, toes
	Gasp, whisper, gabble, scream
	Cold, shiver
Similes/ Metaphors	**Bolts of electricity**, as if fuelled by a lethal poison, like a sponge wrung dry, gripped him like a snake, like a searing heat on his back
Pronouns	**Something**, someone, no one
Adjectives	**Strange**, alarming, disturbing, eerie
	Bad, evil, threatening, dangerous, ominous, menacing
	Shaking, trembling, shivering, quivering
	Cold, clammy, aching
	Breathless
	Wide, staring, bulging
	Urgent, alert, twisted, wild, frantic
	Furtive, fearful
Verbs	**Felt**, sensed, prickled, tingled, warned, paralysed
	Grew, developed, quickened
	Coiled, seized, squeezed, gripped, twisted, stabbed, shot, pounded, slammed
	Gaped, dropped, clenched, gnashed, gasped, gabbled, rushed, tumbled
	Opened, strained, looked, glanced, saw, swept, darted

PHRASES – NOUNS AND ADJECTIVES

- ★ For a brief second . . .
- ★ *Sense of foreboding*
- ★ Tingling sixth sense
- ★ Something inside her . . .
- ★ Something strange and deeply disturbing
- ★ Quivering dread of an invisible presence that . . .
- ★ Some kind of eerie presence in the building
- ★ *No one there*
- ★ No one else in the house
- ★ *Breathless and shaking*

- ★ *All her senses . . .*
- ★ Every bone in his body
- ★ Bolts of electricity
- ★ *Wide eyes*
- ★ Wide and bulging
- ★ Urgent and twisted with terror
- ★ *Arm was cold and clammy*
- ★ An aching cold in his bones

PHRASES – VERBS

- ★ Something was coming
- ★ Something strange was happening in the . . .
- ★ Premonition that something bad was about to happen
- ★ When she looked again . . .
- ★ As if it was waiting. But for what?
- ★ Mind whirled frantically
- ★ Fear of what would happen next
- ★ As if he was making himself speak before he lost his nerve
- ★ Felt its presence
- ★ Sensed something
- ★ Could not see, but knew was there
- ★ Sensed it reaching out to her, drawing her nearer
- ★ Bored into him like a searing heat on his back
- ★ *Thought the light caught someone*
- ★ Aware of another presence . . . of someone watching him
- ★ Lurking behind the curtains
- ★ *Prickled with anticipation*
- ★ Had a strange feeling
- ★ Crept through her
- ★ Tingled at the back of his neck
- ★ Warned him to be alert
- ★ Hairs were standing out on end
- ★ Felt the hairs go up on the back of her neck
- ★ *Made every sense in her body alert*
- ★ Quickened her reactions
- ★ Determined to get to the bottom of it
- ★ *Started to shiver*
- ★ Started at his toes and fingers
- ★ Sweating despite the cold
- ★ Trickled down her forehead
- ★ *Stabbed by a splinter of fear*
- ★ Paralysed with fear

- ⭐ Squeezed tight, like a sponge being wrung dry
- ⭐ Developed a life of its own as if fuelled by a lethal poison
- ⭐ Grew at an alarming rate
- ⭐ Pounded in her temples
- ⭐ Gripped him like a snake
- ⭐ Coiled round his throat, choking his windpipe
- ⭐ Shot up and down her spine
- ⭐ Slammed in his chest
- ⭐ Twisted inside her chest when she stared at . . .
- ⭐ Seized her chest
- ⭐ Moved up into his chest and throat
- ⭐ *Clenched his jaw*
- ⭐ Gaped open in a silent scream
- ⭐ Opened his mouth to cry out
- ⭐ Dropped to an urgent whisper
- ⭐ Gnashed his teeth against each other to stop them chattering
- ⭐ *Came in gasps*
- ⭐ Tumbled over each other in a low gabble
- ⭐ Tumbled out in a rush
- ⭐ *Opened in panic*
- ⭐ Made him take a closer look
- ⭐ Looked furtively over his shoulder
- ⭐ Glanced fearfully around
- ⭐ Swept over the scene in front of him
- ⭐ Strained to pierce the darkness
- ⭐ Darted wildly from side to side

SENTENCES

Something strange was happening in the hotel. Something strange and deeply disturbing. She couldn't understand what, but she was now determined to get to the bottom of it.

It was a quivering dread of a presence that he could not see, but knew was there.

She had had a strange feeling – a premonition that something bad was about to happen.

A sense of foreboding crept through her, and sweat trickled down her forehead.

Something was coming. She felt its presence. It was as if it was waiting. But for what?

She sensed something – some kind of eerie presence in the building. She sensed it reaching out to her, drawing her nearer.

He was suddenly aware of another presence, of someone watching him, its eyes boring into him like a searing heat on his back.

For a brief second, she thought the light caught someone, lurking behind the curtains. She opened her mouth to cry out, but when she looked again . . . there was no one there.

A tingling sixth sense made him look closer.

As the blood pounded in her temples, her brain quickened and all her senses were alert.

She felt the hairs go up on the back of her neck.

He was sweating despite the cold. His skin prickled with anticipation.

Her arm was cold and clammy and the hairs were standing out on end. Bolts of electricity shot up and down her spine.

He started to shiver. It was an aching cold that gnawed at his bones, starting at his toes and fingers, and moving up into his chest and throat.

Something inside her squeezed tight, like a sponge being wrung dry.

The fear grew at an alarming rate, developing a life of its own as if fuelled by a lethal poison.

Katie was stabbed by a splinter of fear, fear of what would happen next.

His heart slammed in his chest. There was no one else in the house.

Her heart twisted inside her chest when she stared at . . .

He looked furtively over his shoulder.

She glanced fearfully around.

His eyes opened in panic and swept over the scene in front of him. Horror gripped him like a snake coiling round his throat and choking his windpipe.

Every bone in his body was tensed and the skin tingled at the back of his neck, warning him to be alert. His wide eyes strained to pierce the darkness and darted wildly from side to side.

His eyes were wide and bulging, and his face urgent and twisted with terror.

Her mouth gaped open in a silent scream.

His voice dropped to an urgent whisper.

Her words came in gasps and tumbled over each other in a low gabble.

The words tumbled out in a rush, as if he was making himself speak before he lost his nerve.

Her voice shook and her words came out in gasps.

Clenching his jaw, he gnashed his teeth against each other to stop them chattering.

Part 3
Atmosphere

13
Silence

Behind her reflection in the mirror was a taller, dark silhouette, standing very still. Watching. *There was a moment of silence, stillness, as if the house was holding its breath.*

Her heart thudding in her chest, she whirled round and was blinded by a ghastly, glinting light flashing onto the wall.

With her wide eyes fixed on the strange shimmering shape, she backed out of the room, slamming the door shut behind her and bolted down the stairs, taking them two at a time, not daring to look back until she was outside the house.

WORDS

Nouns	**House**, room
	Darkness, gloom, echo
	Breath, heartbeat, ears
	Anxiety, suspense
Similes/ Metaphors	**Silence as thick as fog**, wall of silence, like a thick blanket, like a throbbing heartbeat, as if they were in a padded room, as if the world was holding its breath, as if sound had been forbidden to enter
Adjectives	**Quiet**, silent, waiting, secretive, brooding, throbbing, gasping, threatening
	Dark, deep, thick
	Deathly, ghostly, eerie, sinister

Verbs	**Beat**, rang, thudded, pressed, coiled, wrapped, surrounded
	Stopped, waited, stirred, throbbed, surged
	Isolated, forbidden

PHRASES – NOUNS AND ADJECTIVES

* Eerily quiet
* Silent and secretive
* A throbbing silence
* Silence as thick as fog
* Like a thick blanket
* Like a throbbing heartbeat
* A horrible, waiting silence
* Silence of death
* Deathly quiet
* No sound, just a dark, eerie gloom
* Only her own gasping breath

PHRASES – VERBS

* Thudded in her ears
* Pressed in on them
* Coiled around them
* Wrapped around them like a thick blanket
* *As if they were in a padded room*
* Surrounded by a wall of silence
* Came surging back
* *Rang in her ears*
* Beat at her ears
* Nothing stirred
* As if sound had been forbidden to enter
* As if time had stopped
* As if the world was holding its breath
* Quiet of something waiting in the dark
* *Made them feel isolated from the rest of the world*
* Moved in a silence of anxiety and suspense

SENTENCES

The room had gone very quiet, as if time had stopped.

There was a deep silence as if they were in a padded room.

The old house was silent and secretive. Nothing stirred. He was surrounded by a wall of silence.

When the echoes had died away, there was only silence thudding in her ears.

Everything was silent. A silence as thick as fog. A horrible, waiting silence, as if sound had been forbidden to enter.

The house was quiet. The silence of something waiting in the dark, holding its breath.

It was eerily quiet. A throbbing silence, which wrapped around them like a thick blanket.

There was a moment of silence, stillness, as if the world was holding its breath.

The silence was unbearable, beating at his ears. The stillness of something waiting in the dark.

There was no sound. No birds singing. No trees rustling. No voices murmuring. Just an eerie silence and her own gasping breath.

The silence came surging back, wrapping round them, making them feel isolated from the rest of the world.

The world was completely still. Nothing moved, not a leaf quivered, but over the silence brooded a ghostly calm and the whisper of his smoking breath as it rose in gasps and lingered in the frosty air.

14
Eerie light

Someone had walked into his room when he was asleep. He had been woken when the door had opened, and a cold draught had rushed towards him, bringing with it stale, dank air like a cellar that had been locked up for centuries.

A light shone through a gap in the door, making the shadows around him seem darker and more menacing. He sat bolt upright, **his eyes darting frantically from side to side, around the room. Every nerve in his body screamed at him that it was still there.**

WORDS

Nouns	**Sky**, cloud, sun, moon, stars
	Light, moonlight, twilight, dusk, dawn
	Glimmers, glow, beam, shaft
	Shadows, shapes, silhouettes
	Torch, batteries, torchlight, lamp, switch, candle, fire, sparks
	Buildings, rooftops, towers, turrets, walls, courtyard
	Corridor, passage, tunnel, dungeons, room, hall, cellar, basement, attic, ceiling, rafters, door, window, stairs
	Gaps, hollows, crevices, alcoves, recesses
	Trees, branches, trunks, hedges
	Owls, bats
Similes/ Metaphors	**Like thrusting limbs**, like the bars of a prison, fell like a curtain

Adjectives	**Grey**, ashen, dim, dull, gloomy, misty, hazy, shadowy
	Ghostly, strange, eerie, secretive
	Moonlit, ivory, lunar
	Fiery, red, orange, fluorescent, silver, silvery, white
	Chilly, icy
	Leafy, gnarled, jagged
	Fading, weak, faint
	Windblown, shivering, shuddering, flickering, spluttering
	Invisible, silent, nocturnal
	Dangerous, menacing, ominous, malicious
Verbs	**Faded**, sunk, fell, crept, seeped, thrust, stretched, filtered, scattered
	Lit, shone, burned, cast, pierced, penetrated
	Swayed, weaved, whirled, glided, danced, scuttled, scudded
	Flitted, flickered, spluttered, shimmered, glinted, glowed
	Throbbed, whispered, hooted
	Watched, waited, quivered
	Glanced, saw, glimpsed

PHRASES – NOUNS AND ADJECTIVES

* ★ Approach of dusk
* ★ In the fading light . . .
* ★ Dim, grey hour when . . .
* ★ Few hours before dawn
* ★ Grey tint to the outside world
* ★ *In front of him . . .*
* ★ Outside the door . . .
* ★ On the other side of the room
* ★ At the other end of the room
* ★ In a shadowy corner of the room
* ★ On the side of the window
* ★ Through the long window
* ★ On the first landing half-way up the stairs
* ★ Beyond the ghostly white beam of his torch . . .
* ★ Behind the inky fingers of darkness . . .

- *Inky light of dusk*
- First shade of grey
- Gloomy, ghostly grey
- Ashen light
- Darkness on each side like a wall
- *Silver moon*
- Ivory beams of the moon
- Long, shimmering beams
- Deep, silvery moonlight
- Fading moon
- Sideways shaft of moonlight
- Ghostly reflection of daylight
- *Weak glow from the torch*
- Little tongue of flickering light
- Small circle of light from the torch
- Triangle of misty light
- Dull, red glimmers
- Faint light in the tower
- Fading torchlight
- Fluorescent light
- Orange beam of light from the torch
- Spluttering, flickering candle stub
- Dark, save for the light of a branch of candles
- Tunnel of light in the pitch-black
- *Shadows of the trees*
- Trunks of the trees
- Branches like thrusting limbs
- Leafy shadows
- Moonlit hedges
- *Black patches of shadow*
- Strange lunar shadows
- Shivering, shuddering shadow
- Flickering, gnarled shadows like jagged wings
- *Windblown candles*
- Candles in glass shades
- Batteries in her torch

PHRASES – VERBS

- *Time when nothing moves*
- Fear of the unknown . . . of what lurked in the dark
- Everything waiting anxiously for the first light of the new day
- Heralded the night to come

- *Faded into a gloomy grey*
- Choked in the first shade of grey
- Fell like a sinking stone
- *Lit only by the bronze lamp in the ceiling*
- Lit only with sparks from the fire
- Burned with the glow of twilight
- Glinted eerily in the tallow light
- Barely penetrated the darkness
- *Lit the stone walls and beamed ceiling*
- Lit up the long, narrow passage ahead briefly
- Illuminated an arched corridor
- Shimmered on the dark house
- Shimmered from the top of the stairs
- Glistened on the black of the rooftop
- Glinted in the distance like ghostly eyes
- Bathed the garden in a ghostly reflection of daylight
- *When she flicked the switch*
- Before it flickered, faded and died out . . .
- *Flickered on and off*
- Faded and snapped off
- Flickered and then went out
- Flashed on, faded for a moment, flickered back on
- Flickered for a moment from bright light to dark
- Flashed from stair to stair
- Flickered in ghost-like tendrils
- Kept flickering and fading as she moved it from side to side
- *Swayed and weaved in front of him*
- Shone through the gap in the door
- Shone through the curtains
- Seeped under the door
- Filtered through the window
- Cast a thin strip of flickering light
- Cast a pool of tallow light onto the path
- Streamed through the window
- *Cast long shadows like bony, gnarled fingers*
- Framed against the moon like the bars of a prison
- Gathered shadows in the crevices
- Cast leafy shadows on the ground in front of him
- Hidden from her sight
- Spread and lengthened
- Merged into one another
- Scratched at the windows and walls
- Crept across the garden and trees
- Threw a shivering, shuddering shadow across the wall

* *Scuttled across the floor*
* Danced and flickered on the dark walls
* Danced in the grass
* Swayed in the corner
* Leant towards each other in the fading light
* *Glowed behind a lens of cloud*
* Scudded across the horizon
* Came out from behind the torn, black clouds
* Pierced the branches
* Appeared briefly from behind the dark clouds
* Grew dimmer as the clouds drifted across the face of the moon
* *Flitted in the moonlight*
* Swayed outside the window
* Brought nocturnal creatures gliding into the night
* Whirled overhead
* Crept out of the darkness
* *Crept up on the house like a ghostly serpent*
* Drifted up from the tunnel
* Dragged with it a veil of stinging mist through the door
* Hung like a stilled breath on everything they touched
* Slid along the window
* Flicked its tongue into the corners of the house
* Waited a moment and then slipped back along the path
* *Moved his candle from side to side*
* Searched for the bottom step
* Glimpsed in the reflected light
* Imagined all sorts of terrors lurking in the misty night
* *Clung to his heels*
* Wrapped itself around him like a damp blanket
* *Whispered in the silence*
* Moaned and howled

SENTENCES

Twilight danced on the walls and gathered shadows in the crevices.

The sun was falling like a sinking stone and the light was disappearing with it.

It was that dim, grey hour when things were just creeping out of darkness.

It was a few hours before dawn. The time when nothing moves and everything is waiting anxiously for the first light of the new day.

The approach of dusk brought the nocturnal creatures gliding into the night. Owls hooted and bats whirled overhead.

Shadows spread and lengthened. Their fear grew as night fell. Fear of the unknown. Fear of what lurked in the dark.

The shadows were now merging into one another, and the ground was choked in the first shade of grey heralding the night to come – the dark they so dreaded.

There was a small circle of light from the torch, but otherwise the darkness on each side was like a wall.

A fluorescent light dimly lit the stone walls and beamed ceiling.

The light illuminated an arched corridor which led from the opening behind the fireplace.

There were no lamps, just candles in glass shades hanging from the walls.

The light from the torch barely penetrated the darkness.

Outside the door the darkness was thick, the only light from the dull, red glimmers and sparks from the fire.

He imagined all sorts of terrors lurking in the misty night beyond the ghostly, white beam of his torch.

The gloom wrapped itself around him like a damp blanket. The beam from the torch cast a thin strip of flickering light in front of him, whilst behind him the inky fingers of darkness clung to his heels.

Deep, silvery moonlight streamed through the window.

The fading moon glowed from behind a lens of cloud and bathed the land in a ghostly reflection of daylight.

It was a full moon. Its eerie light shimmered on the black of the rooftop.

The silver moon came out from behind the torn, black clouds and its ivory beams pierced the branches and cast leafy shadows on the ground in front of them.

They had only a fleeting glimpse of the moon to guide them, as it scudded across the horizon, appearing briefly from behind the dark clouds.

When she flicked the switch, the light flickered for a moment from bright light to dark like lightning splitting a night sky.

The batteries in her torch were running low and the beam kept flickering and fading as she moved it from side to side.

The moonlight which shone through the curtains gradually grew dimmer as the clouds drifted across the face of the moon.

The lights flickered on, faded for a moment and then flickered back on.

A light came on, lighting up the long, narrow passage ahead briefly, before it flickered, faded and died out.

The only light was a sideways shaft of moonlight through the long window on the first landing half-way up the stairs.

The door to the attic and the stairs up to it were in a shadowy corner of the corridor. His candle was a little tongue of flickering light as he moved it from side to side, searching for the bottom step.

The cloud shrouded the moon which just cast enough light to prevent him from tripping over his own feet.

A torch, a tunnel of light in the pitch black, shimmered from the top of the stairs.

Shadows flitted around her.

There were black patches of shadow to the side of the window hidden from her sight.

In the fading light, he could see the shadows of the trees, which seemed to lean towards each other, whispering in the silence, their branches like thrusting limbs.

The glow from the fire threw a shivering, shuddering shadow across the wall on the other side of the room.

The light overhead flickered in ghostlike tendrils that spread coils of light dancing across the room.

A light shone through the gap in the door, making the shadows around him seem darker and more menacing.

The sun slithered over the horizon, casting long shadows like bony, gnarled fingers scratching at the windows and walls.

Dusk fell like a curtain, and the trunks of the trees swaying outside the window were framed against the moon like the bars of a prison.

The shadows grew, creeping across the garden, and the trees and hedges guarding the drive darkened ominously.

The fog crept up on the house like a ghostly serpent, sliding along the window, flicking its tongue into the corners of the house, waiting a moment and then slipping back along the path.

The wind moaned and howled and dragged with it a veil of stinging mist through the door.

Coils of mist drifted up from the tunnel and hung like a stilled breath on everything they touched.

15
Dark

Kitty was woken in the middle of the night. A hot panting breath had touched the back of her neck . . . as if there was somebody in the room, close to the bed, leaning over her. *She lay motionless in the darkness and listened to the night. It was an unsettling, menacing darkness, full of dancing shadows and the occasional creak and rustle from the house.* **A tingling sixth sense warned Kitty not to move.**

WORDS

Nouns	**Darkness**, dusk, evening, night, midnight, sky, cloud
	Shadows, silhouette
	Buildings, rooftops, towers, turrets, walls, courtyard
	Corridor, passage, hall, tunnel, dungeons, cellar, basement, tomb, room, attic
	Walls, ceiling, beams, rafters, windows, curtains, door
	Light, switch
	Gaps, patches, hollows, crevices, alcoves, recesses
	Gull, bat
	Breeze, draught
	Creaks, rustles
Similes/ Metaphors	**Like a blanket putting out a candle**, like a velvet glove, black wave of darkness, like a curtain, like a hammer, like the shutting of an eye, like thrusting limbs
Adjectives	**Dark**, black, pitch-black, inky, impenetrable
	Cold, icy, frigid

Shivering, shuddering, flitting, thrusting

Invisible, silent, nocturnal, eerie, mysterious

Dangerous, menacing, ominous, malicious, forbidding

Fearful, frightful, ghastly

Solitary, occasional

Verbs

Fell, drew, covered, plunged, drowned

Closed in, thickened, deepened

Covered, hid, shrouded, steeped

Wafted, crept, slithered, filtered, clung, dripped

Pressed, stretched, spread, seeped, poured

Gathered, settled, wrapped, blanketed, enveloped, engulfed, blocked, trapped, forced

Glided, flitted, whirled, moved away

Imagined, quivered, shuddered

Stood, lay, edged, stumbled, raced

Felt, groped, searched

Listened, stirred, creaked, wailed, echoed

PHRASES – NOUNS AND ADJECTIVES

★ Out in the hall
★ Other end of the passage
★ Nearest corridor light
★ *Just after midnight…*
★ Just a few metres away
★ *No lights in the windows*
★ Inky fingers of darkness
★ Curtain of darkness
★ No gap in the dark
★ Nothing but inky darkness
★ Impenetrable darkness
★ Not even a pinprick of light
★ Pitch-black outside the house
★ No more than a shuttered tomb
★ Dark and eerily silent
★ Darkness like a velvet glove
★ Vast cavern of darkness

- Like a wall of darkness on either side of the torch
- Chilly, black wave of darkness
- Dome of menacing darkness
- *Black patches of shadow*
- Ocean of shadows and menace
- Shivering, shuddering shadow
- Mass of shadows in the corners
- Full of dangerous, flitting shadows
- Branches like thrusting limbs
- Forbidding silhouettes
- *Windy, moonless night*
- Night breeze
- *Solitary gull*
- Occasional bat
- Creaks and rustles of the night

PHRASES – VERBS

- Drew a black cloud across the sky
- Drawn across the sky
- Drowned in heavy clouds
- *Fell like a curtain*
- Fell like a hammer
- Faded and snapped off
- Tried the lights. Nothing
- Went out to be replaced by an eerie black shadow
- Plunged the house into darkness
- *Closed in*
- Thickened around the house
- Drew across the castle
- Wafted into the bedroom
- Pressed against the windows
- Scratched to come in
- Filtered through the window
- Poured in through the window
- Seeped under the door
- Like a blanket putting out a candle
- Closed in on him like the shutting of an eye
- *Crept over everything*
- Crept along the corridor
- Stretched its tentacles into every gap and hollow
- Crept into every space around them
- Spread across the ceiling

* Clung to the beams
* Dripped along the walls
* Slithered up the corridor
* *Settled around him like a velvet glove*
* Gathered around her like a cloak
* Stretched around and above him
* Blanketed in a frigid shadow
* Wrapped around her like a damp blanket
* Enveloped her like a blanket
* Wrapped him in a fearful embrace
* Engulfed in darkness
* Clung to her ankles
* Trapped in a dome of menacing darkness
* *Hidden in shadow*
* Covered in darkness
* Shrouded the house
* Steeped in darkness
* Receded into darkness
* Felt as if he was buried deep underground
* *Quivered with anticipation*
* Brought the fear of the invisible predator
* Brought the fear of what lurked in the shadows
* Hid what might lie behind the trees, watching and waiting
* Imagined all sorts of terrors lurking in the inky black of the night
* *Glided into the night*
* Flitted in the moonlight
* Whirled across her face
* Moved away from her in the dark
* *Stood silent in the dark*
* Stood at the bottom of the staircase
* Lay in the darkness
* Edged towards it
* Stumbled on
* Raced blindly past things
* *Blocked her way forward*
* Forced her to grope her way blindly down the stairs
* Groped her way along the wall
* Felt his way by running his hands back and forth along the wall
* Searched until he found another switch
* Until she felt the cold metal of the switch
* Clicked it on to chase away the darkness and the shadows
* *Listened to the night*
* Stirred in the trees
* Creaked somewhere in the house

* Wailed overhead
* Echoed around her

SENTENCES

The evening drew a black cloak across the sky.

The dark closed in, thickening around the house.

A curtain of darkness was drawn across the castle, so thick and dark it seemed to press against the windows, scratching to come in.

The air seemed to be quivering with anticipation as a curtain of darkness was drawn across the sky, bringing with it the fear of what lurked in the shadows.

The darkness of the corridor wafted into the bedroom.

She tried the lights. Nothing. Nothing but inky darkness.

The nearest corridor light was just a few metres away. She edged towards it, groping her way along the wall, until she felt the cold metal and clicked it on to chase away the darkness and the shadows.

He was plunged into darkness. Frozen for a moment, he then stumbled on, feeling his way by moving his hands back and forth along the wall, searching until he found another switch.

The inky fingers of darkness clung to his heels.

The dark enveloped her like a blanket, smothering her, blocking her way forward, forcing her to grope her way blindly down the stairs.

He lay in the darkness and listened to the night. It was an unsettling, menacing darkness, full of dancing shadows and the occasional creak and rustle from the house.

The other end of the passage was an ocean of shadows and menace.

Impenetrable darkness surrounded her, blanketing her as the creaks and rustles of the night echoed around her.

Out in the hall, the light faded and snapped off, plunging the house into darkness, which crept into every space around them.

Darkness closed in on her like the shutting of an eye. There was no gap in the dark surrounding her – not even a pinprick of light to guide her. It had spread across the ceiling, clinging to the rafters, dripping along the walls, and slithered up the passage.

16
Wind

Ahead of him, he saw a flash of white. A torch? It flashed again. He headed towards it. Suddenly, he realised that he had been drawn further into the wood. **It was almost as if it had been done on purpose; some eerie presence tugging him forward.**

He was now in the middle of the wood, and surrounded by blackness on all sides. It was as if the trees and bushes had closed in on him, deliberately preventing him finding his way back. *He struggled to stay on his feet, as the wind shoved and tugged at him fiercely. It seemed to be coming from all directions at once; one moment in front of him, the next behind, whirling around him.*

Unable to shake the feeling of being watched, he kept looking over his shoulder. In his mind, every shadow in the wood grew eyes. Suddenly, his pulse started to race. He had caught sight of a movement out of the corner of his eye. It turned out to be no more than a branch swaying in the wind, but he **couldn't shake off his unease. A strange sensation had gripped the back of his neck, like a cold, skeletal hand tugging at his hair.**

WORDS

Nouns	**Breath**, breeze, gust, gale, whirlwind, hurricane, tornado
	Storm, clouds, dust, snow
	Whisper, moan, groan, shiver, shudder
	House, ruins, courtyard, railings, windows, glass, panes, shutters, curtains, chimney, chimney pot, roof, beams, rafters, door, flowerpot
	Room, corridor, passage, hall

Trees, branches, trunks, bark, leaves, ivy, grass

Skin, hair, head, neck, face, cheek, eyes, ears

Clothes, trousers

Similes/ Metaphors	**Like the touch of cold fingers**, like a gloved hand pressing against the window, tickled her ear like a feather, screeched like a boiling kettle, swirled like a tornado around the walls, tore at his face like stabbing fingers, hunted her like a beast
Adjectives	**Cold**, chilly, bitter
	Strange, ghostly, eerie, moaning, mournful, whining, screeching
	Sudden, invisible
	Shivering, stammering, billowing, swirling
	High, strong, colossal
	Harsh, gritty
	Fierce, fiery, boiling, ferocious, demented
Verbs	**Whispered**, shushed, whined, sighed, whistled, moaned, hooted, groaned
	Tickled, ghosted, prickled
	Rustled, creaked, rattled, grated
	Crept, slithered, prowled, hunted, chased
	Shook, lifted, bent, arched, rocked, overturned, rolled
	Shuddered, quivered, swayed, fluttered, puffed, billowed
	Crashed, banged, slammed
	Howled, roared, screeched, shrieked, screamed, raged
	Shoved, pulled, tugged, buffeted, battered
	Blew, rushed, surged, raged, blustered, swirled, whirled, scudded
	Beat, lashed, hammered, pounded
	Whipped, hit, thrashed, tore, bit, stabbed, caught, stole
	Staggered, struggled, stumbled

PHRASES – NOUNS AND ADJECTIVES

★ *No sound inside the house*
★ Nothing but the . . .
★ *Breath of wind*
★ Quiet whisper of a breeze
★ Quiet whisper and shiver of the ivy
★ Like a gloved hand against the window
★ *Eerie wind*
★ Ghostly, night breeze
★ Cold, shivering wind
★ Like the touch of cold fingers
★ Strange cold breeze on his face
★ *Moaning winds*
★ Mournful wind
★ Thin, whining wind
★ Full of eerie snatches of sound
★ *Sudden gust*
★ Strong gust
★ High wind
★ Ferocious wind
★ Bitter winds and harsh whispers
★ Fiery wind
★ Swirling wind
★ Stammering gusts
★ Colossal rush of wind
★ Unnaturally cold and fierce wind
★ *Billowing clouds of dust*

PHRASES – VERBS

★ As night approached . . .
★ As clouds scudded along overhead . . .
★ Whispered in the breeze
★ Whispered through the window
★ *Fluttered the curtains*
★ Flicked the curtains away from the window
★ *Rustled the ivy*
★ Swayed and tapped at the glass
★ *Sighed into her ear*
★ Sighed among the leaves
★ Sighed and moaned across them
★ Sighed and whispered in the rafters

★ Whistled and sighed as the wind wound itself around the trunks
★ *Crept through the doors*
★ Crept through the gaps in the crumbling walls
★ Slithered through the gaps in the windows
★ Prowled through the rooms
★ *Rushed and leaped around the garden*
★ Sighed through the fir trees lining the drive
★ Tugged at trees, surged through the hedges
★ Rustled the leaves around them
★ Chased the leaves in circles
★ Sent a pile of leaves scurrying round in circles
★ Shushed through the grass
★ *Lifted the trailing vines from the wall of the house*
★ Sent the vines fluttering towards the window
★ Set the leaves of the trailing ivy murmuring
★ *Rattled the chimney pots*
★ Caught an empty flowerpot
★ Overturned the pot and rolled it around
★ *Tugged at the bushes*
★ Bent the tops of the branches
★ Shook the branches
★ Shuddered as they were stabbed by the wind
★ Rattled the bare branches of the shivering trees
★ Sent the branches scraping across the window
★ Arched from side to side
★ Stole the leaves
★ Tore at the bark
★ *Blew snow off the railings*
★ Sent a blanket of snow against the door
★ *Groaned in the trees*
★ Grated together like broken teeth
★ Creaked eerily in the breeze
★ Whined through the trees
★ *Howled around the house*
★ Roared down the chimney
★ Brought eerie snatches of sound
★ Howled and crashed on the jagged rocks of the ruins
★ Screeched like a boiling kettle
★ Whistled and screamed
★ Shrieked down the corridor
★ Groaned and creaked through the beams in the great hall
★ *Rushed through the courtyard*
★ Raged through the ruins
★ Blustered around the house

* Swirled like a tornado around the walls
* Scudded along the passage
* Rattled the windows
* Banged wildly in the wind
* Lashed the panes
* Tore a tile from the roof
* Lashed against the windows
* Hammered at the glass
* Pounded against the door
* Shook the shutter and flung it back against the wall
* Darkened the air with billowing clouds of dust
* Had grown to a thing of force and fury
* *Tickled his ear like a feather*
* Ghosted past him
* Blew on the backs of their necks and ears
* Made the skin at the back of his neck prickle with foreboding
* *Developed a chilling edge*
* Hit like an avalanche of cold
* Whirled around him
* Surged past her cheek
* Buffeted his face
* Bit savagely at them
* Bit him with venom
* Thrashed at her hair
* Tugged at his hair
* Tore at his skin
* Buffeted her face
* Tore at his face like stabbing fingers
* Battered her eyes shut
* *Whipped at his clothes and hair*
* Tore at his clothes with its invisible fingers
* *Hunted her like a beast*
* Shoved, pulled, tugged at him ferociously
* Staggered back and forth, side to side
* Struggled to stay on his feet
* *Lay on his bed listening to the wind outside his window*
* Carried his voice away unanswered into the dark night

SENTENCES

The wind sighed among the leaves.

The eerie wind sighed and whispered, rustling the leaves around them.

A breeze shushed through the grass, rustling the leaves and bringing with it the scent of cigar smoke.

There was nothing to be heard inside the house; nothing but the quiet whisper of the wind and the shiver of the ivy clutching the wall.

The swirling winds caressed the trees, bending their branches and stealing their leaves.

The wind began to whine through the trees and bent the tops of the branches.

A gust of wind lifted the trailing vines from the wall of the house and sent them fluttering towards the window like bony, outstretched arms.

A gust of wind tugged at the bushes and sent their branches scraping across the window.

A breath of wind shook the branches, rattled the chimney pot, and crept through the doors.

A breeze behind him rustled the ivy, which swayed and tapped at the glass. The white sheets covering the furniture fluttered as if suddenly brought to life.

The night breeze sighed into her ear as it whispered through the window.

A thin, whining wind blew through the gap in the window.

She lay on her bed listening to the wind outside the window. Inside, the old house creaked and rattled in the dark.

He could hear the wind like a gloved hand pressing against the window.

A little whisper of a breeze flicked the curtains away from the window.

The ruins creaked and groaned as the wind prowled through the rooms, creeping through gaps in the crumbling walls.

The bitter winds and harsh whispers rattled the bare branches of the shivering trees, which grated together like broken teeth.

The shutters shuddered as they were stabbed by the wind.

The wind shrieked down the corridor.

Moaning winds rushed and leaped round the house.

The window banged wildly in the sudden gust of wind, which roared into the room, swirling like a hurricane from wall to wall, floor to ceiling.

The wind was ferocious, gaining power all the time, until it screamed over the house and beat like a fist against the roof.

The wind lashed against the windows, hammered at the glass.

The shutter in his window shook violently, was flung back against the wall and the door slammed open.

A sudden, ferocious gust of wind caught an empty pot, overturned it and rolled it around.

A strong gust of wind blew through the garden, sending a pile of fallen leaves scurrying round and round in a whirlwind on the patio.

As she reached the house the wind erupted and the temperature dropped to a deathly chill.

As night approached, the wind strengthened, rushing through the courtyard and deepening its roar as it pounded against the doors.

The gale rattled the windows, rain lashed the panes, a single tile was torn from the roof. There was deathly silence as a falling tile clattered on the ground.

The top of the trees were bending, arching from side to side, whistling and sighing as the wind wound itself around the ancient trunks, through the tangle of leaves, tearing at the bark.

The wind buffeted her face like the touch of cold fingers.

A cold, shivering wind blew on the backs of their necks and ears.

A breath of wind ghosted past him, tickling his ear like a feather and making the skin at the back of his neck prickle with foreboding.

The wind carried her voice away unanswered into the dark night.

He was whipped by gusts of warm, gritty wind.

The wind whipped at his clothes, his hair, as leaves flew across his path. The bending branches stabbed at his face.

The wind seemed to come from all directions at once; one moment in front of him, the next behind, whirling around him.

He staggered back and forth, side to side, struggling to stay on his feet, as the wind shoved and tugged at him fiercely.

The wind had grown to a thing of force and fury, darkening the air with billowing clouds of dust and tearing at their clothes with its invisible fingers. Hunting them like a beast.

The wind screamed like a boiling kettle as it tried to lift the skin from her bones, the hair from her head, pulling, tugging, tearing it loose.

The rushing wind hit like an avalanche of cold, thrashing at her hair, whipping her trousers, battering her eyes shut.

17
Rain and hail

As she looked out of the window, she saw that the first heavy drops of rain had started to fall, exploding like spots of ink on the windowsill. She turned back to her computer, and as she clicked through the recent photos of the hotel, **a tingling sixth sense made her look closer at one particular photo**. Her hand froze on the mouse. Standing on the step by the front door was a strange misty silhouette.

Intrigued, she zoomed in to enlarge the image, but just as it came into focus, the computer suddenly crackled and filled with a grey, flickering mist.

As the rain squalled against the hotel, rattling the windows and making the doors creak, **a sense of foreboding crept through her. Something strange was happening in this hotel. From the moment they had arrived, she had sensed something – some kind of eerie presence lurking in the background. After seeing that photo, she was now determined to get to the bottom of it.**

Nouns	**Sky**, horizon, heavens, earth, clouds, rain, sleet, hail
	Showers, drizzle, drops, spots, bullets, downpour, stream, puddles
	Torrent, waves, curtain, veil, blanket, shroud
	Wind, breeze, gusts
	Maelstrom, whirlwind
	Park, garden, forest floor, trees, bushes, blossoms, fern, leaf, ivy, grass
	Street, house, ruins, castle, manor, chapel
	Roof, gutters, chimney, windows, windowsill, glass, door
	Head, face, eyes, neck, hands

Similes/ Metaphors	**Like dark**, **grey streamers**, like a steady downpour of tears, as if they were being blasted by fire hoses, like needles pricking her arms and head, like the rattling of dry bones, like the tick of a very slow clock
Adjectives	**Light**, dark, black, grey, silvery, gloomy, misty
	Icy, cold, chilly, freezing, bitter, stinging
	Heavy, merciless, relentless, monotonous
	Rain-swept, damp, sodden, muddy
	Frothing, boiling, pattering, drumming, spluttering, dancing, swirling
Verbs	**Dripped**, rushed, poured, streamed, squalled, unleashed, flooded
	Formed, clung, hung, spread, arched, blanketed, engulfed
	Splashed, gurgled, rattled, hissed, drummed, crashed, exploded
	Danced, jumped, scattered, spattered, flinched, shivered
	Blew, drilled, pricked, stung, hit, struck, beat, pelted, lashed, slashed, hammered, pounded, pummelled

PHRASES – NOUNS AND ADJECTIVES

- ★ *Every gust of wind*
- ★ Howling wind
- ★ *Spluttering rain and mist*
- ★ A blurred shadow behind the mist
- ★ *Black clouds*
- ★ Layers of heavy clouds
- ★ Huge, boiling clouds
- ★ Heavy, wet clouds
- ★ Clouds like dark grey streamers
- ★ Rain-swept sky
- ★ Swirling maelstrom of cloud and rain
- ★ *First, heavy drops of rain*
- ★ Cold drizzle
- ★ Icy drips
- ★ Chilly stream
- ★ Heavy drizzle

- Showers of heavy rain
- Cords of grey water
- Veils of rain
- Curtain of icy rain
- Drops the size of bullets
- Freezing rain
- Stinging waves of rain
- Constant drumming of rain
- Grey, endless curtain of icy rain
- Like a steady downpour of tears
- Like needles in her arms and head
- *Like the rattling of dry bones*
- *Bitter sleet*
- Dancing hail
- Melting chips of ice
- *Sodden trees*
- Muddy, rutted paths
- *Grey gulls*

PHRASES – VERBS

- Rose in the west
- Crowded over the horizon
- Clung to the hill
- Formed a misty, silver veil
- Hung in the sky
- Hung in a cloud
- *Blanketed the house*
- Engulfed the park
- *Spread darkness and damp*
- Drawn by the wind into an icy curtain
- Trailed veils of stinging rain in its wake
- *Had started to fall*
- Unleashed their load
- Hissed around them
- Splashed and gurgled
- Poured down from the heavens
- Crashed to earth
- Lashed sideways down the street
- Rushed down in torrents
- Hammered down in a steady, monotonous torrent
- Pummelled down mercilessly
- Arched down in stinging waves

- *Rushed towards the house*
- Squalled against the house
- Slashed at the grass
- Hissed on the bushes
- Spattered on the forest floor
- Pelted the trees and beat on the bushes
- Trees flinched, grass shivered
- Hit like fists
- As she shut the curtains . . .
- Silence, except for the beating of rain outside his window
- Hammered relentlessly at the windows
- Spattered the window in sudden gusts
- Lashed against the glass
- Rattled the windows
- Made the front door creak and groan
- Spattered on the gravel path
- Exploded like spots of ink on the windowsill
- Exploded like flung gravel as it struck the windows
- Flooded the gutters
- *Scattered showers of blossoms onto the ground*
- Dripped from every gleaming fern and leaf
- Jumped to life as the rain drummed the surface
- Even after the rain had stopped . . .
- Dripped like the tick of a very slow clock
- Gleamed in the flash of distant lightning
- *Blew straight into their faces*
- Drilled into their faces, blinding them
- Hammered on his face and head
- Stung their faces and hands
- Pricked like needles
- *Poured down his face*
- Poured down his neck
- Streamed down the back of his neck as he ran for cover
- As if they were being blasted by fire hoses

SENTENCES

Clouds like dark grey streamers rose in the west.

Black clouds crowded over the horizon.

Layers of heavy black clouds clung to the hill and blanketed the park.

The sky darkened and showers of heavy rain poured from the heavens.

The rain-swept sky, the sodden trees, the muddy, rutted paths and grey house formed a gloomy background.

The rain fell harder, forming a misty, silver veil; the house a blurred shadow behind it.

The rain rushed down in torrents, gleaming in the flash of the distant lightning.

All he could see was a swirling maelstrom of cloud and rain.

The rain was a steady downpour of tears, crashing to earth, spreading darkness and damp.

The light was almost lost behind the grey, endlessly moving curtain of icy rain, which pummelled down mercilessly.

The clouds rushed towards the house, trailing veils of rain in their wake.

The rain arrived, slashing at the grass in the garden.

The rain hammered down in a steady monotonous torrent.

The trees flinched and the grass shivered in the freezing rain.

The rain lashed sideways down the drive across the grass, drawn by the wind into an icy curtain.

There was silence, except for the beating of rain outside his window.

Raindrops spattered on the forest floor and dripped from every gleaming leaf and fern.

The first, heavy drops of rain had started to fall and exploded like spots of ink on the windowsill. These were quickly followed by drops the size of bullets hammering at the windows.

The puddles jumped to life as pellets of water drummed the surface.

The downpour had flooded the gutters and even after the rain had stopped water dripped like the tick of a very slow clock.

The rain hissed on the bushes. Inside it was silent.

The rain was falling harder now, hammering slantwise against the window as she shut the curtains.

Every gust of wind sent the rain to splatter against the window like the rattling of dry bones.

Rain squalled against the house, rattling the windows and making the front door creak and groan.

With the mist came spluttering rain, exploding like flung gravel as it struck the windows.

The dancing hail hung in a cloud and drove along the path like smoke.

The rain drilled into their faces, blinding them.

A heavy drizzle blew straight into their faces.

The rain was like needles pricking her arms and head.

The rain was coming down harder, relentless. Melting chips of ice hammered on his head and face and streamed down the back of his neck as he ran for cover.

The rain was hammering down and a chilly stream poured down his face.

The rain clouds burst – constant drumming of rain that hit like fists. It was as if they were being blasted by fire hoses.

18
Thunder and lightning

Outside, the sky continued to darken as thunder rumbled in the distance. The staircase was steeped in shadow as it spiralled steeply upwards. Andrew was unable to see even the part that went straight up ahead of him, so there was no way of knowing what waited for him at the top.

Slowly, he started to ascend the narrow stairs, but every step Andrew took was followed by a creaking echo, and *the gusting of the wind against the windows.* **No matter how hard he tried to control the creeping terror spreading through him, his eyes widened and his body jerked at every noise. Goosebumps riddled his body** as the torchlight flickered unsteadily, casting dancing, flickering shadows in front of him. **He began to imagine something hideous in every shadow.**

As the storm moved nearer, the whole house started to shudder with the crack of thunder, quickly followed by a flash of lightning, which briefly lit up the stairs.

WORDS

Nouns	**Thunder**, lightning, sky, air, horizon, heavens
	Bolt, fork, flash, flicker, spears, arrows, blade
	Clap, crash, crack, explosion, echo
	Land, street, ground, path, house, roof, windows, door
Similes/ Metaphors	**Like an exploding firework**, like the echo of a drum
Adjectives	**Huge**, great, torn, jagged, forked, guillotine blade
	Bright, white, brilliant, dazzling, flickering, shimmering

Thunderous, pulsing, boiling, exploding, dangerous, ferocious, menacing, ominous

Verbs

Blew, gusted

Rumbled, crashed, howled, boomed, pulsed

Tore, forked, ripped, pierced

Lit, streaked, flooded, blinded, flickered, illuminated, spattered

Shuddered, shook

Blinded, seared

PHRASES – NOUNS AND ADJECTIVES

* Lightning bolt
* Flash of lightning
* Flash of brilliant white lightning
* Flickering white light
* Ferocious flicker
* Trails of lightning
* Jagged spears of lightning
* Great, forked lightning
* Dazzling arrows of lightning
* Huge, guillotine blade of lightning
* *Pulsing air*
* Clap of thunder
* *Like an exploding firework*
* Like the echo of a drum
* Thunderous echo
* Another much bigger explosion
* *Dangerous and menacing power*

PHRASES – VERBS

* Blew harder
* Gusted against the windows, against the doors
* *Shattered the silence*
* Rumbled in the distance
* Rumbled closer and closer
* Followed almost immediately
* *Crashed and howled overhead*
* Boomed menacingly
* Struggled and howled in fits and starts

- ★ Pulsed and rumbled ominously
- ★ Boomed through the house
- ★ Shuddered with a crack of thunder
- ★ Shook the house to its core
- ★ Felt as if the ground beneath his feet was being ripped apart
- ★ *Streaked across the horizon*
- ★ Tore through the night sky
- ★ Tore the night sky apart and ripped its belly
- ★ Streaked through the streets like an exploding firework
- ★ Forked through the huge, boiling clouds
- ★ Spattered with lightning
- ★ Pierced the sky
- ★ Torn apart by the jagged spears of lightning
- ★ Unravelled across the crest of the oncoming storm
- ★ *Lit up the whole scene*
- ★ Flooded the land
- ★ Lit up the sky above the house
- ★ Touched the roof
- ★ Illuminated the sky with a stark, blue-whiteness
- ★ *Seared his vision*
- ★ Blinded him as it flickered in and out

SENTENCES

The air pulsed as thunder rumbled ominously, and then crashed and howled overhead.

The thunder struggled and howled in fits and starts.

The thunder rumbled closer and closer, until the lightning followed almost immediately.

Thunder boomed through the house, shaking it to its core, lightning streaking through the grounds like an exploding firework.

Thunder like the echo of a drum shattered the silence.

The air shook as the loud, booming wind hammered at the house, and thunder crashed and roared overhead.

Thunder boomed, dull and distant. Flickering white light unravelled across the crest of the oncoming storm.

Thunder rumbled in the distance, the sky continued to darken, and the wind blew harder, gusting against the windows, against the doors.

The windows, then the whole house shuddered with a crack of thunder. Another explosion, but much bigger this time. It felt as if the ground beneath his feet was being ripped apart.

It was as if the heavens were being torn apart by the jagged spears of lightning – the thunder howling their pain.

Lightning tore through the sky, blinding him as it flickered in and out.

An immense guillotine blade of lightning streaked across the horizon and illuminated it with a stark blue-whiteness.

Suddenly, dazzling arrows of lightning tore the night sky apart, ripping its belly, flooding the land. It was an awesome spectacle, but the force of its power was dangerous and menacing.

There came a flash of lightning which lit up the whole scene. A ferocious flicker and then a clap of thunder.

A great fork of lightning pierced the sky, so bright that he was blinded.

A flash of brilliant white lightning lit up the sky above the house.

A lightning bolt forked through the huge boiling clouds to touch the roof.

The sky was spattered with lightning; the thunder boomed menacingly.

Part 4
The ghost

19

The ghost's appearance

SECTION 1 – FACE

WORDS	
Nouns	**Shadow**, figure, skull, hair, face, cheekbones, skin
	Cape, cloak, coat, hood
Similes/ Metaphors	**Pale as marble**, white as alabaster, like marble with hollow sockets, like thin, crumpled paper, like the skin of a lizard, like cruel slashes
Adjectives	**Black**, dark, blue, purple, bluish-white
	White, pale, pallid, colourless, translucent
	Grey, ashen, sallow, deathly, sickly, fragile
	Moon-shaped, oval, narrow, thin, gaunt, hollow, skull-like, skeletal, fleshless
	Shadowy, blurred, faint, dim, ghostly, spectral, swirling, disembodied
	Thin, emaciated, haggard
Verbs	**Dressed**, wore, hooded
	Lined, creased, crumpled
	Hung, sagged, drooped, bulged
	Stretched, twisted, tightened

PHRASES – NOUNS AND ADJECTIVES

- ★ Blood-splattered knight
- ★ Shadowy, hooded figure

- ☆ Black hood
- ☆ Long-coated figure
- ☆ Grinning face of a disembodied skull
- ☆ *Pale, wrinkled face*
- ☆ Pale as marble
- ☆ Like marble with hollow, black sockets
- ☆ White as alabaster
- ☆ White skeletal face
- ☆ Deathly pale
- ☆ Pale, almost colourless skin
- ☆ Pallid, deathly, grey colour
- ☆ Thin, gaunt, shadowy face
- ☆ Grinning, spectral skull
- ☆ Sallow, scarred face
- ☆ Sagging face
- ☆ Face like thin, crumpled paper
- ☆ Folds of leathery wrinkles
- ☆ Like the skin of a lizard
- ☆ Wrinkles like cruel slashes
- ☆ Blue, swollen veins

PHRASES – VERBS

- ☆ As she lifted her head . . .
- ☆ Had seen many battles
- ☆ *Sagged with wrinkles beneath her eyes*
- ☆ Hung in wrinkled folds around her face and neck
- ☆ Drooped from his face
- ☆ Bulged under her deathly, pale skin
- ☆ Stretched tight over his face
- ☆ *Pulled down low over her forehead*
- ☆ Hid her pale, skull-like face

SENTENCES

As she lifted her head, Robert could see her pale face. It was like marble with hollow, black sockets.

A black hood was pulled down low over his forehead to hide his pale, skull-like face.

Her crumpled grey skin hung in creased folds around her neck and arms.

With her pale, almost colourless skin, she looked like a fragile, china doll.

Her skin was a sickly, grey colour and hung in wrinkled folds.

Her pale skin was translucent. It was almost purple under her black eyes.

The colourless skin of his scarred face was stretched tight over his face, giving him the haunted look of someone who had seen many battles.

The wrinkles around his eyes looked like cruel slashes.

Knotted, blue veins bulged under her flaking skin.

The pale skin on her face was covered in wrinkles like thin, crumpled paper.

SECTION 2 – EYES

WORDS

Nouns	**Look**, stare, glare, leer
Similes/ Metaphors	**Like hollow, black cavities**, like two black swirling pools of ink, like dying embers, as small and hard as raisins, piercing like razors, blazed like beacons, sparkled like frost
Adjectives	**Dead**, hollow, cold, icy, frosty, stony, steely
	Sharp, staring, piercing
	Small, little, hard, unblinking
	Sharp, evil, cruel, savage, murderous, pitiless, mocking, sneering, withering, merciless, monstrous, malevolent, demonic, fiendish, demon-haunted
	Buggy, sly, crafty, furtive, cunning
	Gleaming, glowing, glinting, glowering, burning, feverish
Verbs	**Stared**, glared, bulged, squinted, narrowed
	Drilled, blasted, bored, pierced
	Burned, blazed, glinted, sparkled, darkened
	Churned, swirled, flickered, darted

PHRASES – NOUNS AND ADJECTIVES

- ★ Cold, dead eyes
- ★ Steely eyes
- ★ Glowering dark eyes

* Narrow eyes
* Like hollow, black cavities
* Dark, hollow sockets
* Like two black swirling pools of ink
* Glowing eyes like dying embers
* Dark craters for eyes
* As small and hard as raisins
* Frosty and narrowed
* Crafty look

PHRASES – VERBS

* Bored into her skull
* Glinted evilly
* Sparkled like frost – cold and dangerous
* Burned like furnaces
* Burned with a cruel light
* Blazed like beacons
* Drilled into her, piercing like razors
* Darkened warningly
* Flickered in his buggy, little eyes

SENTENCES

Her eyes burned with a cruel light in her skeletal face.

His eyes were hollow and like two black churning, swirling pools of ink.

Burning eyes glinted like dying embers from his sagging face.

His small eyes were as dark and hard as raisins, and had a demonic expression.

Her eyes darkened warningly.

His steely, grey eyes drilled into her, as piercing as razors.

He stared at Kitty for a moment and then a crafty look flickered in his buggy, little eyes.

He stared with unblinking eyes, but his lips twitched briefly.

Drilling into Kitty as if they would pierce her, his cold, staring eyes bulged in his ghastly, pale face.

He stared with eyes that sparkled like frost – cold and dangerous.

SECTION 3 – EXPRESSION

WORDS

Nouns	**Look**, expression, mask
	Mouth, lips, teeth, stumps, fangs, molars, gums, tongue
	Leer, sneer, gaze, squint, smile, grin, smirk, snarl, grimace
Adjectives	**Empty**, cold, chilly, icy, withering, expressionless
	Nasty, cruel, evil, spiteful, vicious, venomous, callous, vengeful, malicious
	Horrible, hideous, monstrous, ghastly
	Sly, cunning, creepy, scary, furtive, sinister, demonic
	Grinning, sneering, arrogant
	Toothless, rotting, jagged, crumbling, crooked, prominent, gap-toothed
	Brown, black, grey, yellow, stained
Verbs	**Glared**, grinned, glanced, grimaced
	Shot, trained, directed, changed
	Curled, twisted, twitched, tightened, stretched
	Stained, jutted, chipped, protruded

PHRASES – NOUNS AND ADJECTIVES

★ *Grinning face*
★ Fiendish snarl
★ Sneering mouth
★ As empty as a carcass
★ Nasty, demonic grin
★ Slow, demonic leer
★ Vicious smile
★ Grisly smirk
★ Hideous sneer
★ Reptilian sneer
★ Leering squint
★ Malicious grin
★ *Cold, sinister look*

* Look of mock concern
* Withering look
* Furtive, viperish expression
* Expressionless, granite mask
* *Toothless smile*
* Two, large, prominent teeth
* Two, jagged rows of rotting, brown teeth
* Stained, chipped teeth
* Mouth full of yellow teeth
* Brown teeth and grey gums
* Crooked teeth and cracked, flaky lips
* Crumbling tombstones

PHRASES – VERBS

* As he drifted through the wall . . .
* As she disappeared back into the shadows . . .
* As she watched him fumbling with the lock . . .
* Glowered at her
* *Twisted briefly*
* Twisted in a knowing grin
* Split into a malicious smirk
* Grimaced at her menacingly
* Stretched her mouth into a grisly smile
* Stretched into a hideous sneer
* *Bared his teeth*
* Bared in a reptilian leer
* Curled his lips into a savage sneer
* Curled in a cunning sneer
* Wrinkled with disgust
* *Jutted out like fangs*
* Chipped diagonally in half
* Worn to yellowing stumps
* Curved down over his lower lip
* Protruded over a gold-capped molar
* Revealed a black, swollen tongue
* *Clicked when she moved her lips*

SENTENCES

His sneering mouth opened wide to reveal a black, swollen tongue.

His icy expression suddenly changed as he curled his lips into a savage sneer.

She leaned forward and grimaced at him malevolently.

His mouth twisted into a knowing grin as he drifted through the wall.

She turned, flicked the lock open and stretched her mouth into a grisly smile.

He directed a look of pure venom at her through the window.

She had an amused, callous look on her face as she watched Robert fumbling with the lock.

His eyebrows were raised and he glanced up from the chest to give Kitty a cold, reptilian sneer.

Her face was an expressionless mask of granite as she disappeared back into the shadows.

Behind the thick, cracked lips she could see his stained and crooked teeth that jutted out like fangs and curved down over his lower lip.

His teeth were bared in a cheerless, reptilian leer and revealed two, jagged rows of brown, rotting teeth.

SECTION 4 – HANDS AND FINGERS

WORDS	
Nouns	**Skeleton**, claw, talons, nails, weapons
	Veins, spots, cuts, wounds, scars
Adjectives	**Bony**, cold, wrinkled, swollen, lumpy
	Black, dirty
	Sharp, long-fingered
Verbs	**Covered**, chipped, blackened, sharpened, encrusted, burnt, twisted
	Felt, shook, held, grabbed, grasped, lunged

PHRASES – NOUNS AND ADJECTIVES

- ★ Wrinkled hands
- ★ Burnt, twisted claw
- ★ Bony hand
- ★ Bony, long-fingered hands
- ★ Cold as a skeleton

- ★ Black talons
- ★ Nails like claws
- ★ Dangerous weapons
- ★ Swollen, lumpy veins
- ★ Filthy with dirt and grime
- ★ Burnt, twisted claw
- ★ Blackened talons for nails

PHRASES – VERBS

- ★ Sharpened to points
- ★ *Felt as cold as a skeleton*
- ★ Backed away from the claw-like hand
- ★ *Grabbed her by the wrist*
- ★ Grasped at the air in front of him
- ★ Lunged at him

SENTENCES

Large, ice-cold hands grabbed her wrist.

His hand was a burnt, twisted claw, with blackened talons for nails.

He backed away from the claw-like hand that was grasping at the air in front of him.

Two, enormous, shovel-like hands lunged at him.

She lunged at him, her nails like claws, sharpened to points and dangerous weapons.

SECTION 5 – INJURIES AND WOUNDS

WORDS

Nouns	**Skull**, face, skin, flesh, jaw, mouth, lip, cheek, eye, eyebrows, socket, hair
	Width, length
Adjectives	**Wide**, thin, huge, jagged, gnarled
	Pink, black, purple, blue, yellow, green
	Peeling
	Terrible, horrible, hideous, battle-scarred

Verbs	**Ran**, covered
	Stretched, pulled, dragged, closed, twisted, puckered, shrivelled
	Scarred, disfigured, scabbed
	Burnt, scorched, seared, singed

PHRASES – NOUNS AND ADJECTIVES

- ⋆ Above his left eyebrow
- ⋆ Left side of his face
- ⋆ One side of her face
- ⋆ Width of his jaw
- ⋆ Around one eye
- ⋆ *Flaking skin*
- ⋆ Peeling skin
- ⋆ Sores around his lips
- ⋆ Swollen, red blisters
- ⋆ Mass of angry sores
- ⋆ Festering, green wound
- ⋆ Thin, jagged scar across . . .
- ⋆ Ugly, wide scar
- ⋆ Hideous scar
- ⋆ Scar tissue
- ⋆ Scarred and scabbed
- ⋆ Huge, pink patches
- ⋆ Singed hair and eyebrows
- ⋆ *Puckered folds*
- ⋆ Gnarled lump of flesh
- ⋆ Mass of seared, scarred skin
- ⋆ Scarred and twisted lip
- ⋆ Burnt, puckered skin
- ⋆ *Permanent snarl*
- ⋆ Curious squint

PHRASES – VERBS

- ⋆ Ran the length of one side of his face
- ⋆ Almost closed one eye in its puckered folds
- ⋆ Twisted his lips
- ⋆ Bunched up
- ⋆ Puckered around the wound
- ⋆ Squinted from a black socket
- ⋆ *Pulled downwards by a scar*

- ✳ Pulled into a permanent snarl
- ✳ Closed in the puckered folds of a jagged scar
- ✳ Pulled his eye into a curious squint
- ✳ Dragged her lip to meet her nostril
- ✳ *Disfigured by fire*
- ✳ Scorched into huge, pink patches
- ✳ Shrivelled into a twisted lump of flesh
- ✳ *Covered his face and skull*
- ✳ Ran across his hip

SENTENCES

His face was a mass of sores and peeling skin.

The swollen, red blisters twisted his lips into a grimace.

The skin on his face and bald skull was scarred and scabbed.

One side of his face was a pocked mass of scars and seared skin.

The skin was bunched up around the festering, green wound.

A thin, jagged scar was just visible above his left eyebrow.

One of his cheeks was dragged downwards by an ugly scar.

The skin around one eye had been pulled out of shape and gave her a curious squint.

He had a scarred and twisted lip, which was pulled up to meet his nostril.

The left side of her face was terribly burned. It was a mass of seared skin and scorched in huge, pink patches.

His face had been disfigured by fire. One eye squinted from a black, empty socket. His eyebrows were singed and sprouted at odd angles, and his ear was a shrivelled, gnarled lump.

His face was disfigured by a hideous scar that ran the length of one side of his face and pulled his mouth into a permanent snarl.

His face was a mass of scar tissue and almost closed one eye in its puckered folds.

SECTION 6 – MOVEMENT

WORDS

Nouns	**Figure**, shadow, shape, mist
Similes/ Metaphors	**Like a dark mist**, as silent as the shadow of a bird, like a figure carved from stone, glided like a shadow, as if pulled by invisible strings, like a predator scenting its prey, like a panther waiting to pounce, landed quietly like a cat, like a scuttling lizard
Adjectives	**Dark**, black, misty
	Quiet, silent, still, motionless, invisible, unseen
	Brief, fleeting, flickering
	Quick, swift, deft, scuttling
	Slow, shuffling
	Threatening, menacing
Verbs	**Wandered**, paraded
	Floated, glided, swished, thinned out, disappeared
	Moved, walked, stepped, shuffled, strutted, ran, galloped
	Poised, leaned, leaped, landed
	Raised, pointed, jerked, clutched, beckoned
	Groaned, moaned, screamed, wailed, howled, shrieked
Adverbs	**Slowly**, stealthily, noiselessly
	Menacingly

PHRASES – NOUNS AND ADJECTIVES

- ★ Where the moonlight . . .
- ★ In the dead of night . . .
- ★ *Like a dark mist*
- ★ Black shadow
- ★ A flickering shadow
- ★ Like a scuttling lizard
- ★ Silent and motionless
- ★ Like a stone figure

* As silent as the shadow of a bird
* Fatal wound in his . . .

PHRASES – VERBS

* When the clock struck twelve . . .
* *Shuffled down the corridor*
* Paraded up and down the stairs
* Wandered around the . . . in the dead of night
* *Glided like a shadow*
* Glided noiselessly
* Moved stealthily
* Swished out of sight
* Floated towards her
* Floated as if being pulled by invisible strings
* Walked right through the door
* Thinned out and disappeared
* *Raised to his full height*
* Leaned forward menacingly
* *Poised on the balls of his feet*
* Like a predator scenting its prey
* Like a panther waiting to pounce
* Crouched on the edge
* Leaped into the air
* Landed on the brick path in front of him
* Landed quietly like a cat
* *Advanced slowly*
* Strutted like a peacock
* Ran in pecking strides
* Galloped off
* *Beckoned them to come to him*
* Jerked her fingers
* *Made no sound*
* Didn't rustle as she stepped on them
* Groaned and clutched his hand to . . .

SENTENCES

She was as silent and motionless as a figure carved from stone.

He stood still and poised like a cobra about to strike.

She made no more sound than the shadow of a bird.

He landed quietly like a cat.

She was tensed, poised on the balls of her feet, like a predator scenting its prey.

He was crouched on the edge, like a panther waiting to pounce.

She glided smoothly, noiselessly in the shadows.

He floated as if being pulled by invisible strings.

She walked right through the door.

It seemed to float towards where the moonlight flooded through the window.

She went into the room, but not through the locked door. It was as if she had thinned out and disappeared.

When he moved closer, he made no sound. The grass didn't bend, the leaves didn't rustle as he stepped on them.

Its invisible feet paraded up and down the stairs.

Suddenly, the black shadow seemed to leap in the air, then land on the brick path and gallop off.

He wandered around the castle in the dead of night, groaning and clutching his hand to the fatal sword wound in his chest.

20

Interaction with and reaction to the ghost

Kitty whirled round at lightning speed and found herself face-to-face with a dark, hooded figure. As the hood fell back, she caught sight of his pale, scarred face. It was like marble with two hollow, black sockets for eyes.

Her breath caught in her chest as she eyed it with alarm. A cold thought began to unfold in her mind, a cold dread that she couldn't force back down. Drenched in sweat and heart pounding, Kitty kept her narrowed eyes fixed to the floor, unable to meet its cold, unblinking stare.

Scrambling to her feet, she started to run, not daring to look back, the **sound of her breath roaring in her ears, her pulse thumping hard. She didn't dare stop. Never once did she turn and look back** . . . just kept on running, arms pumping, her lungs burning.

SECTION 1 – INTERACTION

WORDS

Nouns	**Courtyard**, gate, house, building, ground, floor
	Corridor, passage, hall, room, cellar, bedroom
	Wall, door, handle, lock, bolt, window, sill, drainpipe, curtains
	Stairs, flight, steps, rail
	Furniture, table, chair, dinner gong, dust sheets

Figure, shadow, knight, hood

Face, scar

Eyes, sockets, look, glance, blur

Mouth, lips, snarl, breath, air, lungs

Legs, feet, ankle

Arm, hand, grip, nails, talons

Shoulder, back

Similes/ Metaphors	**Like lightning**, like marble, like a burnt, twisted claw

Adjectives

Unsure, hesitant

Anxious, desperate, frantic

Winded, breathless

Huge, enormous

Flailing, thrashing

Dark, black, white, brass

Hooded, shadowy

Hollow, sunken

Pale, pallid, bloodless, waxy, waxen

Scarred, disfigured

Hideous, ghastly, grotesque

Stained, blood-splattered

Verbs

Warned, urged, knew

Shocked, startled, dazed, jolted

Vanished, disappeared

Stopped, waited, followed

Spun, turned, whirled

Pointed, covered, beckoned

Lifted, raised, peeked, peered, looked, glanced, shot, saw, caught sight of, watched, stared, glued

Seized, caught, coiled, grasped, grabbed, gripped, clenched

Thrashed, kicked, struggled, fought

Pulled, pushed, tugged, yanked, heaved, slammed, smashed

Stretched, wrapped, climbed, descended

Pressed, hugged, edged, inched, manoeuvred, shuffled, crept, crawled

Dodged, ducked, dived, scrambled, swung, bounded, pounded

Broke cover, darted, dashed, ran, sprinted, charged, tore, quickened, exploded

Slipped, slid, skidded, fell, stumbled, tumbled

Adverbs **Suddenly**, silently, gradually

Frantically

PHRASES – NOUNS AND ADJECTIVES

* *Something inside her*
* Every nerve in his body
* No sign of . . .
* No one there
* Not sure which way to go
* *Out in the open*
* Just to her right
* Out of the corner of her eye . . .
* *Dark, hooded figure*
* Like marble with two hollow, black sockets for eyes
* *Huge hand*
* Flailing hand
* Huge hand like a burnt, twisted claw
* With his arm outstretched . . .
* More she fought, the tighter the grip
* Head down, arms pumping, legs a blur of movement
* *Cellar door*
* Huge, brass dinner gong
* White sheets
* Blood-splattered knight

PHRASES – VERBS

* Pressed a finger to her lips, warning Tom to be quiet
* Pointed down to the end of the tunnel
* Caught sight of his pale, scarred face

- ★ Knew that she couldn't stay where she was
- ★ *Desperate to get away*
- ★ *Looked over her shoulder at . . .*
- ★ Saw it hidden in the shadows
- ★ Shot a look over her shoulder
- ★ Peeped around the corner of the building
- ★ Lifted her head above the sill
- ★ Peered out from behind the curtain
- ★ Looked up and down the passage for the hundredth time
- ★ Looked both ways to check that the coast was clear
- ★ Swept the corridor
- ★ Looked from side to side and over her shoulders
- ★ Shot him a warning glance to keep quiet, and not move
- ★ *Spun round at lightning speed to face . . .*
- ★ Whirled round and found herself face-to-face with . . .
- ★ Whirled round but never saw the thing that . . .
- ★ As the hood fell back . . .
- ★ *Stopped when her foot caught on something behind her*
- ★ Coiled around her ankle
- ★ Seized hold of her
- ★ Grabbed her ankle
- ★ Thrashed against its grip as she screamed
- ★ Yanked backwards so quickly, the ground pushed past her in a blur
- ★ Caught something as he went down
- ★ Rested on his hands and knees
- ★ Shocked and winded, shoulders heaving as he sucked in air
- ★ *Disfigured by a hideous scar*
- ★ Ran the length of one side of his face
- ★ Pulled his mouth into a permanent snarl
- ★ *Kept low, hardly daring to raise his head*
- ★ Couldn't move
- ★ Made his way towards the front door
- ★ Pressed himself against the wall
- ★ Hugged the wall with her back
- ★ Shuffled sideways, one foot crossing the other, until . . .
- ★ Dived under the table
- ★ *Crawled over the ground*
- ★ Scrambled on his hands and knees towards the door
- ★ Waited for a moment, then followed
- ★ Had vanished into thin air
- ★ *Kicked the door shut behind her*
- ★ Threw herself against it
- ★ Groped for the bolt
- ★ Grasped the handle

- ⋆ Pulled, pushed, tugged at every door
- ⋆ Dived through the door
- ⋆ Slammed the door shut behind her
- ⋆ Leant against the door
- ⋆ Breathed a sigh of relief as she felt the bolt slide home
- ⋆ *Crouched on all fours*
- ⋆ Manoeuvred around her bedroom towards the window
- ⋆ Ducked behind the . . .
- ⋆ Ran to the corner, waited a moment, and peered round
- ⋆ *Slipped on the damp floor*
- ⋆ Skidded on the marble floor
- ⋆ Blundered and slipped
- ⋆ Almost fell headlong down the stairs
- ⋆ Legs gave way and she slid in a heap down to the floor
- ⋆ *Scrambled to her feet and bolted down the hall*
- ⋆ Broke cover from behind the curtains
- ⋆ Charged towards the door
- ⋆ *Did a backwards roll and sprang to his feet*
- ⋆ Found her legs and ran again
- ⋆ Scrambled to her feet, and began to move
- ⋆ Darted and dodged around the furniture
- ⋆ Scrambled over the furniture
- ⋆ Pushed her way into the great hall
- ⋆ *Quickened until her feet appeared to be flying*
- ⋆ Sprinted wildly down the corridor
- ⋆ Ran down the hall, shrieking and pounding on the doors
- ⋆ Started to run, not daring to look back
- ⋆ Didn't dare stop
- ⋆ Kept on running, arms pumping, her lungs burning
- ⋆ Tore across the courtyard
- ⋆ Exploded through the gate
- ⋆ Tried to put as much distance between himself and the house
- ⋆ Never once did she turn and look back . . .
- ⋆ Sound of her breath roared in her ears
- ⋆ *Sprinted for the stairs*
- ⋆ Threw open the door
- ⋆ Using the metal rail, bounded down the steps
- ⋆ Took them three at a time
- ⋆ Swung herself round flight after flight
- ⋆ Pounded down the steps, faster and faster
- ⋆ *Grabbed a chair*
- ⋆ Smashed the window
- ⋆ Climbed out onto the sill
- ⋆ Stretched out her arm to grab the drainpipe

* Wrapped her arms and legs around the pipe
* Inched her way down to the ground
* *Screamed at the top of his lungs*

SENTENCES

Katie looked over her shoulder at him, put a finger to her lips, warning Tom to be quiet.

Out of the corner of her eye, Katie saw it hidden in the shadows. She glanced at Tom and shot him a warning glance to keep quiet, and not move.

With his arm outstretched, Alfie pointed down to the end of the tunnel. He looked over his shoulder, silently urging them to run.

Kitty whirled round and found herself face-to-face with a dark, hooded figure. As the hood fell back, she caught sight of his pale, scarred face. It was like marble with two hollow, black sockets for eyes.

She spun round at lightning speed to face the ghost, her heart pounding in her chest.

Her heart stopped when her foot caught on something behind her. She shot a look over her shoulder, as a huge hand coiled around her ankle. She thrashed against its grip as she screamed, desperate to get away, but the more she fought, the tighter the grip.

She was yanked backwards so quickly, the ground pushed past her in a blur.

His flailing hand caught something as he went down. He rested there on his hands and knees, shocked and winded, shoulders heaving as he sucked in air.

She couldn't move. Her eyes were glued to his face. It was disfigured by a hideous scar that ran the length of one side of his face, pulling his mouth into a permanent snarl.

He crawled over the ground, keeping low, hardly daring to raise his head.

Pressing himself against the wall, he made his way towards the front door.

Hugging the wall with her back, she shuffled sideways, one foot crossing the other, until she reached the door.

She dived under the table and scrambled on her hands and knees towards the door.

Tom waited for a moment, then followed. He peeped around the corner of the building. There was no one there. No sign of the blood-splattered knight. He had vanished into thin air.

She kicked the door shut behind her and threw herself against it, groping for the bolt and breathing a sigh of relief as she felt it slide home.

Crouching on all fours, Kitty manoeuvred around her bedroom towards the window. Slowly, she lifted her head above the sill and peered out from behind the curtain.

Frantically looking from side to side and over her shoulders, she ducked behind the huge, brass dinner gong.

She scrambled to her feet and bolted down the hall, her heart thudding against her ribs.

He broke cover from behind the curtains and charged towards the door.

The cellar door was just to her right. Her flailing hand grasped the handle and she dived through it. Slipping on the damp floor, she almost fell headlong down the stairs.

They looked up and down the passage for the hundredth time.

She looked both ways to check that the coast was clear.

Her eyes swept the corridor. There was nowhere to hide.

He ran to the corner, waited a moment, and peered round.

He did a backwards roll and sprang to his feet.

She found her legs and ran again, her feet skidding on the marble floor.

She scrambled to her feet, and began to move, not sure which way to go, only knowing that she couldn't stay where she was.

He darted and dodged around the furniture. Blundering and slipping, he fought his way to the door.

Her steps quickened until her feet appeared to be flying.

Sprinting wildly down the corridor, Kitty pulled, pushed, tugged at every door.

He screamed at the top of his lungs, and ran down the hall, shrieking and pounding on the doors.

She scrambled over the furniture, the white sheets billowing as she ran past. Pushing her way into the great hall, she slammed the door shut behind her. She leant against it but her legs gave way and she slid in a heap down to the floor.

She sprinted for the stairs, threw open the door and, using the metal rail, bounded down the steps, taking them three at a time.

She swung herself round flight after flight, pounding down the steps, faster and faster.

He started to run faster and faster, his head down, his arms pumping, and his legs a blur of movement as he tried to put as much distance between himself and the house.

She started to run, not daring to look back, the sound of her breath roaring in her ears, her pulse thumping hard. She didn't dare stop.

Suddenly, she was out in the open, tearing across the courtyard, exploding through the gate.

Never once did she turn and look back . . . just kept on running, arms pumping, her lungs burning.

Grabbing a chair, she smashed the window, climbed out onto the sill and stretched out her arm to grab the drainpipe. Wrapping her arms and legs around the pipe, she gradually inched her way down to the ground.

SECTION 2 – REACTION

WORDS	
Nouns	**Mind**, thoughts, instincts, nerves, shivers, sweat
	Dread, terror, horror, fear, panic
	Scene, image, face, eyes, look, stare
	Heart, pulse, adrenaline, chest, ribs
	Mouth, throat, lips
	Breath, sound, prayer, voice, gasps, gabble, cry, scream
	Body, stomach, head, arms, hands, palms, nails
Similes/ Metaphors	**Tornado of thoughts and fears**, like a sponge being wrung dry, like two black swirling pools of ink
Adjectives	**Alert**, afraid
	Frozen, paralysed
	Shaking, heaving, pounding
	Wet, damp, drenched, soaked
	Wide, staring, unblinking, horror-struck
	White, deathly pale
	Huge, yawning, wide open, cavernous
	Low, tight, choked, strangled
Verbs	**Warned**, knew, urged
	Etched, engraved, imprinted

Bubbled, pumped, strained, clutched, clenched, tightened, twisted, churned

Shut, squeezed

Swept, stared, watched, saw

Sucked, gripped, strangled, choked

Covered, clasped, dug, bit, gnashed, gnawed

Rushed, tumbled, cascaded

Whispered, whimpered, screamed

Adverbs

Suddenly, silently, gradually

Frantically

PHRASES – NOUNS AND ADJECTIVES

* Something inside her
* Every nerve in his body
* Utterly alert
* With instincts on high alert . . .
* Raw instinct
* *Cold thought*
* Cold dread
* A whirlwind of thoughts and fears
* Pulsing, pounding, surging tornado of thoughts and fears
* Horror of what he . . .
* *Wide and staring eyes*
* Wide with horror
* Like two black swirling pools of ink
* Horror-struck
* *White, deathly pale face*
* Urgent and twisted with terror
* Look of sheer terror on her face
* *Words came in gasps*
* Not a sound
* Huge, yawning screams with his mouth wide open

PHRASES – VERBS

* Pulse stopped, heart stood still, her outstretched arm was paralysed
* Chest was heaving, hands shaking
* Drenched in sweat and heart pounding

* *Squeezed tight, like a sponge being wrung dry*
* Bubbled in her throat as . . .
* Clenched behind her ribs
* Caught in her chest
* Pumped through his body
* Strained to breaking point
* More afraid than she had ever been in her life
* Tightened and twisted as a single word roared in her head
* Began to unfold in her mind
* Could hardly process what she was seeing
* Knew that he faced great danger
* Couldn't force the thought back down
* *Saw it at the end of the corridor*
* Engraved with horror
* Found it difficult to look into her eyes
* Kept his head down
* Kept her narrowed eyes fixed to the floor
* Unable to meet its cold, unblinking stare
* Stared into the room in horror
* Stared unblinking, as if in a trance
* Swept over the scene in front of her
* Watched in horror as it moved closer to the stairs
* *Choked him with its murderous hands*
* Clutched at his throat and stopped him breathing
* Sucked in her breath as shivers racked her body
* Gripped at his throat and strangled his breath into deep, unsteady gasps
* Moved her lips silently in prayer
* Twisted in a scream that never came
* Whimpered and covered her face with her hands
* Tumbled over each other in a low gabble
* Whispered in a tight, choked voice
* Began to scream . . .
* Uttered a thin, high-pitched scream
* Bit her lip
* Before he could cry for help . . .
* *Clasped her hands in her lap*
* Dug her nails into her palms to stop them shaking
* *Froze in horror*
* Frozen to the spot
* Paused on the threshold

SENTENCES

Something inside her squeezed tight, like a sponge being wrung dry.

Her stomach tightened and twisted as a single word roared in her head.

Raw instinct took control. He was utterly alert. Every nerve in his body was straining to breaking point.

Suddenly, he knew that he faced great danger. His instincts were on high alert as adrenaline pumped through his body.

Panic bubbled in her throat as suddenly she saw it at the end of the corridor.

His chest was heaving, his hands, one still holding on to the door, were shaking, and his eyes were wide with horror.

She was suddenly more afraid than she had ever been in her life.

Her breath caught in her chest. She eyed it with alarm. A cold thought began to unfold in her mind, a cold dread that she couldn't force back down.

She could hardly process what she was seeing as her heart clenched behind her ribs.

His mind was a whirlwind – a pulsing, pounding, surging tornado of thoughts and fears.

Her pulse stopped, her heart stood still, her outstretched arm was paralysed.

She was white, deathly pale. Her face was engraved with horror.

He found it difficult to look into her eyes. They were like two black swirling pools of ink. He kept his head down and his eyes fixed to the floor.

Drenched in sweat and heart pounding, Kitty kept her narrowed eyes fixed to the floor, unable to meet its cold, unblinking stare.

Her eyes swept over the scene in front of her and her face froze in horror.

Pausing on the threshold, she stared into the room in horror.

His eyes were wide and staring and his face urgent and twisted with terror.

She was horror-struck. She stared unblinking, as if in a trance and frozen to the spot.

Her words came in gasps and tumbled over each other in a low gabble.

Fear choked him with its murderous hands. It gripped at his throat and strangled his breath into deep, unsteady gasps.

The horror of what he had just seen clutched at his throat and stopped him breathing.

His mouth was twisted in a scream that never came.

Clasping her hands in her lap, she moved her lips silently in prayer.

There was a look of sheer terror on her face. She sucked in her breath as shivers racked her body.

His mouth twisted in a scream that never came. Before he could cry for help, she had thinned out and disappeared through the locked door.

She whimpered and covered her face with her hands.

He whispered in a tight, choked voice, watching in horror as it moved closer to the stairs.

She uttered a thin, high-pitched scream, which echoed through the house.

He began to scream . . . huge, yawning screams with his mouth wide open, but no sound coming out.

She bit her lip and dug her nails into her palms to stop them shaking.

Appendix

Appendix

Planning a ghost story

There should be a *mystery* surrounding the ghost and its unfinished business. When the hero meets the ghost, the reader should feel the:

- ★ anticipation
- ★ tension
- ★ fear.

Think of:

- ★ things that you would not want coming at you from the shadows;
- ★ what might happen if they did.

1. The beginning of the mystery

Something *changes* in your character's life to introduce the *mystery* of the ghost. Maybe:

- ★ Move to a new house
- ★ Inherit an old property from a distant relative
- ★ Go on a school trip
- ★ Go on a journey
- ★ Go on holiday
- ★ Visit an ancient historical site
- ★ Start a new school
- ★ Arrival of a mysterious invitation.

2. The character has a strange experience

(a) Hint that something is going to *happen* which will kick-start the story. For example:

- ★ It was quiet . . . perhaps a bit too quiet.
- ★ . . . the first of that day's strange occurrences.

★ . . . had a strange sense of foreboding.
★ My iPhone . . . impossible . . . ! How did it get there? Who took those pictures?
★ Strange handwriting . . . it's my grandfather's name. What does it mean?
★ There was no sensible reason why she was so desperate to go up into the attic; she just knew she had to. It was as if she was being drawn by an invisible force.

(b) Describe the haunted place where the story is going to take place. Think of:

★ Where would the ghost like to live?
★ What does your character see, hear or smell in this place?
★ What does it feel like to be there?
★ Are there any ghostly signs, sounds, smells, a change in temperature?
★ Are there any curious rooms, locked doors, strange objects, paintings or marks?

3. The character encounters the ghost

★ More strange occurrences indicate there is a mysterious presence in the setting, *or*
★ Character comes face-to-face with the ghost, *and*
★ Ghost disappears again
★ Character explores the setting/investigates the mystery.

Remember:

★ Use description. Don't just tell the reader what is happening. Let the reader know how your character is feeling (reaction). How does the character move (interaction)?
★ Dream up scenes and events where the character is tested.
★ Describe the presence/ghost. Imagine where it comes from.

4. The character has a second encounter with the ghost

This is different from the first one, perhaps:

- ★ More of the ghost is revealed.
- ★ It is more threatening.
- ★ Your character learns more about the ghost's history and discovers the threat of the ghost's enemy.

Think of what things or plan the hero might need to tackle the ghost or its enemy.

5. The key point in the story

Your character does some digging and finds out:

- ★ The ghost's identity;
- ★ Why it is haunting the place;
- ★ Hero meets the ghost once again.

Your character may meet an ally or someone who has lived in the area for many years and knows a lot about the history of the place. Think of:

- ★ What the ghost might smell or sound like;
- ★ Does the ghost have any distinguishing features? For example, if it was poisoned it may have a swollen, black tongue. Injured in battle, it may have a jagged sword wound etc.

6. The ghost or its enemy tries to harm your character

The character is in great danger, either from:

- ★ The ghost, *or*
- ★ The ghost's enemy who is also trying to recover the lost object or prevent his/her crime being discovered.

Think of:

- ★ Ways in which ghost/enemy could harm your character;
- ★ What sort of defence will the character put up? Will he have any help?

7. The ending

Your character uses knowledge of the ghost to:

- ★ Overcome it or help it to defeat its enemy;
- ★ Help it to resolve its unfinished business.

Think of:

- ★ How the problem of the ghost might be sorted.
- ★ A memorable ending – a sudden plot twist or an eerie discovery!
- ★ You don't have to explain what happened. Provide some hints, but leave the rest up to the reader's imagination.

Plot planning sheet

What happens to get the hero/ heroine involved in the mystery?	
Describe the setting. *Are there any curious rooms, locked doors, strange objects, paintings, marks?* *Hint at a strange experience.*	
What strange events take place to indicate a mysterious presence?	
What additional events occur to confirm suspicion that a ghost is present and is now a more threatening presence? What does the main character learn about the history of the setting and the ghost, or the ghost's enemy, e.g. the ghost's identity or why it is haunting the setting?	

The ghost is revealed! *What does it look like?* *How does it move? Does it have* *any distinguishing features?* *(Check the ghost planning* *sheet.)*	
The character is in great danger, either from the ghost or the ghost's enemy. *How could the ghost/ghost's enemy harm the main character?*	
What will the main character do to protect himself/herself? *Does he or she have any help?*	
How is the problem of the ghost sorted? *Is there a sudden plot twist at the end or an eerie discovery?*	
Additional notes	

Hero planning sheet

Name Age Is he or she related to, or does he or she know, the ghost? How?	
Physical description: face, eyes, voice, hairstyle, clothes Distinctive features	
What is the hero most afraid of?	
Does the hero have any secrets, skills or unusual traits?	

What are the hero's main interests?	
Who are the members of their family? What do they do? Do any of them have a secret?	
Who are their close friends? Will any of them help/hinder the hero?	
What has the hero got to gain by resolving the problem with the ghost? What has the hero got to lose if he or she fails? How does the hero change?	
Additional information	

Ghost planning sheet

Why is the ghost haunting the setting? What is the unfinished business?	
Is the ghost: ★ adult? ★ child? ★ male or female?	
When did they live? How did they die? Are there any distinguishing features, e.g. a swollen black tongue if they were poisoned?	
When and where does the ghost appear, and to whom?	

What is the signal to the reader that the ghost is present, e.g. a change in temperature, a movement, sounds, smells?	
How does the ghost: ★ sound? ★ move? ★ look?	
What can the ghost do?	
Can the ghost help or hurt the main character?	
Will the main character help or defeat the ghost?	

Setting

SETTING/CHARACTER	INTERACTION	REACTION

The ghost

SETTING/CHARACTER	INTERACTION	REACTION

Suspense: smells

SETTING/CHARACTER	INTERACTION	REACTION

Suspense: temperature

SETTING/CHARACTER	INTERACTION	REACTION

Suspense: sounds

SETTING/CHARACTER	INTERACTION	REACTION

Suspense: touch

SETTING/CHARACTER	INTERACTION	REACTION

Suspense: eerie presence

SETTING/CHARACTER	INTERACTION	REACTION

Suspense: strange events

SETTING/CHARACTER	INTERACTION	REACTION